Of German Ways

Of German Ways

By LaVern Rippley

Illustrated by Henning B. Jensen

Dillon Press, Inc., Minneapolis, Minnesota

E
184
G3
R5

Dillon Press, Inc.
Minneapolis, Minnesota 55401

International Standard Book Number: 0-87518-013-2
Library of Congress Catalog Card Number: 75-76194

To Barbara Jean

TABLE OF CONTENTS

Introduction

The Land 7

Why They Came and Why They Left 31

The Great Minds: The Last Immigration Wave 49

Patriotism and Its Symbols 65

The Language: High German, Low German,
              Dialects of German 83

Artistic Achievement 107

Life's Milestones 123

Education and Learning 145

Legend, Folklore, Folk Wisdom 165

Christmas and Other Holidays 193

Sports: Paths to Glory 213

The Sweetness of Work 227

German Food 241

About Drink 259

Music, Theater, Song 283

Conclusion 299

INTRODUCTION

IN TODAY'S GENERATION, millions of German-Americans
are curious about the habits and customs that made their
German-born grandparents seem foreign. Too often, perhaps, the children of German immigrants were hasty in
shrugging off their cultural ties with the Fatherland. These
first-generation Americans wanted to belong, and to be
known as Americans. The quicker they could shuck off
Old Country traits the better. Usually it was the second
generation, the grandchildren of Germans, who were inspired to rekindle an interest in the lands and traditions of
their forefathers. In the process they have raised a bundle
of questions about "strange" German ways.

This book seeks to provide answers to their curiosity. It
focuses on the German heritage delivered intact to American soil. This does not mean that the Germany of today is
excluded from consideration. Rather our view includes
present-day Germany only insofar as the present reflects
what has always been typically German. Indeed, much that
is German is ageless. Today's traditions and rituals as often
as not are derived from the misty past of pagan times.
Pagan tribesmen, early Christian missionaries and medieval
knights and noblemen helped make the composite of
German ways. For our purposes, past is telescoped into
present so that we may focus on the continuing habits, customs and traditions that form the German-American heritage of today.

The name "German" has never coincided with political boundaries. Writers from Switzerland, Austria, Czechoslovakia and parts of eastern France all belong to "German" literature. We make far greater distinctions between English and American literature than German-speakers do among theirs. It is also curious that the French believe the real Germany is only the Rhineland and Southern Germany, in other words, that which inherited the Latin civilization. Prussia is Slavic in origin, yet Prussia is held to be the most typically German part of Germany. The Swiss who live in the Italian-speaking part of Switzerland are generally referred to as Tedesci, that is, as "Germans." But in Zürich, Bern or Basel where the mother tongue is German, the native Swiss would be highly insulted if you classified them as Germans. As late as 1933 the official statistics of the Police Department in New York City listed the nationalities of their officers either as "German" or as "Bavarian." During the thirties, the same two distinctions were used in various editions of *Who's Who*.

Yankee Americans of the nineteenth century broadly categorized all German immigrants as "Dutchmen." Why? After all, most of them had never even set foot in Holland, and they were certainly not Dutch. The reason is simply that the German refers to himself as *deutsch* (doitsch as in oil) and to his country as *Deutschland* (doitschlant). Yet the speaker of English refers to him as a German and to his country as Germany, a derivative of the Latin word, *Germania*. In the days of Rome's glory when Germany stood on the fringes of history, the Romans had already established forts and trading posts on and beyond the Rhine. It was in describing these tribes living east of the Rhine and north of the Danube that the Roman historian Tacitus coined the name *Germania*, giving us the first clear information about the land and people of Germany. To this day the English language persists in using the Latin term. Yet in French, a language which has Latin for its parent tongue, the word for Germany is *Allemagne,* originally the name for a tribe of Germans that lived in the southwest corner of Germany bordering on France. The German word *Deutsch* dates from the year 700 when the Old High German word *tiutsch* meant simply "people" or "folk." Slowly the term expanded in meaning and came to include a whole tribe of people, and eventually the whole nation. The German immigrant in America was at first not miffed to hear *Deutsch* mispronounced as "Dutch." Gradually, however, the word changed until the mid-nineteenth century when to call a German a "Dutchman" was a good way to pick a fight.

Despite two World Wars fought against Germany, Americans still retain a friendly attitude toward Germans. In many communities in the United States, even where Germans have never made up the predominant ethnic group, it remains a matter of pride to be "German." Through their newspapers, cultural offerings, music and social mores the German immigrants managed to win the respect of their new countrymen. Rightly or wrongly, most Germans felt themselves culturally superior to the existing American culture. No matter how things were in the country they left, nostalgia soon transformed hard times and bitter memories into glowing reminiscence and patriotic devotion to the country they called home.

Thus a parent's cruel fortune and wretched life evolved in the child's eye as a blissful, romantic existence. A desire to preserve the good traditions from the Old World, when spiced heavily with nostalgia, caused countless German customs and ways to lodge permanently in the American soul. If we realize that there are approximately fifty million Americans who have descended directly from German im-

THE LAND

THE LAND

THE RHINE RIVER is so German that it virtually flows in the veins of every German alive. Mention the Rhine and a German is suddenly transported to the cool valleys and verdant landscape of his homeland. *Vater Rhein,* he thinks, and immediately uncontrollable emotions well up. More than any other river in the world, the Rhine pulsates through the body and soul of every German no matter where he lives. To him it's the greatest river in the world. And to him it's, of course, a *German* Rhine. In fact, you even find Germans who believe the Rhine is the only river in the world. A word of caution: one thing you never want to argue with a German about is the Rhine. To counter his feelings about this river would be tantamount to cursing his mother and father.

Let's agree. The Rhine is a German river and it's certainly the greatest. It isn't the longest, to be sure, nor the broadest, nor the deepest. It may carry the most traffic (more than the combined total of the Mississippi and the St. Lawrence), but it does not flow the swiftest, nor flood the most, and it may not even be the prettiest—though there is room for argument here. If we want to be really technical about it, the Rhine isn't even a German river. It begins high in the Swiss Alps and flows basically northeast, forming natural borders on its eight hundred and twenty mile race to its mouth on the North Sea.

The members of every German singing society in America have at one time or another leaped to their feet, stood erect like soldiers and with tears streaming down their cheeks thundered forth Max Schneckenburger's *"Die Wacht am Rhein."* The first three verses of the poem provide a sample of its flavor:

Es braust ein Ruf wie Donnerhall
Wie Schwertgeklirr und Wogenprall:
Zum Rhein, zum Rhein, zum deutschen Rhein,
Wer will des Stromes Hüter sein?
Lieb Vaterland, magst ruhig sein,
Fest steht und treu die Wacht am Rhein!

Durch Hunderttausend zuckt es schnell,
Und aller Augen blitzen hell.
Der deutsche Jüngling, fromm und stark,
Verschirmt die heil'ge Landesmark.
Lieb Vaterland, magst ruhig sein,
Fest steht und treu die Wacht am Rhein!

Er blickt hinauf in Himmelsau'n
Wo Heldengeister niederschau'n
Und schwört mit stolzer Kampfeslust:
"Du, Rhein, bleibst deutsch wie meine Brust."
Lieb Vaterland, magst ruhig sein,
Fest steht und treu die Wacht am Rhein!

There rumbles a cry like thunder,
Like the clanking of swords and crashing of waves.
To the Rhine, to the Rhine, the German Rhine,
Who wants to be the stream's protector?
Dear Fatherland, may you rest quietly,
Firm and true stands the watch on the Rhine!

Through a hundred thousand it thrills quickly
And the eyes of all glitter brightly
The German youth, pious and strong
Is covering the holy landmark.
Dear Fatherland, you may rest quietly,
Firm and true stands the watch on the Rhine!

He looks up into Heaven's meadows
Where the souls of heroes look down
And swears with proud desire for battle
"You, O Rhine, will remain as German as my breast."
Dear Fatherland, may you rest quietly,
Firm and true stands the watch on the Rhine!

When Schneckenburger wrote his poem in November,
1840, there was no question of the Rhine's functioning as
one of Germany's borders. Germany was then only a collection of states where German was spoken. Still the sentiment
of his poem was the same then as now: if the Rhine is safe,
all of Germany is safe. To appreciate the mystical power
of the river over the German people, you must sit beside
it with companions, drinking glasses of chilled Riesling
wine, eating loaves of dark German bread, and singing of
legendary knights and beautiful maidens. You should view
the ruins of castles hauntingly gazing down the cliffs high
above the current. Not least, you must get up early some
morning to glimpse the panorama of a drowsy river seeth-
ing with ghostly mist, penetrated only occasionally by a
Rhine steamer's bell piercing the fog. Go anywhere in Germany, or even among second-generation Germans in America and you will hear the phrase, *"es fliesst noch viel Wasser den Rhein hinunter."* The wisdom in the proverb is approximately this: time will go on despite what has just happened. Literally it means, "a lot of water will yet flow down
the Rhine."

Prejudice and romanticism aside, the Rhine is truly a great river. In all, it washes the borders or heartlands of six countries: Switzerland, Liechtenstein, Austria, Germany, France, and the Netherlands. Yet even though it touches so many shores, all the people who live on its banks speak German, of one dialect or another. Even the name "Rhein" isn't German; it stems from an old Celtic word used by the people who inhabited the Rhine area before history began. To the Celts the word *Rhein* simply meant "stream."

Since the beginning of literature the river has charmed German poets and thinkers—and not only Germans but foreigners as well. To cite two of them, the English author John Ruskin wrote of it, "Music for the eyes and melody for the heart." Traveling the mountain stretch of the Rhine, his countryman, the poet Lord Byron, penned sad words about the crumbling fortresses, "chiefless castles breathing stern farewells."

Again and again in discussing German ways it will be necessary to return to the Rhine. For the time being, suffice it to say that to the German-American, nothing is more synonymous with his image of the homeland than the River Rhine. Once it literally gave him food to eat. Now the Rhine is still his home, his heritage, his myth, his national make-up, his epic, his pride, his very soul—even though a good many Germans or German-Americans have never even seen the Rhine.

The other major German river is the Danube. But despite the near worship paid the Danube in Vienna, it flows along quite unnoticed in Germany. This is not easily explained since the Danube's distance of flow within German territory is only a few miles shorter than the Rhine's four hundred fifty German miles, and the Danube also has served frequently as an important border, even in Roman times. From its source in the Black Forest, a scant few miles from the Rhine, the Danube flows in the opposite direction, eastward through Austria, Yugoslavia, Bulgaria and Rumania to the Black Sea. Perhaps because the river turns its back on Germany, or for reasons lost in the dim past, the Danube remains to the German just another river, while the Rhine has always triggered fierce loyalty among German peoples. Some rivers like the Neckar have been eulogized in song. Others like the Elbe, Oder, and Main have nourished local legend and popular dedication. But no matter which one, all German rivers are personified by the German people; like grand old relatives, rivers never taste death.

After the Rhine, the next greatest single cause for *Heimweh* (homesickness) for the German in a new mother country is his native region. Unlike other major European countries, Germany has never had a permanent capital. London, Paris, Rome and Vienna have always been centers of their respective countries but Berlin was the capital of all of Germany from 1871-1945, a mere seventy-four years. Moreover, many of our German ancestors had arrived in America long before Berlin ever gained the status of a capital city. Consequently it is understandable that Germans abroad often show devotion to their *Heimat* rather than to their country or its capital. In fact, for a time the U.S. Census Bureau listed all German immigrants according to national origin, not as arriving from Germany, but from Saxony, Bavaria, Prussia, Mecklenburg, etc. Really, there was no alternative, for until 1871 the word "Germany" was rather vague. Some would say it was less a state than a state of mind. The German *Reich,* as united by the statesman Bismarck, existed from 1871 to 1918. It represented a territory of almost 209,000 square miles. This pre-World War I size is approximately equal to the

combined territorial size of Minnesota, Wisconsin, and
North Dakota. If we take the German borders existing in 1937, just
before Hitler began his expansion policy, then the West
Germany of today comprises about fifty-three percent of
the former territory. In 1945 twenty-four percent of the
former territory was ceded to Poland and the balance of
twenty-three percent makes up present-day East Germany. In regard to size, West Germany is best compared
to our state of Oregon, both having roughly 97,000 square
miles of territory. On January 1, 1967, the population of
West Germany was 59,824,000.

The West German Federal Republic is made up of eleven
states called *Länder*. Three of these are actually only city-
states. Beginning in the north the *Länder* are Schleswig-
Holstein, Niedersachsen, Nordrhein - Westfalen, Hessen,
Rheinland-Pfalz, Saarland, Baden-Württemberg, and Bayern. The city-states are Bremen, Hamburg, and West Berlin. In 1957 the German government declared that Berlin
will remain the official capital of the country but that Bonn
will serve as its temporary seat until the question of a
divided Germany can be resolved.

German-Americans are familiar with most of the state
names although the list of states and duchies was much
longer when most of our German ancestors left their country. Some of these additional states were: Silesia, Mecklenburg, Brandenburg, Pomerania, East and West Prussia,
Saxony, Alsace, Lorraine, Hanover, Oldenburg, Thuringia,
and others. Today these areas have either been lost through
German territorial forfeiture, or they have been eradicated
by reorganization of state boundaries. The latter was carried out extensively after World War II by the Russian oc-
cupational forces in East Germany.

The geographic sections of Germany divide up nicely

into four basic units of terrain. Moving from north to south we find the low, flat lands in the north referred to as the North German Plain, *Norddeutsches Flachland.* Once this area was covered by the glaciers that pushed down from Scandinavia during the second to the last glacial period. Next comes the Middle German Hill Region, *Deutsches Mittelgebirge,* a well-eroded section with alternating hilly areas and small plains thoroughly cut through in spots by rivers which form narrow passes as in the most scenic section of the Rhine. Thirdly we have the Swabian and Bavarian Plateau extending roughly from the foothills of the Alps northward to the Danube. In effect, the Danube flows along this plateau region as it makes a bed from west to east in southern Germany. Finally there are the German Alps. A narrow Alpine belt stretches from the *Bodensee* (Lake Constance) in the west to the city of Salzburg, Austria, on the eastern border of Germany. The two highest mountains on the German side of the Alps are the Zugspitze and the Watzmann, both under ten thousand feet.

It is often said that specific types of ˌpeople fit naturally into a given geographical region. Whether in such cases the geographic terrain attracts personalities or whether the land and the climate form the people no one can say. But it is a fact that personalities in the northern provinces vary considerably from those farther south. In the North they are somehow more withdrawn and restrained. In the South they are more folksy, jovial, and outgoing. On the surface the southerners seem to enjoy life a great deal more than the northerners.

Let us look at the four geological sections in more detail.

The North German Plain is less than six hundred feet above sea level. Formerly perhaps a mountain area, the structure has been leveled by glaciers and smoothed by runoff. The ice actually advanced and retreated several times, each time causing erosion and alluvial fill. Today the Elbe River serves as a north-south demarcation line between two distinct glacial periods, and between two clearly distinguishable areas of the plain. The last glacier never advanced west of the Elbe; thus the terrain is predominantly flat with little sand. East of the Elbe, however, the last glacier deposited moraine reliefs while it carved sharp depressions and basins. In front of these moraines there are heavy deposits of sand and gravel left by the melting ice. In this North German Plain the people are, of course, geared to a specific kind of life. A lot of river and canal traffic bolsters trade in the towns while large farms dot the landscape. Windmills once speckled this skyline especially in the territory East of the Netherlands. In the sandy regions even today the soil is stubborn and life does not treat its inhabitants kindly. The result is that legend and superstitions which were sown long ago still are thriving among the rural people of the heath.

Contributing to the general flora of the plain are the knotty oaks, the slender birches, and especially the juniper clumps that manage to grow in the coarse soils. Here, too, one finds the European species of our cranberry, the *Preisselbeere*. The city that gives its name to this sandy region is Lüneburg. Once a booming city of the Hanseatic League of cities, Lüneburg is now a quaint, old-fashioned town. Formerly it was also prominent for its position in the commercial salt markets. Today the salt deposits are largely depleted, but the *Lüneburger Heide* remains as stark as before.

The largest city in the area is Hamburg on the Elbe. All three major cities—Hamburg, Bremen and Lübeck—are situated inland from the North Sea, back on the plains but along large rivers. All were once members of the sea-faring Hanseatic League established as a trade union in the Middle

Ages. So flat is the terrain that where rivers do not reach, canals were easily constructed so that today the entire heath is literally tied to the sea. Thus, when the North Germans are accused of being stand-offish, stern and overly rigid, it is probably because their patterns of life have been unwittingly tempered by the sternness of the North Sea. That, plus the monotonous lowland, alternating only between huge bogs and broken-down dunes, must have profoundly affected their personalities. In this area, commonly called the *Geest,* the population today is sparse.

Before moving south, a word about the Jutland peninsula which projects up from the mainland from a line drawn between Hamburg and Lübeck. In Jutland the coasts are beautiful. They are uniformly low and are intricately embroidered with thin coastal chains of dunes. Here Germans of all classes love to spend their summer vacations. The winds from the sea are brisk and chilly, but the swimming is invigorating. Nevertheless, bathers don't usually last too long in the chilly waters of the North and Baltic Seas. Instead they prefer to sit in the sun. Frequently they dig deep hollows in the sand to avoid the frigid northeasterly winds. Or, they rent wicker-basket chairs with carriage-type hoods. These swivel away from the wind allowing two people to lounge gracefully and track the sun's warm rays all day long. Inland there is a fertile plain interspersed with elongated lakes and basins. Off the western shore are several islands which have been virtually extracted from the sea by the extreme effort of the inhabitants. Isolated farmers on the islands have developed a lore all their own, some of which has been immortalized by the North German novelist, Theodor Storm of Husum.

At the southern edge of the North German Plain lies a rich, highly developed agricultural area famous for its good soils, the *Lehm.* Here farmers raise large quantities

of wheat, sugar beets, and other fodder root crops, as well
as alfalfa and vegetables. Along this line we find such
cities as Hannover, Magdeburg and Berlin, all highly developed commercial centers. These cities enjoy great advantages in today's industrial age because they are situated
on the *Mittelland Kanal,* a great man-made waterway which
binds together the girth of Germany in one commercial
unit. Ships of up to one thousand tons haul freight on the
canal from the Rhine to the Weser, to the Elbe, and even
to the Oder River east of Berlin. In effect, this canal provides all the major cities of northern Germany with access
to the sea. Traffic can move north and south on the rivers
and east and west on the *Mittelland* and other smaller
canals.

Adjacent to the desolate Geest lands to the east, the
Münsterland offers rolling hills, woods, meadows and a
lively rural scene. The Ems River flows northward through
the *Münsterland* and the Dortmund-Ems canal ties the city
and the plain into the Rhine basin. In the city of Münster
stands the beautiful gothic *Rathaus* (city hall), where the
peace of Westphalia was signed in October, 1648. After
thirty years of religious wars, Protestants and Catholics
gathered in its now famous *Friedenssaal* (hall of peace) to
sign the treaty. Today the hall remains exactly as when the
last envoy departed, preserved as a memorial to the sense-
lessness of the Thirty Years' War which ravaged nearly all
of Germany.

Jutting skyward on the Münster plain is the *Teutoburgerwald,* a northeast-southwest lying hill region. The *Teutoburgerwald* is legendary in German history. In this forest
dedicated to German independence, stands a statue of the
tribal German General Arminius, who stopped the advance
of the Roman armies under their General Varus. The immense image of the German general, according to his

tribal name, Hermann der Cherusker, symbolizes all the patriotic defenders who, in 9 A.D. and ever since, have fought to prevent the fall of the Fatherland to a foreign invader. Today the forest offers a pleasant respite from the hustle and bustle of modern life in the cities of that region. Hermann der Cherusker has not been confined to his home in the Teutoburgerwald. Indeed Minnesotans have known him for over a half century to be in their back yard. High atop Hermann Hill just south of the city of New Ulm stands the Hermann Monument in a park by the same name, near the ruins of the Old Waraju Distillery. The helmeted Hermann is a bronze figure with sword raised protectively, standing watch over this city of German immigrants.

Southeast of the Teutoburgerwald rise the chimneys of the Ruhr, the single most industrialized region in the world. Once a meadowy area speckled with small lakes and rolling fields, it is now a jungle of cement and steel, railroads, and huge stockpiles of material. South of the Ruhr River estuary lies the Cologne basin, a closed plain resembling the neighboring Netherlands with their windmill dotted farmlands. Here, too, are the poplar-lined canals, dikes, and quiet villages.

Moving to our second geographic section, the *Deutches Mittelgebirge* (Midland Mountains) we find a rugged belt of uplands and basins. In reality these uplands are not true mountains. They are former mountains that have been virtually eroded, then lifted again in the period when the Alpine foldings occurred. Interspersed in this landscape are isolated rock masses such as the Harz, and several volcanic outpourings like the Rhon, Eifel and Vogelsberg. Nowhere in this region is there a mountain over five thousand feet. The highest point in the northern part is the Harz with 3,747 feet.

Of greatest interest in the northern section is the pene-
plain that cradles the Rhine. Again during the period of the
Alpine foldings, this level area was pushed up, and as it
rose, the Rhine continued to cut its way through the bed
rock, forming the beautiful Rhine gorge. Thus divided into
a western and an eastern block by the Rhine, the plain is
further divided from north to south by the Mosel on the
west, creating the Eifel Plateau on the north (2,447 feet)
and the Hunsrück Mountains (2,677 feet) on the south.
On the right bank of the Rhine, the Lahn and the Sieg
Rivers trisect the eastern portion of the plain separating the
Sauerland Hills from the Westerwald (2,155 feet) in the
center, and forming the Taunus (2,877 feet) in the south.

Lying on the Rhine, the central artery of this region is
the famed Lorelei Rock. This rocky projection is situated
at the narrowest point of the Rhine a little downstream from
Bingen. There is not a single German at home or in an
adopted mother country who has not heard and sung of
the Lorelei. Like a mammoth ship's bow, the Lorelei Rock
juts into the Rhine obstructing the navigator's view. On top
of the precipice a beautiful maiden with golden hair has
traditionally reared her head to lure medieval rivermen to
their destruction. Actually, of course, it is the whirlpool
formed by the sharp bend in the current and the invisible
crags projecting from below the surface that have wrenched
down ship and shipman in years gone by. However, the
phenomenon defied reasonable explanation for over a thousand years, during which time the legend of the siren's melody sung by a bewitchingly beautiful lady blossomed among
the populace.

The latest version of the ballad was written by Heinrich
Heine in 1827. Its first two stanzas are as follows:

Ich weiss nicht, was soll es bedeuten,
Dass ich so traurig bin;
Ein Märchen aus alten Zeiten,
Das kommt mir nicht aus dem Sinn.

Die Luft ist kühl und es dunkelt,
Und ruhig fliesst der Rhein;
Der Gipfel des Berges funkelt
Im Abendsonnenschein.

I know not what it should mean
That I am so sad;
A fairytale from olden times,
Which won't come out of my mind.

The air is cool and it's getting dark,
And quietly flows the Rhine;
The peak of the mount glitters
In the evening sunshine.

Flanking the Lorelei (Celtic for Lei-stone) are the ruined fortresses and castles of the medieval robber barons. A favorite hobby of theirs was to plunder the commercial traffic on the Rhine. The booty in goods was appropriated and rich merchants were tossed into dingy cellars or walled towers until they purchased their freedom by heavy ransom or withered away in death. In 1250 the cities along the Rhine formed the *Rheinische Städtebund* (confederation of Rhine cities) for protection against the marauders. The principal contributions of the alliance were larger palaces and new armies which eventually triumphed over the lawless breed. Soon the mountain-top fortresses were abandoned. Those that were not ruined in the struggle soon fell into decay. In ruins, however, they retain stark and haunting contact with that period known as the Middle Ages.

The plateaus overlooking the Rhine are poor in resources and in general they suffer from a feeble economy. However, the slopes immediately adjacent to the various rivers are rich and populous. In particular, the Rhine and the Mosel are blessed with good soils and a temperate climate favorable to the growing of grapes. From this region come the world-famous wine brand-names: Liebfraumilch, Riesling, Niersteiner, Scharlachberger, Markobrunner, Johannisberger. No less well-known are the Mosel wines, the Moselblümchen, Bernkasteler, Piesporter, Graach, and Zell. We'll visit this wine land in a later chapter.

East of the Rhine in the Mid-German Hill section lies the gently rolling plain of Hesse. This region includes the Vogelsberg (2,540 feet) and the Rhone mountains (3,117 feet) which tower above the landscape. Farther east still are two raised ranges, the *Thüringerwald,* and the Harz. Of greatest interest in this region is the Harz with its highest peak, the Brocken (3,747 feet). On a clear day you can see from the peaks of the Brocken over three hundred cities, villages, and castles. Rising like a pyramid from the plain, this mountain is the home of countless German legends. Here the rural families, both superstitious and religious, frequently sing the hymnic melody:

> *Es grünen die Tannen.*
> *Es wachse das Erz;*
> *Gott schenke uns allen*
> *Ein fröhliches Herz!*

> May the fir trees green
> May the iron ore increase
> And may God give us all
> A happy heart.

The *Walpurgisnacht* (Sabbath of Witches) is the most significant legend associated with the Brocken mountain. It has become known in the world primarily through Goethe's long poetic drama, *Faust.*

In pagan times the Germanic tribes believed that on the evening from April 30 to May 1, the god Wodan had married the goddess Freya. Centuries ago this feast was celebrated yearly for twelve consecutive days. During the entire time the gods had special powers over men. Hoping to placate the gods' anger, people decorated their homes with green bows, sang songs, and offered ritual dances of praise to them. The name for the night of April 30th does not come from a pagan god but from the Christian patron saint, Walpurgis, who was declared by the Church to be the protectress against evil spirits. Appropriately she is called on at this time of the year.

Going southeast from the Harz through Leipzig one soon reaches a long ridge of mountains stretching some eighty miles along the Czech border. This range is called the *Erzgebirge,* the Ore Mountains. The Elbe River cuts through this range on the way from its source in Bohemia to the North Sea. At the river's mountain cut, there is a scenic and geologically interesting district of rocky pinnacles, steeples and mushrooms, bridges and arches, as well as caverns all eaten out by the heady river currents of a bygone period. Often this area is called Saxon Switzerland.

Shifting to southwestern Germany we find a large depression between the Vosges Mountains of France and the Black Forest which is called simply the Rhine depression. It runs from Basel in Switzerland to Mainz, a length of nearly two hundred miles and a width of some twenty. Fertile soil and excellent transportation facilities have helped this area develop a flourishing commerce and agriculture. The Black Forest, *Schwarzwald,* has been named for the dark color of the fir trees which blanket its slopes. For as long as people can remember this has been the center of a highly technical industry, the building of cuckoo clocks. The *Kuckuck Uhr,* bringing joy and fascination to homes around the globe, represents the very livelihood of many a village in the Black Forest. Whole villages appear on the surface to have no jobs for their occupants. But if you visit one of the homes the true state of affairs will soon be obvious. In nearly every house members of a family are busy producing parts for the brand of cuckoo clock manufactured in their particular town. Little wheels come from one house, the chassis from another, tiny pivots from another, bellows from this one, carved birds from that one, until in the last house all the parts are assembled into those dark-brown little birdhouses known as cuckoo clocks.

Between the Black Forest and the Thuringian and Franconian Forests lies the large Swabian-Franconian Basin noted for its terrace look. Two rivers flow through this basin, the Neckar and the Main. Forage crops and tobacco along with fruit orchards make up the produce of these valleys. Around Nürnberg is the Naab River which flows into the Danube near Regensberg. It is contained to the west by the *Bayrischer Wald,* Bavarian Forest. In general this is a rather unfertile, hilly region interspersed with marshes.

More interesting is the Swabian-Bavarian Tableland made up of the out-gliding Alps as they slope toward the Danube. Pine forests and blue lakes offer more variety than is available in most of Germany. This sub-alpine region extends all the way from Geneva in western Switzerland to the gates of Vienna. Farthest south in Germany, but nearest the Alps, is the highest portion of this tableland. It is easily identifiable by the large lakes (Bodensee, Chiemsee, Ammersee, Starnbergersee, Würmsee) and the many peat bogs. The north shore of the *Bodensee* (Lake Constance) is an exception, having fine soils and vineyards blessed by a warm climate. North of this region stretching to the Danube the soils are quite good: sometimes sandy, other times covered with heavy layers of pebbles, with abundant forests and pasturelands.

Territorially the German Alps represent the smallest of the four geographic sections. Technically they are only the northernmost slopes of a massive range that stretches in a grand arc from Nice on the Mediterranean to Vienna on the Danube. Vienna lies on what is called the *Donaudurchbruch,* that point where the Danube divides the Alpine from the Carpathian Ranges. Having such a small portion of the secondary Alps, the Germans are so proud of their mountains that they have divided them up into three sections: The *Algäuer Alpen,* the *Bayerische Alpen* and the *Salzburger Alpen.*

From the natural demarcation of Lake Constance to the Salzach River in the vicinity of Salzburg, Austria, the political frontier between Germany and Austria runs a most capricious line. Sometimes the border follows the crest of the divide, at other times the center of a valley. The meandering border was plotted in the past when local families arbitrarily fixed property lines without consideration of natural definitions. The German Alpine strip consists substantially of harsh and jagged peaks that culminate in the Zugspitze (9,720 feet) near Garmisch-Partenkirchen and in the Watzmann (9,333 feet) which towers over the village of Berchtesgaden. Nestled under the latter mountain is the beautiful *Königsee,* (the king's lake). No other lake in the Alps can compare to its starkly handsome, cavernous walls rising seven thousand feet above the crystal-clear, quiet waters. Travelers can take battery-powered boat rides on this lake. At one point everything stops and the driver heaves a blast on his trumpet which resounds harmoniously in seven distinct echoes. On a little isthmus at the lower end of the lake the excursion stops to permit visits to the St. Bartholomew Chapel, or for a dinner of delicate trout caught in the deep blue lake. With luck and a telescope one can also observe the mountain goats traipsing about on crests of limestone walls high above.

What about the climate in Germany?

German immigrants to the United States usually feel uncomfortable in our country's climate of extremes, for such weather is not the case in Germany where "moderate" is the rule the year round. Since Germany stretches from below the forty-eighth parallel in the south to well above the fifty-fourth parallel in the north we might want to conclude that she has severely cold winters. After all, the northern border of the United States, the forty-ninth parallel, is almost the southern border of Germany and the fifty-fourth parallel in North America runs through the southern end of Hudson Bay in Canada. Nevertheless, during the winter it gets much colder in the heartland of the United States than in any part of Germany. The same comparison might be made for the summers. Even north of the Canadian border it is frequently much hotter on this continent than at any place in the German nation.

Thus Germany is situated in what is called the central portion of the temperate zone. Its mean temperature is a mild fifty degrees, much higher than the world average for its latitude. By contrast, Minnesota has a forty-four degree annual mean, but the climate is more dramatic. The winters are much colder while the summers are cursed by intense heat waves. In Germany it would be unthinkable to have winter temperatures of thirty-five degrees below zero and 105 degrees in the same city during the summer.

Warm moist air from the Atlantic Gulf Stream is responsible for this moderate climate. Occasionally during the winter, blasts of Siberian cold air masses can chill the European continent but generally the pattern of weather flow is from west to east. Bavarians experience relatively harsh winters with heavy snowfalls and cool, wet summers. On the other hand, the valleys of the Rhine and the subsidiary rivers enjoy a very mild climate. There the mean winter temperature is around thirty-two degrees while in summer it is sixty-six degrees. The average rainfall calculated for the whole of Germany is twenty-seven inches, which is approximately the same as in central Minnesota.

The natural vegetation of regions in the United States often determined where German immigrants chose to settle. It is a fact that the Germans sought those areas where the countryside resembled their native Germany. But over and above this, they seem to have had an uncanny sense of geography when they selected their farms in America. In Pennsylvania, for example, it is interesting to examine the geological maps of countries where there were both German and Irish settlers, such as Berks or Lancaster. In areas where there is a limestone base, the Germans settled. Where slate comprises the basic foundation, the Irish appear. Did the Germans have some early scientific knowledge of geology?

In his book, *The German Element in the United States,* Albert Faust postulates rather that they had a better eye for the vegetation as a clue to productivity than did other immigrant groups. Thus while the Irish took the well-watered land near the big rivers, the Germans chose land which grew the best trees, the oaks and the other hardwoods. Needless to say, of course, the similarity of the new terrain to that of the homeland was a powerful factor in the selection of farm lands. The hilly regions of the *Rheinland-Pfalz* are mirrored in the areas of heaviest German settlements in the eastern United States. Even more remarkable are the cases of family after family who migrated farther and farther west with each succeeding generation. Invariably their homesteads retained an identical appearance to the farm owned in the original locality.

In Wisconsin and Minnesota, the German immigrants generally preferred the wooded districts since these promised better soils. Throughout much of the nineteenth century the Germans left the prairie land and the bigger farms to others. They concentrated instead on the long pull. They developed the acreage and built up the land. They were interested in permanence, so they constructed houses of stone or brick. Traveling in the United States in 1905, the German historian Earl Lamprecht wrote that in the whole country he had seen only two prosperous farming areas, Utah and Pennsylvania. In the former, the result of religious enthusiasm, he maintained, and in the latter, the product of the German nationality. Concerning his passage through Wisconsin, however, he also wrote favorably: "rich farms abound, and the prosaic frame cottages are replaced partly by stone houses; mowing machines and merry harvest wagons present a sumptuous picture. In the prettiest parts it seems as if we had come into a land such as the German farmer might dream of—an improved Germany—a region of which the poet had a vision when he said: 'And like a garden was the land to look upon'."

Decades earlier, before German farmers began spilling out into the American Middle West, other Germans had already paved the way. Perhaps most famous among these was John Jacob Astor who was born in the small village of Waldorf near Heidelberg in 1763. Poor, his parents migrated to America after the Revolutionary War. On board ship from Germany the young Astor heard about the fur trading possibilities in America. In New York he sold some of the musical instruments he got from his brother and set up a store for such instruments. From their meager capital he established the American Fur Company in 1809 and became immensely wealthy. To this day his name remains in places as distant from each other as the city of Astoria, Oregon on the Pacific, and the Waldorf-Astoria in New York on the Atlantic.

WHY THEY CAME AND WHY THEY LEFT

WHY THEY CAME AND WHY THEY LEFT

WHAT IS a *Neuländer?* Literally translated it means a New World man. Actually the *Neuländers* were Old Worlders, generally representatives from the large shipping companies of England and Holland. Many were one-time immigrants to America who found immigrant-hunting in the Old World more profitable than making a living in the New World. Gottlieb Mittelberger, who came to America in the latter half of the eighteenth century, recorded his experiences in a book entitled *Journey to Pennsylvania:* "The *Neuländer* receive from their merchants in Rotterdam and Amsterdam for every person of ten years and over, three florins or a ducat; The merchants in Philadelphia pay sixty, seventy, or eighty florins for such a person, in proportion as said person has incurred more or less debts during the voyage."

Thus the *Neuländer* were agents who obtained commissions from the shippers for the bodies they supplied. Moving through Germany, these *Neuländer* dressed gaily to give the appearance of great wealth. Supposedly it had been earned in America where, they pretended, the streets were paved with gold. Pocket watches dangled from golden chains and stories about immigrants moving from rags to riches were spun from their mouths. According to the *Neuländer,* "The maid had become a lady, the peasant a nobleman, the artisan a baron, the officers of the government held their places by the will of the people," wrote Mittelberger. Even state officials occasionally published pamphlets describing the brilliant prospects for German immigrants in Pennsylvania, the Carolinas, Ohio, or Wisconsin. So bad did the situation become at one time in the *Pfalz* (Palatinate) that its Elector issued a ban on all Newlanders. Nevertheless, by moving secretly from house to house under the guise of fellow countrymen returning from America to tell about it, they still accomplished their purposes. Speedy arrangements often whisked away the gullible overnight. They were transported via the Rhine to the Netherlands where large ships awaited them.

An example of the literature used to lure settlers are the pamphlets and books printed by the state of Wisconsin. Several such titles are given here: Ziegler, *"Skizzen einer Reise durch Nordamerika und Westindien mit besonderer Berücksichtigung des deutschen Elements, der Auswanderung und der landwirtschaftlichen Verhältnisse in dem neuen Staat Wisconsin"* (Sketches of a Journey Through North America and the West Indies with Special Emphasis on the German Element, the Emigration and the Agricultural Prospects in the New State of Wisconsin) (Dresden, 1849); Freimund Goldmann, *"Briefe aus Wisconsin in Nordamerika"* (Letters from Wisconsin in North America) (Leipzig 1949); Wilhelm Dames, *"Wie sieht es in Nordamerika aus?"* (How does it look in North America?) (1849); Kennan, *"Der Staat Wisconsin, seine Hülfquellen und Vorzüge für Auswanderer"* (The State of Wisconsin, Its Provisions and Advantages for Emigrants) (Basel, 1882); Gustav Richter, *"Der Nordamerikanische Freistaat Wisconsin"* (The North American Free State of Wisconsin) (Wesel, 1849).

For many reasons early waves of German immigrants remained in Pennsylvania and the Carolinas. Later Ohio was a favorite spot. Wisconsin, too, gained prominence as soon as its territory was opened up. In 1835 a society called the "Germania" was formed to maintain German customs, speech, and traditions as well as to assist German immigrants and refugees arriving in the United States. This society once asked Congress to set aside land to be claimed exclusively by German fugitives, but Congress rebuffed the request. Later, when Wisconsin was admitted to the Union in 1848, an attempt was made to reserve Wisconsin completely as a German state, but this, too, proved unsuccessful. Similar efforts also failed to make Missouri and Texas German states within the Union. During each struggle, however, heavy percentages of Germans settled in all three states. Wisconsin was the latest and enjoyed advantages over the other two because its climate and soil were virtually identical with what the Germans had left behind. Wheat, rye, oats, and garden vegetables grew well there. Summers were moderate and the landscape picturesque. Furthermore, there was no competition from slave labor before emancipation and from cheap Negro help after it.

Other things favored Wisconsin too. A foreigner could vote after a single year of residence—a privilege won through the struggle of German spokesmen when the state was admitted to the union in 1848. A similar clause was added to the Indiana constitution and later incorporated into the Minnesota document of statehood in 1857. Minnesota thereafter had the most liberal laws of any state in the Union for enfranchisement of immigrants—four months after applying for citizenship. Wisconsin also had a liberal land policy. Federal acreage granted to support the University and maintain schools was sold to immigrants for the minimum price allowed by the government, $1.25 per acre.

Perhaps most influential in attracting Germans to Wisconsin and a few other states was the appointment of a state commissioner of immigration. In the first two years of operation (the law passed in 1852) the commissioner distributed nearly thirty thousand pamphlets acquainting potential emigrants with the soil and climate of Wisconsin. He was helpful in other ways too. For example, often settlers in the state were able to funnel travel money through him back to friends and relatives in Germany. Another positive step was taken when the Wisconsin Central Railroad sent its agent, K. K. Kennan, under state auspices to search for emigrants in Germany. From the forest lands of Bavaria he was able to procure over five thousand who were then settled on the railroad line from Stevens Point to Ashland. The inducement Kennan used was primarily the good wages in lumber camps and the opportunity to buy land with the quick money earned by lumbering. Provisions for free shelter were also offered. For example, in Medford around one hundred immigrants were housed free for several weeks until they could establish their own accommodations.

The success of these policies can be seen from the statistics which show that between 1850 and 1900 Wisconsin received a far greater proportion of German immigration than any other state in the Union. As a result the 1900 U.S. Census shows that the German population of Wisconsin was an astonishing 34.3 percent of the total, and if we include under "German" those who had at least one German parent, the figure jumps astonishingly to over 50 percent.

Although some immigrants received state-sanctioned help in adopting their new mother country, the difficulties of passage and reestablishment had to be borne by individuals. Early in the history of colonization a system of transportation was evolved by which a shipping company often transported an immigrant free of charge. In return, the immigrant would agree to work in bondage for from three to seven years. Usually a company or an individual in the United States "bought" the immigrant and retained him in service without pay until his passage had been earned. Faust, in *The German Element in the United States,* quotes from a letter describing a ship's arrival in Philadelphia: "Those that have paid their passage are released, the others are advertised in the newspapers for sale. The ship becomes the market. The buyers make their choice and bargain with the immigrants for a certain number of years and days, depending upon the price demanded by the ship captain or other 'merchant' who made the outlay for transportation, etc. . . . The young unmarried people of both sexes are very quickly sold, and their fortunes are either good or bad, according to the character of the buyer. Old married people, widows, and the feeble, are a drag on the market, but if they have sound children, then their transportation charges are added to those of the children, and the latter must serve longer." Hence the term redemptioner or "indentured servant" became a household word in the American vocabulary during the days of heavy immigration.

This system of course led to many abuses. Unscrupulous shippers sometimes plundered their regular paying passengers by leaving baggage behind to be loaded on other vessels which was then intentionally "lost." They then charged merciless tolls and fees retroactive from their point of departure somewhere on the Rhine to their arrival at a destination in the United States. Destitute, these immigrants had no choice but to become redemptioners in order to get started in the new country. The system of redemptioning was not always bad, however. Some immigrants who had paid their passage in advance nevertheless offered themselves for sale to ease their transition into a new world. They worked for a master without compensation but gained a knowledge of the language and customs, and had time to make plans for a career in their new home.

Other nearly insurmountable problems in reaching the Atlantic shores were the shipwrecks due to storms, substandard equipment, and diseases such as dysentery, smallpox, and scurvy. Simple starvation was a problem because provisions on board were rarely proportional to the number of people squeezed into a hulk. This being the situation, it is surprising that so many still came. The many reasons why they did come in spite of the difficulties can be reduced to two: one economic, the other religious. And yet these two separate causes are strangely combined into one remote cause in German history, the Thirty Years' War.

For two hundred years and more after the Thirty Years' War, Germany did not recover economically. What happened to the economy, of course, was the result of vast destruction in a war fought for religious reasons. For thirty years, from 1618 to 1648, Protestants fought against Catholics, each allying themselves with foreign nationalities professing similar creeds until every major country of Europe was dragged into the fray. It is estimated that in many sections of Germany 75 percent of the inhabitants were killed in the struggle. Equally bad, 66 percent of the houses, 85 percent of the horses, and 82 percent of the cattle were wiped out. Statistics show further that until 1850 the number of houses and inhabitants in these German territories had not yet been regained.

During the war, undisciplined armies roamed at will foraging and plundering through the countryside. Moral degradation was even worse. Famine drove people to cannibalism; graves were robbed for the flesh and wolves prowled at will. As if this were not enough, ruling potentates authorized the systematic persecution of religious groups. Wherever Protestants gained the upper hand they killed Catholics and when Catholics regained control of the same territory they brutally exterminated the Protestants. Fortune was wholly capricious. Whatever the status one day, it was likely to be reversed the next. Furthermore, in the Germany of that day, the land was held by hundreds of sovereign princes who did nothing to alleviate the process of trade between territories. As a result the economy was mercilessly strangled and even primitive bartering for food was frequently impossible. Clinging to something that was not destructible by rust, dust or the lust of princes, the German peasantry remained fanatically religious.

Thus, when reports and rumors of a promised land reached Germany, potential emigrants everywhere were willing to listen to the shipping agents and the semi-official government representatives who encouraged them to leave their country. What therefore began as a trickle soon swelled to a flood and finally reached tidal wave proportions.

A few statistics gleaned from the 1900 census of the United States show that up to the turn of the last century, Germany had given vastly more immigrants to the United States than any other country except perhaps England. If we restrict the figures to the period 1820-1920, Germany even outstrips England. Using the 1910 census, let us calculate the number of Germans who were living in the United States before World War I sealed off the source. Including Austria and Switzerland as well as the German sections of Poland and Russia in the calculations, we arrive at a total figure of between eighteen and nineteen million persons who were either German-born or had at least one German parent. Faust, in *The German Element,* uses numerous long and complex calculations to determine how many Germans were in the United States in 1910. Taking his most conservative count, we have a figure of 18,500,-000 persons of German blood. This figure represents 27.5 percent of the total American population alive in 1910. We know that after 1910 German immigration slowed down dramatically and that southern and Slavic Europeans comprised the bulk of the new arrivals. Still, if the proportions remained even relatively parallel to the 1910 figures, then today's United States may have even more German than English blood coursing its veins. Comparing the proportions in another way, we learn that in the year 1910, for example, there was more German blood in the population of the United States than the total volume of Spanish and Portuguese blood in all of South America.

An isolated but fascinating story of why German immigrants settled in the United States concerns the Hessian mercenary soldiers who fought for the British during the American Revolutionary War. Writing just after the War, the famous German playwright Friedrich Schiller wrote a tragedy called *Kabale und Liebe* in which a butler tells how a certain German lord in one day had seven thousand of his German subjects sent to America to fight with the British army. The only reason the nobleman had for sending troops was to get enough money to buy precious gems for his female sycophants. When the butler, whose two sons were also in the troop, was asked whether the young men were being sent by force he answered sarcastically, *"O Gott—Nein—lauter Freiwillige!"* (O God no, all volunteers). Surely this story is an exaggeration, but it does tell the basic truth.

One reason why the British government needed the Germans was that the British faced a particular problem in putting down the rebellious colonies in America. Namely, the English soldiers were not completely trustworthy in

firing on their own countrymen, sometimes their own relatives. Thus the government put out feelers at several courts
on the continent offering to hire mercenary soldiers. The
Russians and others declined but several German princes
were only too eager to sell the services of their subjects.
Outstanding for the numbers they sent are the duchies of
Braunschweig (5,723), Hessen-Kassel (16,922), Hessen-
Hanau (2,422), Anspach (2,353), and others. In all there
were about thirty thousand Germans fighting for the English in America.

A curious formula was used to appraise the value of
these soldiers. Taking the Duke of Braunschweig as an example, we find that the ruler received thirty thalers for
each soldier he delivered. But if the soldier died in battle
he received five times that amount. Also, three wounded
soldiers were to be reckoned for pay purposes as one dead
soldier. Unconfirmed reports attributed to Benjamin Franklin state that Duke Friedrich of Hessen-Kassel ordered his
generals to let the wounded die because a dead man was
worth a great deal more to him than a live one.

In an age when every prince wanted to erect his own
sumptuous little "court in Versailles," it is understandable
that the need to obtain funds sometimes took hideous turns.
But these princes were not the first to sell human beings
into battle. The practice of using mercenaries existed among
the Germans for ages. Already in Roman times Germans
hired out to fight Roman wars, and they continued to appear on both sides of virtually every conflict that was waged
in Europe until 1870. During the devastation and starvation of the Thirty Years' War the German peasant fought
for whoever would pay him—one day for the Swedes, the
next for the French, then for the Holy Roman Emperor.

The tactics for pressing young men into service as mercenaries varied but none lacked for brutality. Deserters

were punished frequently with severe public beatings if not death. After all, no ruler wanted to send men to a foreign army only to find that his remuneration was decimated by a failure of his subjects to show up for embarkation.

As for America the Hessians at first enjoyed a reputation of cruelty and invincibility. They were well led and the mere fact of their survival under the awful conditions of shipment attests to their physical strength. Rumor spread among the colonists that Hessians never took prisoners. It was said that they killed civilians without discrimination, and plundered the captured land mercilessly. Generally speaking this was untrue. And a great reverse in popular belief came on December 24th, 1776. It was Christmas eve and late that night Washington crossed the Delaware River to attack Trenton, New Jersey, which was being defended by Hessians. To everyone's great surprise the Hessians were caught unarmed and in many cases intoxicated. This situation resulted in a stunning victory for the Americans, a victory that tremendously nourished the morale of the recruits, dispelling the legendary invincibility of the Hessians.

The Hessian prisoners proved to be respectable men. Even Jefferson enjoyed their music. Many Hessians found life among their captors very civilized, the more so when they discovered that their captors were German immigrants of a few years back. When the Hessian prince heard about the Trenton outcome he was, of course, furious because he feared that his soldiers would no longer bring such an excellent price as mercenaries to the British.

Thereafter the American mood toward the Hessians changed rapidly. Congress even had leaflets printed in German and smuggled into the Hessian camps, promising every Hessian fifty acres of land if he would desert his army and settle in the United States. When such desertions became commonplace there was even a movement (later abandoned) to form a regiment of volunteer Hessians in the American service. Because desertion from any army is a clandestine affair, it is impossible to know exactly how many Hessians chose to remain in America permanently. According to the most reliable estimates, though, the figure is above twelve thousand. In addition, it is believed that thousands initially sent back with their regiments returned later as regular immigrants.

A final major reason why Germans abandoned their Fatherland for the American shores is that of political revolution, specifically, the revolutions of 1848. These revolutions swept Europe in March and through the summer of 1848. Their cause lay deep in the intellectual and social soil of that time. They represented the forces of liberalism on one hand, and the fundamentals of monarchical rule on the other. Politically the revolutions represented the last in a series of struggles to bring democratic rule to Germany. Socially, the revolutions concerned the first rise of the proletariat against the middle class property holders. The 1848 uprising was, in a sense, the first outburst of a movement that was not to gain a single victory until its stunning victory in Russia during the October Revolutions of 1917. In 1848 the rulers in power triumphed over all the upstart elements of the revolution. The result was that intellectuals and political activists were either expelled or they fled from the country.

These Forty-eighters, as they came to be called, brought tremendous gifts to the American scene. They were not numerically great nor were they kneaded into a compact group, but they did possess a capacity for political and military activity unknown in immigrants prior to their arrival. In the book *The Forty-Eighters* edited by A. E. Zucker, one can read about their importance in politics and later in the

Union cause in the American Civil War.

Before 1848, the German immigrant was usually a farmer, artisan or laborer accompanied by a few intellectuals. A Forty-eighter who observed his fellow countrymen from an earlier period of German immigration characterized them as *Stimmvieh*—voting cattle, dull followers who never took any interest in politics beyond the obvious issues that affected them such as temperance and Sabbath laws. For the pre-1848 group it was considered proper to be a Jacksonian Democrat, because the Democratic Party was "friendly" to the Irish and German immigrant. A Wisconsin German newspaper counseled in 1847, "Don't trust the Whigs, they have always opposed the rights of the foreign-born." All these early German immigrants wanted nothing more than to be left alone, to live with their fellow immigrants, and to enjoy the fruits of their labor. Naturally they did not understand the English language nor, to be sure, the importance of voting. After all they came from a system where political experience did not belong to farmers and workers.

When the political revolutionaries arrived after 1848, however, they simply transplanted their old opinions into new soil, planting much of the ideological strife as well. Very shortly they discovered that in American politics voting power was a thing to be bargained for. With enthusiasm they therefore organized party maneuvers, platforms, and demonstrations to counter threats and to extract promises. Besides, as Carl Wittke has pointed out, the Forty-eighters "took keen delight in flaunting their Continental tastes in the face of Americans whom they regarded as little better than barbarians—men without music, culture, or refinement, who were suppressed and crushed by the bigotry of Puritanism." Two vociferous spokesmen for the group of Forty-eighters were Karl Heinzen and Carl Schurz. As a general rule they adamantly opposed slavery and espoused the Republican party with great zeal. Counting scores of learned editors of German newspapers in their following, the Forty-eighters increasingly moulded the German-Americans into a solid block and soon developed a powerful political machine.

After his election in 1860, President Lincoln appointed many Forty-eighters to diplomatic and consular posts abroad to show his appreciation for their support. President Lincoln also wrote to Carl Schurz, "to the extent of our limited acquaintance, no man stands nearer my heart than yourself," and shortly appointed him ambassador to Spain. He even sent many of them back as ambassadors to their own states in Germany against which they had rebelled in 1848. One of them, Gustav Struve, was not accepted as consul to the Thuringian State because of his earlier record, but in all other instances they worked out admirably.

The other area where the Forty-eighters excelled in American life was the military, especially on the side of the Union during the Civil War. In reality, Germany suffered a great intellectual and military loss in the 1848 migrations, and their loss was truly America's gain. Accustomed to attacking, these leaders struck fiercely, not at crowned tyrants this time, but at the slaveholders. Once the war broke out they quickly took to the field to continue the fight and if necessary to die for their ideals. Through the brilliant recruiting leadership of the Forty-eighters, Germans enlisted in the army by droves, far in excess proportionally of any other immigrant group in America.

Partly because the German Forty-eighters possessed expert military skills and partly because the government wanted to reward individuals for getting out the enlistees among their ethnic following, Germans held more than half of all the major generalships allotted to foreigners. Although none of them made truly distinguishing military careers, some of the best known German major generals were Franz Sigel, Carl Schurz, Peter Osterhaus, and Adolf von Steinwehr. Of the nine German-immigrant brigadier generals we mention the following: Alexander von Schimmelpfennig, August von Willich, and Max von Weber.

Von Weber was the colorful commander of the Turner Rifles, the Twentieth New York, having gained experience in the Baden revolt and valuable training in the Karlsruhe Military Academy. Von Willich organized fighting units from Ohio and Indiana and later merited a descriptive entry in General Lew Wallace's *Autobiography* where he reported on the Battle of Shiloh. After fighting in many other famous battles, von Willich received spectacular distinction at Missionary Ridge where his nine regiments scaled the summit before Grant ordered it, thereby generating such enthusiasm that the neighboring troops were swept up the heights with him. Von Schimmelpfennig commanded the Eleventh Corps at Gettysburg where the Confederates overwhelmed two of his divisions driving them back into the streets of the town. But the General hid in a basement to escape capture and later went on to lead his troops at the surrender of Charleston.

The contributions made by German immigrants to the preservation of the Union during the Civil War is commendable. The extent of German participation can be read in the painstaking study published in German by Wilhelm Kaufmann, *Die Deutschen im amerikanischen Bürgerkriege* (Munich, 1911). Kauffmann limits his statistics to men actually born in Germany. Accordingly, he states that 216,-000 German soldiers fought in the war, a figure which Faust, *The German Element in the United States,* finds to be conservative. Moreover, Faust points out that in 1864 there were no more than 1,300,000 German-born people of both sexes residing in the Union states. Dividing the sexes equally, that leaves 650,000 males. If over 200,000 enlisted in the Union Army, that means roughly one in every three German-born males offered his life for his adopted country—a rather remarkable record.

There were, of course, advantages. Bounties for volunteering were attractive. Often immigrants were met at their arrival in northern ports by recruiting officers and induced to sign up. There is even some evidence that recruiters were sent abroad. Senator Wilson of Massachusetts once stated publicly that about one thousand Germans were imported to fill up four regiments from his state. The Germans who served were promised, and eventually got, full rights of American citizenship without the usual papers and delays, providing they received honorable discharge.

Yet regardless of the unnatural stimuli, the fact remains that the Germans made a striking contribution to victory for the North. They vindicated themselves before the charges of nativist newspaper editors and for that matter before their own papers in Germany who frequently referred to the U.S. Civil War as "an overseas orphanage for cracked-up German officers."

This ground-swell of support does not mean that every German immigrant rushed into the fray. Draft riots occurred among the Germans of Milwaukee and other Wisconsin counties. In fact, Milwaukee County voted for McClellan in 1864, in spite of Carl Schurz' preaching for Lincoln. Nevertheless, the German farmers were gradually educated to support the War, especially by the Forty-eighters among them, who struggled valiantly to bring to their countrymen a national consciousness.

There is a final ingredient that set the Forty-eighter apart from earlier German immigrants: in religious matters, he was a freethinker if not an outright atheist. A substantial migration of Germans before 1848 was made up of *Altlutheraner,* orthodox Lutherans who left Germany because King Frederick William III had ordered a combination of the Lutheran and the Calvinist creed into a new "Evangelical" creed. The *Altlutheraner* were staunch conservatives who felt strongly enough about the king's fiat to depart their native land. By contrast, the Forty-eighters were humanists committed to liberalism on all fronts, political and religious. Yet in rejecting dogma in both areas, they made a phenomenal contribution to the climate of personal and religious freedom and to the progressive climate of church-state democracy in America.

In the middle of the nineteenth century, to America's great benefit and to Germany's great misfortune, many of Germany's best minds came to the United States to make their life's contribution. Americans had a deep sympathy and understanding for revolutionary efforts to overthrow despised monarchs. Therefore, those who fled in the aftermath of revolution were received in America as heroes, temporarily defeated of course, but with great vigor for the ideals of freedom that were yet to be contested in the United States.

THE GREAT MINDS

THE GREAT MINDS: THE LAST
IMMIGRATION WAVE

THE FORTY-EIGHTERS would have many things in common
with the latest group of German immigrants to the United
States. Whether we call them refugees, the illustrious immigrants, or the intellectual's migration, the fact remains that
the Forty-eighters and those who arrived on our shores in
the years after the rise of Hitler shared a similar plight.
   Both groups were small. Numerically the Hitler refugees
perhaps exceeded the total we would classify as the Forty-
eighters. But in comparison to the millions of Germans
who came to the United States during a similar period in
the nineteenth century, the statistic of a couple hundred
thousand is almost negligible. Like the Forty-eighters, the
Hitler refugees represented a richly talented and highly
trained group of individuals. Consequently, they had an
impact on the host country far in excess of their numerical
significance. Again, as was the case with the Forty-
eighters, the victims of Nazi upheaval also arrived from
an ordeal charged with intense excitement and heroic
drama. Most experienced privation and hardship; many
narrowly escaped with their lives, and all underwent the
cruel hazards of assuming a meaningful life in the New
World. Virtually every immigrant in the 1930's and 1940's
was forced to emigrate.
   A migration such as this can be termed a hybridization
of nations which has both desirable and difficult social side

effects. Bridging two cultures can result in broadened intellectual horizons—it may even bring a biological enrichment of the fused population. However, it can incite conflicts, tensions and economic hazards. Moreover there can occur a disintegration of social values and ideals both on the part of the immigrants and the native population. A sample study of these effects can be found in Donald P. Kent, *The Refugee Intellectual: The Americanization of the Immigrants of 1933-41* (New York, 1953).

Some data on the number of refugees who arrived in America are available in Kent's book. One of the difficulties we experience in arriving at an exact figure is that the U.S. Government has never classified incoming migrants under the heading "refugees." However, if we take all German immigrants who arrived after the advent of Hitler we have at least an optimal number. It is likely that almost all were genuine refugees since it was not particularly easy or desirable to emigrate from Germany or Austria during the 1933-41 period. Accordingly, we have a total of 104,098 immigrants from Germany-Austria. The highest number for a single year is in 1939, with a heavy accumulation during the months immediately before the outbreak of World War II.

While the immigrants from these countries prior to 1930 tended to be young and unmarried, the refugees arriving during the Hitler period tended to be much older. A full 25 percent were over 45, and nearly 50 percent of them were married. This indicates that the Hitler migration was primarily a family movement and reconfirms the theory that it was a forced transplanting. Of those immigrants who chose to register a profession with the U.S. Immigration Service, only 7,623 can be categorized as strictly professional. The two largest groups were the medical doctors with 2,352 followed by educators with 1,090.

This is not to minimize the fact that an unusually large proportion of the immigrants were well-educated and possessed special skills or knowledge.

Hardly surprising is the fact that a full 76 percent of the incoming aliens from Germany and Austria listed their race as "Hebrew." The true percentage is probably even higher since the Immigration Service does not include a classification for religion and Jews would not universally think of "Hebrew" when announcing their race. Kent, in his book, indicates that the total percent of Jewish immigrants may well have been over 80 percent. The balance of immigrants listed themselves sometimes as "non-Aryans," or even as non-Jewish. Frequently they were the wives and husbands of Jews.

It is hard to generalize about the German-Austrian immigrant-refugee. Laura Fermi, *Illustrious Immigrants: The Intellectual Migration from Europe 1930-41* (Chicago, 1968), draws a few broad generalizations about the Germans, which are probably valid for the Austrians as well. For instance, while still in Germany, the emigrés (with the possible exception of those in the natural sciences) all looked down on the status of American culture. This attitude was not so much the result of despising American civilization as it was of the positive opinion they held regarding their own *Kultur*. They had never bothered to pay attention to a society and culture as young as the American. As Fermi puts it, "German scholars were then convinced, as some openly admitted much later, that there was only one humanism, one Protestant theology, one philosophy, and one way to look at social questions—the German."

Once in the United States, though, the open-minded German scholars adapted quickly. Generally they were overwhelmed by the friendliness, tolerance, and even the high

academic competence of their American colleagues. There
were other surprises. Generally the refugees were horrified
by what they witnessed in the American "child-centered
home." Catering to the child's desires was damned by the
German authoritarian paterfamilias as "American softness."
As a matter of fact, however, the vast majority of immigrant families who had children soon acceded to the wishes
of their children, particularly on the matter of language. It
is astounding how few of the children in immigrant families
grew up speaking German. Usually, even when their parents addressed them in German, the younger generation
would respond only in English.

At Ohio State University I knew a German immigrant family intimately. In the home the professor and his
wife tried with the best of intentions to raise their two boys
bilingually. It did not work. Not only did they refuse to
utter a word of German once they began junior high school,
but the one boy actually failed his Ph.D. examination at
Harvard because he could not pass the qualifying section
in German.

Learning English was of course one of the primary tasks
of the intellectual if he were to continue to function in his
adopted country. Many refused to speak, read, or think a
word of German until they could handle English ade-
quately. One refugee remarked that he experienced great
difficulty with such phrases as: I'll let you know, I'll keep
in touch, That would be unwise, I'm afraid there are, Do
call on me some time, I'll be seeing you.

Another refugee made observations, as reported in Kent's
book, page fifty-four, about finding work in America: "An
employer never says 'No job! I don't want you! You are
not able enough for this job.' Rather he says, 'I'm awfully
sorry but right at this time we just don't have a vacancy in
your line. However, we'll keep you in mind, and something

may develop shortly. And we do appreciate your applying and are aware of your fine qualifications.' As Europeans we left feeling elated. Our qualifications were good. He'll keep us in mind. When something develops which he thinks will in a short time, he'll get in touch with us. Now we recognize that this was a refusal just as much as the blunt rejection of a German employer. However, we left feeling good; not angry and bitter. The American way of softening all social contacts prevents this. This is the genius of America."

Similarly, a German professor employed as a guest lecturer at a large American university in the mid-1960's once told the following incident: At a fall coffee hour for the new faculty the president of the university stood in a receiving line with his wife to be introduced to the new professors. Chatting later with the president's wife, the German professor received an invitation to visit at the president's house. According to the professor's version of the story, she said: "Do drop in and see us." When? "Oh, just any time, we'd love to have you." One fine Sunday afternoon a couple of weeks later my friend, in typical German fashion, went strolling and decided to drop in at the president's house. He came away knowing the meaning of still another American phrase: "Do drop in any time" really means, "It was pleasant to meet you at this social hour."

One German scholar-refugee described his impressions of America as a land of the harmonious collective life. He felt that whereas the European newcomer seeks culture in depth, Americans emphasize the faculty of adjustment, the peace of the community, the genius of compromise. "Europe with all her astounding achievements in human genius has not been able to preserve her heritage because she did not equally develop the art of social solidarity. I would advise him to study the way in which the American people, in their daily lives, practice this art and are continuously concerned with its perfection."

Not long ago I was on an airplane returning from Germany. Next to me sat a dapper young German who held a Ph.D. in economics from Berlin University. Upon graduation he had visited the United States and toured different corporations and factories here. His dream was to apply the genius of American industrial management to industries in his native country. Frustrated in his attempts, he wrote a book about the growing management gap afflicting German industry today, had it accepted for publication in Germany, and was returning to America to accept a position in management at International Business Machines.

Eventually we must ask ourselves what the infusion of immigrant intellectuals from Germany and Austria has done for America. On a scientific and technical basis, of course, the contribution has been enormous. Most who entered the professions in the United States were forced in one way or another to assimilate in order to survive. This necessity coupled with good intentions enabled the German-Austrians to have a solid influence on America. Advising his fellow immigrants, one refugee from Germany wrote: "Realize that personal recommendations, neat appearance, readiness to work over and above your regular duties, and willingness to become Americanized mean more than any number of degrees or previously acquired fame. Think of what you can give to America, not of what you can get out of her." The last sentence is hauntingly reminiscent of President Kennedy's famous phrase in his inaugural address, "Ask not what your country can do for you, ask what you can do for your country."

Certainly the most recent wave of German immigrants to our shores has made spectacular infusions to our culture

and civilization. We can point with great pride to Albert
Einstein, Thomas Mann, Bertolt Brecht, and Bruno Walter.
Yet, one could question whether any previous wave of immigrants was so little integrated into American life as these
illustrious ones. The "Latin Farmers" of a century earlier
put their hands to the plow and dug into the soil. The
Forty-eighters as a rule became towering statures in the
fields of American politics, journalism, music and literature. In contrast, the immigrants of the 30's and 40's were,
to a considerable extent, anxious to get back once their
hostile governments had been eradicated.

Having come primarily for physical safety and only sec-
ondarily out of love for democracy and hate for tyranny,
numerous intellectual immigrants might well have agreed
with one of their colleagues: "We are difficult arrivals. We
do not know how to till the soil, we are not fellers of trees,
and only a few of us are masters of a craft. We shelter li-
braries and phonograph records in our much too narrow
rooms, and we cling fondly to the pleasures and arts amid
which we have grown up. With every fiber we are still tied
to the tragedy beneath which Europe is still collapsing."

So after the War many did return to Europe, often for
substantial reasons. Lawyers and other professionals wanted
to continue their work without completely retraining. Writers found it difficult to live in an English-language atmosphere and write about a German one. Hans Sahl, however,
found that he could observe his people better from a distance, claiming that a writer isn't at his best in the language
he uses to order a cup of coffee. Some professors returned
because they missed the high social status. Laura Fermi
points out in her book that Paul Tillich commented on
his shift from a German to an American university by
claiming "he had come down seven steps on the social
ladder."

Others like Arnold Bergsträsser could truly maintain, "Germany is where I am." Departing from the Fatherland in 1937, Bergsträsser taught in Claremont, California. Later, in 1944, he headed a specialized program at the University of Chicago, training soldiers to operate the coming military government in Germany. Through his influence and publications he attracted many of his countrymen to the University. Believing himself a part of Germany abroad, he arranged the Goethe Festival at Aspen, Colorado in 1949, the first in a long series of Aspen summer programs. One year later he, too, returned to Germany where he died in 1964.

There were brighter stars who stayed in the United States or died before they could leave. As Laura Fermi recalls, Albert Einstein was the "man with jet-black eyes, a big halo of white hair, and no socks." Fermi remembered little of her dinner with him except for the strong impact of his presence. Not just to Fermi but to all Americans, Einstein's presence was in itself all-important, not his actions or his words. He was really a symbolic figure after his arrival in the United States. He did not teach and seldom lectured. He just spent his solitary and aloof existence at home in Princeton, New Jersey.

The story of Wernher von Braun is quite different. Born on an estate in Posen in eastern Germany, his father was Secretary of Agriculture in one of the last cabinets of the Weimar Republic. At the age of fourteen when Wernher was confirmed, he received a prophetic gift from his mother, a telescope. Ironically, in the French *Gymnasium* in Berlin he got such poor grades, worst of all in physics and math, that his father decided to send him to an agricultural boarding school near Weimar. There he went to school in the morning and worked on a farm in the afternoon. One day he bought a book, *The Rocket to the Interplanetary*

Spaces. His heart nearly stopped when he opened it to find it full of mathematical formulae. From that moment on he resolved to master math, the gateway to his love.

After study at the Institute of Technology in Berlin, Wernher von Braun and some colleagues procured an old weedy ammunition dump near Berlin and grandiosely named it "Rocket Field Berlin." One day in 1932 some officers of the German Army stopped at the "Field" and from then on von Braun became a civilian employee of the Army, entitled to the handsome proving grounds at Kummersdorf. At the tender age of twenty he had unlimited facilities for experimentation at his disposal. In 1934 von Braun launched his first successful rockets, a team called Max and Moritz, the German models for the American comic strip characters known as the "Katzenjammer kids." Subsequently, in 1937 the rocket team received new quarters and a 250-mile missile range at Peenemüde on the Baltic Sea.

After war broke out in 1939 the scientists were commissioned to forget space travel and to concentrate on the long range delivery of weapons. Thus in October, 1942, under the strictest secrecy precautions, they tested a rocket that soared over sixty miles and traveled a distance of over one hundred and twenty miles. This became the infamous V-2, the *Vergeltungswaffe,* which means "weapon of revenge" or "retribution." One night, about a year later, the Gestapo awakened von Braun and whisked him off to prison in Stettin, under charges that he was still thinking only of space and was therefore guilty of sabotaging the war effort. Only the last minute intervention of Hitler himself saved von Braun's life. When the V-2 rockets were first sent over England in 1944, von Braun remarked, "We designed it to blaze the trail to other planets, not to destroy our own."

With Germany in a near state of collapse despite the V-2

weapons, von Braun and his team decided that only the vast resources of the United States could ensure the future of space travel. He and his team therefore packed what they could into trucks, abandoned the Peenemünde range and headed west. In our country, simultaneously, there was a program underway known as "Operation Paperclip" whose purpose was to lure German scientific men and equipment to our shores. Under the leadership of Wernher von Braun, about 120 scientists, chemists, aerodynamicists, metallurgists, etc., signed contracts with the American Army to go to the United States and work on rockets.

Sixteen shiploads of captured documents and hardware came with them. Until 1950 von Braun and his fellow scientists sat under the hot sun of Fort Bliss, Texas, tinkering with their captured German equipment. Finally, after the outbreak of the Korean War they were moved to Huntsville, Alabama. There they developed the Redstone missile, first tested at Cape Canaveral (now Kennedy) in 1953. By 1955 the United States had publicly announced that they would launch an earth satellite for the International Geophysical Year in 1957. The Russians were faster, however, launching their satellite on October 4, 1957. Von Braun and his team were immediately given more assistants and accomplished the same task with Explorer I on January 31, 1958.

The story of space exploration since then is well known. Caught repeatedly in the crossfire of questions about cost and "What is the use?" of rocketry and space travel, Wernher von Braun has tirelessly explained and instructed our whole population. Perhaps his best answer to queries is when he asks a question in return: "What is the use of a newborn baby?"

Early in 1969 we saw still another scientist of German origin, this time a political scientist, elevated to the pinnacle of American life. He is the personal foreign affairs adviser to President Nixon, Henry A. Kissinger. Born in Fürth, Germany in 1923, he came to the United States at the age of fifteen. Graduating from Harvard *summa cum laude,* he stayed on there to become a distinguished professor. By 1958 he had already achieved distinction in the form of a citation by the Overseas Press Club for his writings on foreign affairs and, in the same year, the Woodrow Wilson prize for the best book in the field of government and politics. Once again in 1965 Kissinger was acclaimed for his writings concerning a reappraisal of the Atlantic Alliance, which did much to win him selection by the President of the United States as a foreign policy adviser.

The scientists were by no means the only contributors. There were many, many others in all areas of the arts as well. The world of the Austrian theater and letters was transported to America in the person of Max Reinhardt. From his arrival in 1933 until his death ten years later, Reinhardt was a titan on the theatrical scene. His assistant, John Reich, is still the head of the Goodman Theater of the Art Institute in Chicago. Bruno Walter became director of the New York Symphony Orchestra. Walter Gropius arrived to teach at the Massachusetts Institute of Technology and profoundly influenced the world of American architecture. Mies van der Rohe designed the Illinois Institute of Technology in Chicago. Marcel Breuer has gained fame for his conception of the St. John's University campus at Collegeville, Minnesota. There were painters such as Max Beckmann and Wassily Kandinsky, the cartoonist and critic Georges Grosz, literary critics like Ernst Cassirer and Oskar Seidlin, and the writers Mann, Werfel, Brecht, Beer-Hoffmann, and Zuckmayer. Who can forget the remarkable list of Austrian musicians? Arnold Schoenberg, Erich Leinsdorf, Erich Korngold, Karl

Geiringer, Hans Tischler and Artur Schnabel. Of Schnabel the *Boston Globe* recently reported the following anecdote: After a performance of Beethoven's *Moonlight Sonata* one critic viciously panned Schnabel who in turn phoned the critic the following morning at 2 a.m., shouting, "Who are *you* to say Schnabel played the Moonlight poorly? I say he was superb." Half asleep the critic demanded, "Who is this?" to which Schnabel snapped, "This is Beethoven," and hung up.

In passing we ought to mention Rudolf Flesch, a Viennese who turned his back on European law because the training was useless for the United States, to become a guardian of the English language. Six months after being admitted to the bar, Flesch came to America—Hitler had taken over Vienna. Flesch was later to write to Lauri Fermi, "Without resources — and certainly without the chance of going through an American law school all over again, I worked in the School of Library Science at Columbia University." Later he earned a Ph.D. with a dissertation on the "Marks of a Readable Style." It made available a statistical formula to test the readability of English prose. There followed numerous books, among them *The Art of Plain Talk* and *The Art of Readable Writing,* about which Alan Gould, editor of the Associated Press wrote ". . . the impact of Dr. Flesch's ideas on simpler, clearer ways of writing represents one of the most significant developments of our journalistic times." Many more books followed, including *The ABC of Style* and the sometimes controversial *Why Johnny Can't Read.*

From the years 1933 to about 1950 American shores were again, in the words of Crevecoeur, "every man's country." With open arms America once again took in the hungry, needy, well-educated, but poor refugees, without asking a price. But for her efforts she has been rewarded many times over by the exuberant creativity and restless experimentation of her adopted children.

Deutschland, Deutschland über alles

1. Deutschland, Deutschland ü - ber al - les, ü - ber al - les in der
2. Deut - sche Frau - en, deutsche Treu - e, deutscher Wein und deut - scher
3. Ei - nig - keit und Recht und Frei - heit für das deut - sche Va - ter -

Welt, wenn es stets zum Schutz und
Sang sol - len in der Welt
-land! Da - nach laßt

-lich zu
al -
-lich mit Herz und Hand

Me - mel, von der Etsch bis an den Belt Deutschland,
-gei - stern un - ser gan - zes Le - ben lang. Deut - sche
Frei - heit sind des Glü - ckes Un - ter - pfand. Blüh im

al - les in der Welt!
Wein und deutscher Sang!
deut - sches Va - ter - land!

T Heinrich Hoffmann von Fallersleben
M Joseph Haydn
„Gott erhalte Franz, den Kaiser"

PATRIOTISM AND ITS SYMBOLS

PATRIOTISM AND ITS SYMBOLS

THE UNITY OF the Kaiser's Empire and the monolithic facade created for Hitler's Reich have obscured a very significant fact about the Fatherland—its lack of unity. One hundred years ago there was no such thing as a political Germany, only a cultural tradition and an unfulfilled hope. Few countries in history have seen such tortuous division as Germany. Foreign influences, dynastic struggles, international storms, divergent ethnic backgrounds and not least, religious quarrels have rent the family of the Fatherland for as long as history can remember. Even the German language has varied so much from locale to locale that it has never become a cohesive force in the country.

Against this somber background one must bear in mind Germany's geographic position. Carved out of the heart of central Europe, Germany more than any other country on the continent has forever been accessible to foreign domination. In fact, Germany has only one natural boundary, the Alpine range with Austria. Yet paradoxically Austria is the only country on Germany's frontiers that is culturally, linguistically and ethnically identical to her. Paradoxically also, Germany has never yielded to a Latin culture directly, despite her situation of swinging doors throughout all of recorded time. Countless ancient tribes and innnumerable foreign armies have crossed and recrossed her at will. Like America, through the course of history, Germany became a melting pot. Each time new ingredients were thrown in a new mixture resulted, altering the temperature and pressure erratically. The difficulty is that the contents of the German pot never fused into a homogeneous unity. As if weary of a unity forged from too many variants, again today Germany is torn asunder.

No one would deny that Germans long for reunification, but one must admit that they like their local traditions and ways of life even more than unity. East Germany is of course still sealed off, but in West Germany the citizens are at least free—freer on the whole than they have ever been before. Still, moving around in this new climate one is not as impressed by the freedom as a whole, as by the regional differences. In the west there is plenty of Latin stock and in the east enough Slavic blood, but what about the composite? For centuries dissimilar families have remained in their specific towns. Thus, from generation to generation the characteristics of each locale have grown stronger, and loyalty to the community has taken on "patriotic" proportions. A German is above all proud to be a Müncher, Frankfurter, or Schwarzwälder. To be a "German" is fine, too, but it is secondary.

Today, however, one can no longer trust first impressions in West Germany, not so much because in our modern world people tend to move around more, but because of Russia's policies of expulsion of ethnic Germans immediately following World War II. At that time approximately eight million refugees of German stock were driven out of the territories east of the Oder and the Neisse Rivers. By a West German decree these refugees were injected into the regional territories of the West in numbers proportional to the population. Thus people from Silesia, Pomerania, East Prussia, Danzig and from the many pockets of *Volksdeutsche* are now mingled with the "native" West Germans.

By *Volksdeutsche* is meant the millions of Germans who had emigrated from their homeland to settle and colonize throughout eastern Europe, especially in southern Russia and in Rumania, Hungary and Czechoslovakia. In addition to these we must include in the total of eastern stock now living in West Germany, the over three million refugees from East Germany who managed to reach the West before the Berlin Wall finally plugged the escape hole in 1961.

Naturally Germans are patriotic and love their Fatherland, but they love their own particular region much more. After almost twenty-five years in exile expellees still long for the day when they may be permitted to return to their own *Heimat,* which to them means not necessarily East Germany, but their native regions. The Silesians, Sudeten Germans, Pomeranians, etc., assiduously maintain their societies and clubs. They even vote in blocs for the party which supports what they feel is a legitimate claim to their *Heimat.*

Because of strong regionalism, each state, kingdom or principality has always had its own flag and coat of arms. There was no Germany for centuries, hence, there wasn't a national flag of Germany until 1871. When suddenly one was needed, they chose the flag which had been adopted four years earlier by the North German Confederation— three horizontal stripes of black, white and red. These three colors had a twofold source representing on one hand the black and white coat of arms of Prussia and on the other, the white and red in the flag of the Hanseatic League. The black, white and red stripes remained in the flag until after the birth of the German Republic in 1918. At that time the colors were changed to black, red and gold, representing a flag used in the abortive revolutions for democracy in 1848. During the rule of Hitler the black *Hakenkreuz* (swastika) on a red banner served as the flag, but it was replaced again after the war by the black, red and gold stripes, used today by both the Federal Republic of West Germany and the German Democratic Republic in East Germany. The latter has, however, superimposed a circle in the seal of the flag which displays a hammer and compass surrounded by a wreath of grain with a black, red and gold ribbon woven into it.

Of course, there is nothing particularly German about the use of flags. The origin of flags rests on an ancient religious practice which called for the exhibition of insignia which later became flags. Mounted on the top of a pole, this military standard was intended as a sacred symbol to give discomfort to an enemy. Later the Romans had a similar practice of carrying the vexillum, a cavalry flag, into battle. The vexillum is still used today in Roman Catholic religious ceremonies. Because the vexillum manifested a cross it was spontaneously adopted by the early Christians. After Constantine's conversion in 312, the flag displaying a cross quickly gained prominence. When the crusades were being waged in the eleventh and twelfth centuries, Europeans widely copied the use of flags by proclaiming the cross as their motto and even by wearing crosses sewn on their chests and backs. Wearing the flag by the crusading knights came to imply a semi-religious vow to bear arms for the Christian cause not only in the Holy Land but everywhere.

From this medieval tradition came the practice still prevalent in many European countries of using some form of the cross in their flags. A few such nations are: all five of the Scandinavian countries, Switzerland, Greece and, though less obviously, Great Britain.

From 1871 until 1918 Germany had a special national flag of war which exhibited the ancient pattern of a cross. It had a white background with a black cross on the front and the German eagle fixed in a circle at the intersection of the cross. In the upper left hand corner were the black, white and red stripes, a miniature of the regular flag. Over the tiny flag was superimposed the traditional black iron cross. Far from anything associated with a Nazi cause, the German iron cross is simply another ramification of the crusaders' cross. For centuries Germans who had distinguished themselves in battle were given the iron cross, much as Americans are given medals for bravery, merit and honor. Today the figure of the iron cross is the recognized insignia on all West German military equipment, similarly as the star is the American insignia for our military hardware.

Nationalism vs. regionalism — these seeming contradictions are still the two sweeping generalizations that can be made about Germany. Bismarck forged a unity out of the regions in 1871 by means of "Blood and Iron." Through sinister and clever tactics Hitler was, however, even more successful. At convocations of youth and soldiers during the Hitler regime, individuals repeated one after another, *"ich komme aus Preussen, ich komme aus Bayern, ich komme aus dem Rheinland,"* etc., and then they chanted as one loud chorus in unison, *"ein Volk, ein Reich, ein Führer."* (One people, one empire, one leader.) The idea behind the slogan had but one purpose—to brainwash regionalism from the common people and motivate them to a strong sense of national unity. In part, of course, the technique was successful. The great irony is that the final legacy left to the German people by this program is total and perhaps permanent division. What is more, many states, Prussia included, have been rubbed completely off the map.

In the states that have survived, deep-rooted regional loyalty has not been eradicated or transcended. A Bavari-

an's dislike for the Prussians (sows, he calls them) is unbelievable. His intense love for his native Bavaria would
shame any Texan. In part because the Prussians have dominated the military training procedures of the nation the
southern Germans dislike them. Furthermore, for hundreds
of years Prussians have been Lutherans while the south
German states have always been Catholic. The Bavarians
like to take life easier, and this in turn has elicited much
scorn from the Prussians.

In fact, the Main River is a kind of Mason-Dixon line
in Germany. Those who live north of it consider themselves
more cosmopolitan, industrial and hard-working. South of
the Main and west of the Rhine, the people, their lives, and
their architecture are different. Like the southern Germans
the Rhinelanders are Catholic, and religion determines
dress, social habits, and political party affiliation. Wayside
shrines of crucifixes or madonnas speckle the landscape in
these areas. The holy days are state holidays that have to
be observed by Protestants as well as Catholics. *Fasching*
or *Karnival* festivals on the eve of Lent, though celebrated
all over Germany, are by far the most elaborate in Catholic
areas. Although we shall have more to say about these festivals later, it is well to note here that these cities dominate
the pre-lenten season by their gaiety: *München* (Munich),
Mainz, and *Köln* (Cologne), and to a lesser extent also
Düsseldorf.

In southern Germany and in the Rhineland we find the
strongholds of the Christian Democratic Party which is
heavily Catholic. The party's great leader, Konrad Aden-
auer, the architect of post-war Germany, was himself a
Catholic Rhinelander. Religious division also influences
state politics. Although local states are in a federal republic, they retain sovereign control over their educational system—a legal tactic which nourishes stark regional differ-

ences in attitudes and training. What is more, the states still have much to do with the religious instruction in the schools and this tends to perpetuate the religious split along the state boundaries.

This "authority" over religion goes back to the Peace of Augsburg, of 1555. In that year a compromise was reached between the Catholic Holy Roman Emperor, Charles V, and the supporters of German Lutheranism. The formula laid down read *"cuius regio, eius religio."* Whoever has the territory, he determines which religion. Thus the prince could decide which religion was to be practiced in his country and for a time those who did not like it were invited to move elsewhere. But after the prescribed time for changing, entire states became either Protestant or Catholic, a phenomenon which to a large extent still persists to this day.

Separating the states along religious boundaries produced other cultural disparities. One of the obvious ones was the sympathy of the Catholic states to the Hapsburg rulers of Austria and to the Renaissance architecture of Catholic Italy. A gay and gracious Baroque style drifted across cities like Munich, Regensburg, Passau, Würzburg and many others. Even now, stucco curlicues still laugh with color, bathed in the light from big windows. Everywhere the *Zwiebeltürme,* onion-shaped slate-covered steeples, puncture the skies of the Bavarian landscape. Even older Gothic structures like Freiburg, Ulm and Köln are now more richly ornamented than their counterparts farther north. *Oberbayern,* the Bavaria mountain regions, has numerous Benedictine abbeys decorated in fine Baroque patterns.

North of the Main and east of the Rhine the Protestant Reformation has scrubbed away much of the ornamentation and in a sterner mood has put a premium on simplicity.

Also, northerners have a flaxen-haired, blue-eyed look and they prefer their formal approach to things. Whereas the southern German likes his folksongs, yodelling, and beer drinking music, the northerner is more austere, and believes himself too sophisticated for these antics. Likewise, the northerner believes that he is more industrious and efficient, somehow more orderly in all of life. Seemingly because of this bent, the rural people in the North are also more superstitious, less reassured by participation in the formalities of religion than is true in the South. Considering these tremendously divergent characteristics, it would, of course, be silly to try to describe what constitutes the German national character.

Probing the German national character is an endless pastime, one which inspires awesome admiration and bitter hatred. There is an abundance of childlike tenderness alongside monstrous cruelty—or at least so writers have charged. Journalists complain that everything is *verboten* (forbidden), and historians of democratic systems bemoan the German's servility to the state and obedience to the petty official. Proverbs extoll the cult of order: *"Ordnung ist das halbe Leben"* (order is half of life), *Wohlerzogen hat nie gelogen"* (a good up-bringing never deceives), *"Kein warum ohne darum"* (no why without its because), *"Erst besinnen, dann beginnen"* (first think, then begin), and *"Heilige Ordnung, segensreiche Himmelstochter"* (holy order, the richly blessed daughter of heaven). In a way there is an even more pronounced way of expressing the German penchant for order. It is by the phrase which in English means "everything's O.K.," for which the German says *"Alles in Ordnung,"* literally, everything is in order. What does all this prove about the Germans and their deviation from their neighbors? Well, let us agree. The Germans have a point, maybe an obsession, about wanting even routine matters in their places and running smoothly, but that is about all that can be said about *the* German character.

Instead of more analysis, let us turn to some of the methods by which all people, including the Germans, symbolize their regional loyalty, namely, by the use of coats of arms. Sometimes called "Heralds," or more correctly "Armor," the coat of arms is a system of symbols on a shield developed during the medieval period to give personal recognition. Soon the practice became hereditary and a certain shield then belonged to a specific family. At a time when only clerks could read, of course, it was essential that markings be devised to document ownership. It is thought that at one time the coat of arms was truly a garment of recognition worn in battle as a uniform and serving the same purpose as our insignia.

By the end of the twelfth century, that is after many European nations had fought together in the crusades, coats of arms and seals bearing arms became common. They developed out of necessity during the common conflict when large armies had to be marked by visible signs. Soon the practice of heraldry became an essential part of the official and ceremonial functioning of feudal society. Civil as well as martial affairs required it. The German word for "coat of arms" is *Wappen,* low German for the High German word, *Waffe,* which means "weapon." Notice that in English we say "arms," that is, we use the Latin word whereas the medieval instigators could have selected the English word "weapon" which is of Germanic origin and is directly related to *Wappen.*

An entire system of language is necessary to describe the art of making and using the *Wappen.* Naturally since arms are essentially coded messages conveyed by pictures and symbols, the reader or viewer must know how to interpret them. Without going into technical terms, one might note that colors, animals, plants, the division of the shield, use of cogged wheels, borders, crests, braids, geometric patterns, wreaths, streamers and countless other devices are employed to impart the complex meaning in a coat of arms.

In most countries there were legal restrictions established by the Crown which governed the issuance and the use of *Wappen* and which prevented them from being assumed by just anybody. Only the nobility used arms and people were given the status of nobility only by authority of the Court. In a case where the central authority was weak, or as in Germany where it was virtually non-existent, many non-noble burghers and patrician families also practiced the custom of displaying coats of arms. In some territories it was even possible to buy the privilege and often unscrupulous princes used the technique to raise money. In certain sections of Germany and Austria even the peasantry commonly used arms as part of the family heritage.

Thus in Germany we have both the *bürgerliche Wappen* (Civil Coats of Arms) and the *adlige Wappen* (Nobility Coats of Arms). Even more surprising, *Bäuerliche Wappen* (peasant use of a coat of arms) have occurred in Germany from as early as the thirteenth century. From this loose adaptation of the coat of arms to show personal identity, there developed the widespread use of the territorial arms and state arms. Sometimes these derive from a prominent family in that area, at other times from state seals. Usually if the coat of arms is for a city it includes some feature from the state in which the city lies. For example, Stuttgart(*Stute Garten* or Horse Farm) has a horse on its shield and the imperial cities of Germany have always included the imperial eagle in their crests. It is interesting to note that before 1920 the county divisions of Prussia were forbidden to use arms because it symbolized decentralized authority, whereas in Bavaria, Baden, Würtemberg and the other states, counties and cities had always used such symbols of local allegiance.

Prussia, the state where military and noble correctness was a long defined ritual, forbade the ill-defined use of the arms symbolism. Likewise, Prussia fostered and enjoyed far greater state loyalty and centralized patriotism than was ever developed in the remaining states of Germany. In other words, the everyday symbols of unity have, in Germany, often characterized the local region as more worthy of altruism than the centralized government. Today the official coat of arms for the Federal Republic is a simple black eagle on a yellow shield. Many of the states and cities have far more elaborate and imperious looking arms all fixed on shields. Only Prussia has no shield and no complicated symbols, only a true-to-life image of a gray eagle.

For purposes of tending the uses of arms as well as for scientific study of their importance in the past there is the *Deutsche Zentralstelle für Heraldik* founded in 1946 and located in Stuttgart.

No discussion of German partiotism and its symbols would be complete without mentioning the national anthem. The music of the national anthem was composed at a time when the German nation still did not exist, in a country that was never incorporated into the German nation, for a Kaiser who never ruled Germany, by a man who almost never set foot in Germany—Franz Joseph Haydn. Born in lower Austria in 1732, he died in Vienna in March, 1809. In the year 1797 when the imperial court in Vienna was worried about the revolutionary influences touching Austria from France, Haydn was persuaded to compose a melody that would be appropriately patriotic for a national anthem. So it was that Haydn wrote what was considered by many to be one of the best national songs ever written. Its title was *"Gott erhalte Franz den Kaiser"* (May God Uphold

Emperor Francis II). The anthem was sung for the first time on the emporer's birthday, February 12, 1797.

Haydn's melody was appropriated by the German Republic for its national anthem in 1922 and the words were taken from a poem by Heinrich Hoffman von Fallersleben (1798-1874). Once a professor of German literature in Breslau, the poet became mixed up in the early student demonstrations for a more liberal government there, and was dismissed from his position at the university and forced to flee the state of Silesia. Living in semi-exile on the island of Helgoland off the northern coast of Germany, he wrote the spirited *Deutschlandslied,* a poem which to its author was a heart-felt outpouring of the spirit of freedom and love of country. Ironically, during World War II many people outside of Germany came to view the poem as a threat to the freedom of all other nations simply because they misunderstood the first verse, "Germany above all else," being interpreted as "Germany over everybody." Sensitive to world opinion, the Federal Republic in 1950 voted to adopt the third verse as the official national hymn and to abandon the "offensve" first verse. Following is the poem as Hoffman von Fallersleben wrote it in 1841:

Das Lied der Deutschen

> *Deutschland, Deutschland über alles,*
> *Über alles in der Welt,*
> *Wenn es stets zu Schutz und Trutze*
> *Brüderlich zusammenhält,*
> *Von der Maas bis an die Memel,*
> *Von der Etsch bis an der Belt—*
> *Deutschland, Deutschland über alles,*
> *Über alles in der Welt!*

Germany, Germany above all else,
Above everything in the world,
If in matters of defense it
Will forever stick together,
From the Maas to the Memel,
From the Etsch to the Belt—
Germany, Germany above all else,
Above all else in the world.

Deutsche Frauen, deutsche Treue,
Deutscher Wein und deutscher Sang
Sollen in der Welt behalten
Ihren alten schönen Klang,
Uns zu edler Tat begeistern
Unser ganzes Leben lang—
Deutsche Frauen, deutsche Treue,
Deutscher Wein und deutscher Sang!

German women, German loyalty,
German wine and German song
Ought in all the world to
Retain their beautiful old tones,
And inspire us to noble deeds
Our whole life long—
German women, German loyalty,
German wine and German song.

Einigkeit und Recht und Freiheit
Für das deutsche Vaterland!
Danach lasst uns alle streben
Brüderlich mit Herz und Hand!
Einigkeit und Recht und Freiheit
Sind des Glückes Unterpfand—
Blüh' im Glanze dieses Glückes,
Blühe, deutsches Vaterland!

Unity and Justice and Freedom
For the German Fatherland!
To that goal let us all strive
Brotherly, with heart and hand!
Unity justice and freedom
Are the pledge of this good fortune,
Bloom in the glow of this good fortune,
Bloom, German Fatherland!

As the fortunes of the world would have it, the author of the poem was banished from his country for writing this and other "overly liberal" political poems. In effect the poet's government was too right-winged for his kind of free, left-wing sentiment. A hundred years later, however, the world judged the poem itself to be too far right—believing that the words were a statement of Hitler's official policy of world domination. In the face of this dichotomy, the German people today do not respond with enthusiastic patriotism when they hear their national anthem.

When the post-war West Germans selected the third verse of the poem as their national anthem, they truly chose words that express a wish that has for two thousand years represented the seemingly unattainable dream of the German people for: unity, justice and freedom.

The problem of unity, justice and freedom—that is really the German problem. Germans sometimes say they are not responsible for their country's history and to a point they are right. Outside pressures have frequently determined their destiny. During the Thirty Years' War, Spanish armies ravaged central Germany. Danes invaded south into Braunschweig. Catholic France intervened along the Rhine to prevent the Austrian family of Hapsburg from taking control of northern Germany. The Swedish king Gustavus Adolphus marched through the north at will until he was killed in a battle near Leipzig. All sense of unity, justice and freedom disappeared.

During the eighteenth century the dream of a German nation persisted, but the leadership was impotent. Bavaria was one of many states with fierce patriotism, but only to itself. Hanover was linked with England when its George Ludwig became George I of England. A great many cities retained their imperial autonomy until recent times. States such as Mecklenburg, Hessen-Darmstadt, and Würtemberg wasted their energies maintaining courts of fairy-tale irrelevance. Other states like Hessen-Kassel squandered their manpower on the British armies for money to support their profligate ways of life. Austria was the logical source of German unity but its traditions were too dynastic and its interests too closely centered around the lower Danube. Worst of all, Austria was Catholic and the northern state of Prussia was Lutheran and powerful. Hence Austria could have done little to unify the German states even if she had wanted to.

What Bismarck accomplished in 1871 lasted but a short seventy-five years. In a way today's divided Germany is more historically natural than Bismarckian unity ever was. But in many ways the lasting division is for the German people more bitter than their defeat. Today especially the Germans in the eastern zone must still dream the words of their former national anthem, "Unity, justice and freedom/ For the German Fatherland!" To the East German Communist regime the German national anthem of the Weimar Republic smacked of the Right and Nazism, and so both the poem and the music were rejected. In its place they sing a melody composed by Hans Eisler for a poem *"Auferstanden aus Ruinen"* (Ressurrection From Ruins) written by Johannes R. Becher, one-time cultural minister and poet laureate of the East German state.

THE LANGUAGE

THE LANGUAGE
HIGH GERMAN, LOW GERMAN, DIALECTS
OF GERMAN

PECULIAR AS IT MAY SOUND, correct German is never really spoken. One might say there are in effect two German languages: the one, standard German, is spoken as a "semi-foreign" language on the radio, stage and television, as well as by people who don't understand each other's dialects. The other German is a composite of all the countless local dialects that exist in each region, village and city in Germany. In a sense, then, Germany is a polyglot nation where standard German exists only in an artificial and formal way.

Many times an American of German descent is heard to say, "Oh, my parents spoke German but not very well, it was Low German." The implication for the listener is that Low German is somehow of lower quality or more debased than High German. I have even heard a German teacher say "Low German is a mixture of bad German and worse English." However, this is not true. In German we distinguish broadly between *Niederdeutsch, Mitteldeutsch,* and *Oberdeutsch.* Actually these names—low, middle and high—are strictly geographical in origin and they haven't the slightest thing to do with social class. So, if you are uninformed as was the German teacher, best you take to heart the proverb, "Besser stumm als dumm," (better to remain silent than show you're stupid).

How do we get High German and Low German then?

High German is more or less the common denominator between *Oberdeutsch* (upper, or mountain German) and *Mitteldeutsch* (midway German or middle upland German). Low German has been spoken only north of what language historians call the Benrath line. Benrath is the name of a town near Cologne through which the line happens to run. This line is imaginary, of course, and runs almost straight across the country from just north of Cologne in the west, north to Kassel, south of Magdeburg, through Berlin and continues eastward through East Prussia.

Although Low German is not spoken officially today, it lives on as *Plattdeutsch* in the rural and small town areas north of the Benrath line. Historically, Low German shares with English the common parentage of Saxon, and to this day *Platt* sounds very much like English.

Likewise, if one moves westward in northern Germany toward the Dutch border the language spoken on the street begins to sound more and more like Dutch but a noticeable barrier is never crossed. The dialect just drifts gradually to a point where the speaker of High German simply finds himself unable to understand the local dialect. W. B. Lockwood, *An Informal History of the German Language,* page 188 reports: "Many German girls cross the frontier every morning to work in Dutch factories a few miles away. They mix easily with the Dutch employees. But these girls haven't learned the Dutch language. It isn't necessary. A Dutch farmer with land adjoining the frontier can stroll up to the dividing wire and have a word with a German farmer working on the other side. These two can talk about their workaday business in the Saxon dialect with perfect mutual comprehension and no feeling that they are foreigners to each other. Yet the one will have a Dutch-language newspaper in his pocket, the other a German one."

Farther south there is the Low Franconian dialect which

extends unbroken over the state boundary where, going eastward, it merges with the Rhenish Franconian dialects forming one continuum. Nowhere else on the German frontiers
do we find this kind of gradual language transition. In passing, it is interesting to note that Low German exerted enormous influence on the Scandinavian languages. Particularly
in Swedish and Danish, Low German loan words are common. Scholars in fact compare the effects of German words
on the Scandinavian tongues to the influence of French on
English resulting from the Norman conquest of England
in 1066. The occasion for this linguistic borrowing into
Scandinavia was not military but commercial conquest.
During the Middle Ages and especially in the heyday of
the Hanseatic League, North German merchants dominated
the whole Baltic area. Scandinavian guilds were organized
on German lines. Whole Scandinavian towns were founded
by Germans. The German businessmen posed such a threat
that the city of Stockholm stipulated in its City Law of that
period that not more than half of its aldermen could be
Germans.

This being the situation, why didn't Low German become
the accepted dialect for the entire German speaking territory? The reason is quite accidental. In the early 1500's the
duke of Saxony was making an attempt to standardize the
dialects used officially in his duchy. Out of this effect developed the so-called *Kanzleisprache,* the language for state
affairs. This program by itself would have been ineffectual
except that another coincidence occurred simultaneously—
Martin Luther translated the Bible from Latin using the
same German dialect. Defining his problem, Luther wrote:
*"Ich habe keine gewisse, sonderliche, eigene Sprache im
Deutschen, sondern brauche die gemeine deutsche Sprache,
dass mich beide, Ober- und Niederländer verstehen kön-
nen."* (I have no special, definitive language in German,

but I am using the common German tongue so that both High German and Low German will be able to understand me.) In other words Luther sought a compromise between upper and lower German and in effect he chose the middle tongue that could be largely understood by both extremes. The real coincidence is that Luther was from the Saxon area and wrote the Bible as well as his many other manuscripts in the *Kanzleisprache.*

Out of this blend of dialects developed what is today called New High German, the standardized grammar learned by all Germans in elementary and secondary schools. Sometimes it is called the *Bühnensprache,* the language of the stage, or *Schriftdeutsch,* written German. Yet it remains a fact that almost no one speaks High German all of the time. Everyone writes it but at home and among friends Germans are proud to be speaking their local dialects, just another example of the deep-seated devotion of the German to his local region, his hometown and his beloved territorial district.

To speak a sub-standard brand of English in the United States is to betray oneself as a hayseed or as uneducated. Not so in Germany. If a young man studies at the university using only High German and returns to his hometown he is under considerable social pressure to revert to the use of the local dialect. If he does not he is an intolerable snob. Or take politics. In the United States, a good way for the candidate to endear himself to the local electorate is to speak about local problems, shake hands, kiss babies and remember the names of other office seekers. In Germany about the same thing can be achieved by a spiel in the regional dialect.

English and German, once again, are the products of the common parent, Saxon. Naturally they also share a single grandfather, namely Gothic. Hundreds of years before the

Romans entered German territory, many Germanic tribes roamed the continent of Europe. One of these tribes was called the Goths. After the beginning of the Christian era this tribe migrated to southern Russia where in about 350 A.D. the Bible was translated into Gothic by their Bishop Wulfilas. From this single document written in Gothic we are able to compare the Gothic language with the later Saxon documents and determine that Saxon indeed evolved from the root language of Gothic. Thus the parent language of modern English was Anglo-Saxon—of modern German, Saxon.

Much undocumented evolution occurs in German between 350 and 750 A.D. when a second work was written, the *Hildebrandslied,* or Lay of Hildebrand. Between 750 and 1050 the German language can best be described as a collection of monastery dialects. That is, there is a certain uniformity in the writings of any given monastery but no common denominator for all of them. To teach the natives and convert them to Christianity the monks struggled to express alien concepts in native German much as missionaries were forced to do in the case of the American Indians. Often the monks made up Latin-German word lists, or they made interlinear translations of the Latin by writing the German words above the Latin, making a kind of medieval schoolboy's pony. Below is a list of words which have come into both German as well as English from the parent Latin words. Borrowed early, these words underwent all subsequent vowel and consonant changes along with the German or English patterns of development. Professionally we refer to them as Latin loan words.

German	Latin	English
Birne	*pirum*	pear
Esel	*asinus*	ass
Feige	*ficus*	fig

German	Latin	English
Kammer	*camera*	chamber
Keller	*cellarium*	cellar
Lilie	*lilium*	lily
Markt	*mercatus*	market
Meile	*mille*	mile
Munze	*moneta*	money
Pforte	*porta*	portal
Pfund	*pondo*	pound
Rose	*rosa*	rose
Rettich	*radix*	radish
Siegel	*sigillum*	seal
Schindel	*scindula*	shingle
Tafel	*tabula*	tablet
Wein	*vinum*	wine

Since both Germany and England were populated by unstructured societies, the sophisticated Roman civilization usually imposed its own vocabulary for the sophisticated life on the more primitive German language. Thus many legal, medical, civil and religious terms were threaded directly into German and English from Latin. In subsequent evolution these borrowed words also changed within the new framework. Examples of these professional and technical loan words follow:

German	Latin	English
Abt	*abbas*	abbot
Altar	*altaria*	altar
Fieber	*febris*	fever
Kanzel	*cancelli*	chancel
Kaiser	*Caesar*	Caesar
Kloster	*claustrum*	cloister
Kreuz	*crux*	cross
Münster	*monasterium*	minister
opfern	*offere*	offer
Pflaster	*emplastrum*	plaster

Priester	*presbyter*	priest
Propst	*propositus*	provost
Tempel	*templum*	temple

Much later in history, English and German borrowed an equally large number of words from French. For example:

German	French	English
Abenteuer	*aventure*	adventure
Banner	*bannière*	banner
Chance	*chance*	chance
fein	*fin*	fine
galoppieren	*galoper*	gallop
Lanze	*lance*	lance
Manier	*manière*	manner
Partie	*partie*	part
Platz	*place*	place
Preis	*prix*	price
Prinz	*prince*	prince
Tanz	*danse*	dance

Some English and German words have been imported via the Crusaders who borrowed them from the oriental languages then spoken in Jerusalem, mostly Arabian:

German	Arabian	English
Kampfer	*kafur*	camphor
Reis	*vrihi*	rice
Sirup	*scharab*	syrup
Spinat	*isbanakh*	spinach
Zucker	*sokkar*	sugar

In more modern developments hundreds of words were borrowed from Latin, the official language of instruction at the universities until relatively recent times. A few of these words are listed without their obvious English counterparts: *Arithmetik, Atlas, Botanik, Aktiv, Disziplin, dividieren. Echo, Examen, Geographie, Klima, Mineralogie,*

Nominativ, Objekt, Passiv, Physik, Reformation, Skelett (skeleton), *Student, Universität.*

Likewise in more modern times both German and English have borrowed heavily from the French for their military terminology: *Armee, Artillerie, Bataillon, Batterie, Brigade, Division, Fort, General, Infanterie, Kanone, Kapitulation, Kommandeur, Kompanie, Korporal, Korps, Leutnant, Major, Munition, Offizier, Parade, Parole, Pistole, Quartier, Regiment, Rekrut, Sergeant, Train, Uniform.*

Finally, English has also given many words to German. Since all nouns in German are capitalized, capitalization is the only change they undergo. In clothing German has acquired: *Cape, Plaid, Pullover, Sweater;* in foods: *Beefsteak, Cocktail, Pudding, Punsch, Roastbeef, Rum, Sherry;* in sports: *Bobsleigh, Boxer, Finish, Golf, Hockey, Meeting, Sport, Team, Tennis, Trainer;* and in other areas: *Baby, Babysitter, Boykott, Clown, Garage, Hobby, Job, Lift, Lokomotiv, Manager, Pony, Propeller, Revolver, Scheck, Snob, Streik, Teenager, Trick, Tunnel, Waggon.*

Some words that German has donated to enrich the English language are: blitzkrieg, dachshund, ersatz, echt, frankfurter, hinterland, kindergarten, rucksack, sauerkraut, wiener.

Learning the German language has many pitfalls, even for the German-American son or daughter who grew up in a German-speaking home in the United States. A few years ago a friend of mine serving in the Air Force was stationed near Bitburg, Germany. His parents, now living in Milwaukee, had come from Paderborn and the family spoke only German at home. Naturally outside the home my friend always spoke English. One weekend, having decided to visit his uncles and aunts in Paderborn, he boarded a train and began to converse with an elderly gentleman. Using his "family" German he repeatedly said *du* and *dein* for the English "you" and "your." The trouble is that anywhere but in family situations or with very close friends, one always should say *"Sie"* and *"Ihr."* To reverse the formalities is to offend and embarrass.

Suspecting some misconception rather than bad intentions the gentleman simply explained that my friend should use *Sie* and *Ihr*. Painfully rectifying the "bad" linguistic habit he arrived at the home of his relatives. Now, wanting to appear erudite and high-classed, my friend continued to say *Sie* and *Ihr*. That is, until the cousins and their parents began to wonder what had suddenly come between the two families. A little explanation, of course, and the two extremes were ironed out in my friend's speech.

There are plenty of other quirks about the German language. The most obvious is the use of three articles—*der, die, das*—while English has only "the." We usually say these articles denote the gender of a word as masculine, feminine, or neuter. However, these designations of gender have little correspondence in real life. For example, we have *die Arbeit* (job) but the English loan word becomes in German *der Job*. It is *der Teenager* whether boy or girl, and *das Fotomodell* no matter how feminine and beautiful the model. It is *das Fräulein* (Miss) and *die Frau* (Mrs.) but when speaking about places in New York it is *die* Wallstreet but *der* Broadway. Soldiers are always masculine but German genders for military terms are usually feminine. It is *die Bundeswehr, die Uniform, die Kaserne, die Luftwaffe, die Polizei,* etc.

The American tourist soon learns that *die Strasse* means "street" but he is in Germany for quite awhile before learning that it also means a country road as well as a major highway. And an *Allee* is anything but an English alley; it is a broad avenue built originally on a dam that led through swampy fields. A *Gasse* is a narrow street bordered by houses. If there are no houses it is a *Weg*. In most cases cars cannot drive up these passageways but sometimes they are expanded keeping the same names, and then cars may be seen.

Because English and German are two peas from the same linguistic pod there are many words that have not been borrowed in either direction and yet are very similar: *Der Arm, die Hand, der Ball, das Gold, der Finger*. One does not have to be a genius to see that the following unborrowed German words are similar to their English counterparts: *Die Mutter, der Vater, das Bier, der Mann, die Maus, das Haus, gut, lang, Ende*, etc.

If all is going well in learning German try the real cliff-hanging booby trap, the idiomatic expression. Sitting in a cafe one evening with friends, I was both amused and embarrassed for an American diplomat's wife. She had studied a little German in college before arriving in Germany and was struggling along quite well until she felt a draft and muttered *"Ich bin kalt."* In German one says, *"Mir ist kalt."* Not I'm cold, but it's cold for me. Smiles flashed across the faces of her German friends because what she said is, "I am sexually frigid." I also heard the story of a young American lady who said to a distinguished German gentleman at a party, *"Wenn Sie nichts an haben, dann kommen Sie mal vorbei."* Dead silence resulted from a simple switch of the syllable *an* in place of *vor*. What she intended to say was, "If you have nothing planned, drop in at the house sometime." But what the lady actually said was, "Come over to my house whenever you have nothing on."

The German language ranks sixth in the world for the number of people who speak it—about 100 million. The languages spoken more frequently than German are in this order: Chinese, English, Hindustani, Spanish, and

Russian. Ranking below German in order are Japanese, Arabic, Bengali, Portuguese, French and Italian. Some languages have gained speakers in great numbers when overseas possessions were acquired. Notable is the English language. But Germany was a Johnny-come-lately to colonization, primarily because there was no nation of Germany until the time when unclaimed territory had already been gobbled up. The few colonies she did get were lost during World War I.

Nevertheless, the German language did get overseas in force through German immigrants, but only when they constituted a very large majority was the language able to survive. Thus there are today enclaves of German-speakers in much of South America and in parts of Africa. The large numbers of Germans in Australia and the United States, however, were so anxious to become accepted, normalized citizens that they hastened to assimilate into the English-speaking communities. Regarding assimilation the principle applies that when the immigrants feel superior to the existing culture, they resist assimilation and maintain their own language as a means to isolation. When the immigrants feel equal to or inferior to the native society, their desire to belong to the community is so strong that love and care for the mother tongue quickly fall by the wayside.

The only force strong enough to prevent assimilation and thereby to preserve the German language in the United States has been religion. In eastern Pennsylvania even today German-speaking communities include more than one-half million, and another half-million understand that brand of German. The Quaker, William Penn, invited German Mennonites (a Quaker sect) to found a colony at Germantown, Pennsylvania in 1683, and thousands afterwards fled Europe in favor of Pennsylvania to avoid military service. Once in America these people practiced an extrinsic apartheid which in turn preserved their German mother tongue.

Being "people of the Book" these masses of immigrants were determined to hold to the language in which Luther's Bible was written. Once Benjamin Franklin even wrote to a friend, "They, the Germans, will so outnumber us so that all the advantages we have will, in my opinion, be not able to preserve our language, and even our government will become precarious." Ironically, at that time it was the Germans of Pennsylvania, not Benjamin Franklin, who spoke the language of their sovereign. In Buckingham Palace the first generation of the German Hanoverian line of kings was in power and the royal family never learned to use English.

Franklin's worries soon proved ill-founded. The German immigrants in the Quaker State preferred the simple life based on the Bible and bothered little with politics or the outside world. All their energy was dedicated to living as good members of their own community. Writes Dr. Benjamin Rush, in *An Account of the Manners of the German Inhabitants of Pennsylvania,* "such has been the influence of a pious education among the Germans in Pennsylvania that in the course of nineteen years only one of them has even been brought to a place of shame and punishment. . . In the towns as weavers, millers, glass-blowers, iron and paper manufacturers, they exhibited the same thrift and uprightness of character." In American literature two poets, William Cullen Bryant and John Greenleaf Whittier, have celebrated the beauties and charm of German-Pennsylvania in poems.

Scattered throughout the United States and Canada there are also many colonies of Mennonites or offshoots of this religious sect, such as the Amish, the Hutterites, Moravians, Dunkards, and Schwenkfelders, all of whom retain a dialect of German for dealings in the community, at school, and above all for religious services. Whenever two of these Germans meet they will understand each other perfectly, even though they may always have lived a thousand miles apart. If two speakers suddenly break forth in Pennsylvania German a felicitous bond of friendship is spontaneously cemented. A few years back, Dr. William Frey of Franklin and Marshall College even suggested in a public address that Pennsylvania Dutch be adopted as the official language of the United Nations since it automatically establishes rapport and good will.

What is Pennsylvania Dutch, you may ask. Actually it is a fusion of the divergent dialects of German which, about 1830, began to coalesce into a single, new German dialect. This occurred when the importance of English in official American life relegated German to the level of a language spoken only in the German sections of Pennsylvania, while even there, English became the literary tongue of the inhabitants. Fortunately, the Pennsylvanians then wrote down their brand of German and even published grammars for use in their German schools. The result was a standardized Pennsylvania German built from the dialects which was unlike any dialect used anywhere in Germany. Parenthetically, it should be mentioned that only High German dialects comprise Pennsylvania German. It follows, of course, that many words differed from standard High German or didn't even exist in German. English words were borrowed and Germanized, illustrating what happens when a language of the minority is daily in contact with a language of the majority. Yet English loan words by actual count do not exceed seven percent of the Pennsylvania German vocabulary.

Pennsylvania Dutch is not the only hybrid of German spoken in the United States. Far older—in fact more than a thousand years old—is the Yiddish language which is the spoken language of half the world's Jews. Yiddish, before the Nazi debacle, was spoken by more than eleven million people. As a language Yiddish evolved into a distinct entity between the years 1100 and 1350. As with Pennsylvania German, Yiddish emerged as a superdialect among many, in this case from dialects of Middle High German. In the *Judengassen* (ghettos) along the Rhine and Danube a motley bunch of Middle High German dialects fused simply because the Jews communicated with each other at a time when they were excluded from intercourse with gentile culture. There resulted, therefore, a language which was far more uniform and universal than any single German language of the day. To be sure, the gentiles considered their jibberish to be corrupt German, but the Jews simply referred to it as *teutsch,* the medieval word for "German."

Two incidents forced the speakers of this superdialect to adopt a name (Yiddish is the Hebrew word for "Jewish") and flee to the eastern countries of Europe. One factor was occasioned by the First Crusade. Christian soldiers rehearsing for their mission against the Saracen infidels went about massacring Jews in Germany. The second factor was the Black Death. Frustrated and angered in finding no reason for the catastrophe, the populace of Germany was easily persuaded to blame the Jews; and in droves these Jews fled to eastern Europe where Yiddish became their earmark.

Special conditions favored the growth of Yiddish in the Slavic countries. Most eastern empires were already multilingual and easily accepted a new foreign tongue. Also, the Jews frequently formed a majority in a multilingual metropolis; they brought with them a superiority in economics, fine arts, and urban civilization. This superior feeling, when intertwined with a strong religious insularity, prevented assimilation with the more primitive pagan-Christian populace.

From 1350 to 1750 Yiddish developed in the Slavic countries to a language whose vocabulary was at least seventy percent German but otherwise independent of German sound and form changes. The grammars of each language also underwent changes independently. But then around 1750, when Jewish community life was already sprouting in America, the tide of refugees began to reverse itself. Jews began fleeing from the frenzy of the Cossacks unleashed against them in the Ukraine and Poland with the blessings of local czars and kings. Thus the Jews escaped back to Germany where they were welcomed with open arms. The freedom and tolerance accorded them under Frederick the Great impelled many of them to remain in Germany, ironically, until their annihilation by the German Nazis in World War II. It is a fact, though, that their Yiddish language in the Germany of 1750 was already so distinct as to sound strange, if not foreign, even to their co-religionists.

The expellees from eastern Europe did not all return to Germany. Many in fact went to England and especially in succeeding years to America. Those who emigrated to the United States were largely from the lower classes, speaking now a language 70 percent German (some say 80 percent), 20 percent Hebrew and Aramaic, and 10 percent Slavonic. Yiddish to world Jewry at this time was the tongue of the home, the street and the market place. Only the roaming preacher through the big city American ghettos held forth in Yiddish, finding it a matchless medium for his quaint parables and picturesque fulminations against sin. But the higher class Jews held it in disdain, fit only for the writings of the ignorant, for folk tales and the prayers of women. The educated Jew used Hebrew.

Yet by the middle and later nineteenth century, certain writers in America realized that the message for the multitude could be conveyed only in Yiddish. So they "stooped to conquer," publishing their ideas in the "uncouth" vernacular. Simultaneously, secularist and laborist movements in Germany gave impetus to the acceptance of Yiddish as a world language. Eventually twentieth century Jews split over which language they would use, some considering Yiddish mere jargon and clinging to Hebrew, others adhering to Yiddish as a matter of tradition. Out of the controversy there developed the Yiddish Scientific Institute (YIVO) founded at Vilnyus, Lithuania, in 1925. For the first time the Yiddish language achieved an academy to establish norms and regulate usage. The Institute extensively standardized the spelling and grammar in 1936 and achieved world-wide acceptance of its regulations. During World War II the academy was moved to New York City and in 1956 it was given an English title, the Yivo Institute of Jewish Research.

Yiddish offers a gold mine of insights for the professional philologist. Numerous university curriculums in the United States offer courses in Yiddish for this very reason. Yet Yiddish in twentieth century America is relegated primarily to the library and the scholar's study. As a practical tool for communication in our country, Yiddish has been dying a slow death. It is a fact, of course, that the American Jew does not live in a ghetto. He has, moreover, been assimilated into the very warp and woof of American society up to the heights of government, industry and power. This is wonderful for the human being but it is pernicious for the identity of a language.

The real death blow to Yiddish was not dealt in America, however. That came in 1948 when the new state of

Israel adopted Hebrew as its official language. Yet, due to a new nostalgia and love for the literary treasures contained in the Yiddish language, it can be assumed that Yiddish will linger on for centuries.

Finally, a chapter on the German language would scarcely be satisfactory without mention of the German-language press in America. Living in an unfamiliar land, our German-American ancestors seldom knew English the first day they touched these shores. The vast majority of German immigrants did, however, possess at least an elementary education and they were curious to know something about their new country, about its novel political system, and about their new neighborhood, while they also wanted to read the news from their native Germany.

To fulfill this need, the German press in America eminently performed a twofold role. First, it carried much news from the old country to alleviate the feeling of homesickness and isolation from everything the immigrant had known. Second, it became the bridge to Americanization by integrating and instructing the German into the new political, economic and social life of this country. Two books which tell the story of and catalogue the German press in America are: Carl Wittke, *The German-Language Press in America* (Univ. of Kentucky, 1957) and Karl J. R. Arndt and May Olson, *German-American Newspapers and Periodicals 1732-1955* (Heidelberg, Quelle and Meyer, 1961).

Summarizing a few statistics about the German press as given in Howell's *American Newspaper Directory* and reported by Wittke, it is found that in 1876 there were German publications in the United States as follows:

Dailies 74	297,037 circulation
Weeklies 374	1,022,100 circulation
Monthlies 31	156,800 circulation

Two and one-half German newspapers were Democratic to every one Republican.

To evaluate the significance of these statistics, note the circulation at that time (1876) for a few prominent English language newspapers.

Boston Transcript	8,000	circulation
Cleveland Plain Dealer	2,400	circulation
Ohio State Journal	2,500	circulation

The end for the German-American press came abruptly in 1917 when Congress passed a law forcing the papers to print parallel columns of English and German so the United States censor could determine whether or not the German newspaper was printing anything pro-German regarding World War I. The immediate result of the law was an astronomical cost squeeze that choked off most German newspapers.

The few that survived immediately after World War I embarked on a vigorous campaign to revive the German press. The livelihood of many an editor and printer depended on it. Their strategy was to revitalize the German clubs, music, drama and literature, for without a German heritage in the community the German-language newspapers were doomed. There were other tactics too. Emphasis on festivals and celebrations shifted to heroes from the German-Americans of yesteryear. The birthday of Carl Schurz became important; there was a Franz Sigel Society, a Steuben Society, and once again there was sauerkraut and German potato salad.

The German papers now saw themselves exclusively as the vehicle of Americanization. This meant in effect reporting the *Vereinsleben* and the activities of the German social organizations. Editorial comment faded from sight. Driven farther onto the ropes during the depression, the papers by 1935 had virtually ceased all comments on public affairs. A few statistics pinpoint the reasons. At their highwater mark the number of German papers in the United States totaled more than eight hundred. This figure decreased sharply during World War I and in the decade following.

In the 1920's and 1930's there was considerable influence of the German press on American newspaper publishing, but not on the German-language press in America. For example, the art of the comic strips was taken over by men who mimicked such talents as Wilhelm Busch. Rudolph Dirks for years wrote the strip called the *Katzenjammer Kids,* characters patterned after the Busch creations, Max and Moritz. Although that particular strip has disappeared, other institutions including a dance band today have appropriated the name, "Katzenjammer Kids." Also, the highly successful publishing enterprise of Time-Life took its philosophy of photo-journalism from the Berlin newspapers of that time. Former correspondents of the New York Times serving with the Berlin bureau left after Hitler seized power. They tell how their ideas formed the thrust of Henry R. Luce's mid-thirties launching of *Life* magazine. The new philosophy and technique proved so successful that the styles of both *Time* and *Life* have been exported back to Germany especially to the magazines *Spiegel* and the various *Illustrierte.*

By 1930, Ayer's *Newspaper Annual* reported a mere 172 German publications of all kinds. In 1950 this had dropped to sixty, including the seven dailies still in existence. At latest count, in 1966, the German-language press was maintaining this level with about fifty-five publications, including several with both English and German sections.

In most cases the papers are independent, both politically and with respect to frequency of publication. Although there were twelve dailies in 1939 (Chicago *Abendpost,* Baltimore *Correspondent,* Detroit *Abendpost,* St. Paul *Tägliche Volkszeitung,* Omaha *Tägliche Tribune,* New York *Statszeitung und Herold,* Rochester *Abendpost,* Cincinnati *Freie Presse,* Cleveland *Wächter und Anzeiger,* Philadelphia *Gazette-Democrat,* Philadelphia *Tageblatt,* and the Milwaukee *Deutsche Zeitung*), today there are only three dailies left in the entire United States. There is in New York the *Staatszeitung und Herold* with its circulation of 15,200; in Rochester the *Abendpost* with 13,300; and in Chicago, the *Abendpost* whose circulation is not reported.

Throughout the history of the immigrant press in the United States, the German press has consistently held the lead considering both number of publications and circulation. This status continued until World War II. Since then German has yielded first place to Spanish, due no doubt to the heavy influx of Latin immigrants from our neighbors to the south. However, if one takes into account that the Spanish press in large measure is simply a translation of the English-language papers (e.g. Los Angeles *La Opinion,* Berkeley *Post,* Miami Beach *Voice,* Chicago *Revista Rotaria, Christian Science Quarterly, Life En Espanol*) then even now the German-language press maintains its leading position.

The rise of Hitler had little direct effect on the German press readership in the United States. Only a very few papers turned out to be pro-Nazi, such as the *Deutscher Weckruf und Beobachter* in New York. However, this sheet never achieved a circulation over five thousand. Most of the papers were embarrassed by the progress of the *Führer,* and remembering World War I all too vividly, the editors and publishers again feared for their lives. Some remained studiously neutral; others quickly turned decidedly anti-Nazi.

One new German paper came out of the German catastrophe, namely the *Aufbau,* launched and published by the German-Jewish Club (now the New World Club) of New York. A weekly, it reported and commented on current problems, expressed viewpoints on the forced migration of German Jews, and still thrives on a circulation of about 30,000. Undergirded by healthy advertising support and good editing, the paper seems to have an optimistic future.

Thus the German-language press in the United States, covering nearly two and a half centuries, is still doing what it has nearly always accomplished eminently: aiding immigrants in the process of assimilation. Incoming Germans may still get a few of their impressions of America and her institutions through the papers published in their native language; in these days of mass education and instant diffusion of information, the *raison d'etre* of the German-language press continues to decline, and nostalgia for its former greatness will not reverse that fact. Assimilation of the readers is what always dooms a foreign language press. This is not to minimize the death-blow dealt to the German-American press during World War I.

Hysteria against German-Americans during World War I, in fact, reached unbelievable proportions. Using German on the telephone was a betrayal of loyalty; German teachers were investigated; pacifists were considered pro-German; ministers who preached in German were challenged in their pulpits. Super-patriots killed the "Hun" language in the school curriculum; German textbooks were burned in public squares with the American flag flying. Symphonies refused to play works by German composers; German names were anglicized; German foods were banished; occasionally Germans whose patriotism seemed lukewarm were forced to kneel in a public place and kiss the American flag, or else submit to a public flogging. Several counties in Iowa denied Germans use of the mails.

Elsewhere vigilantes sponsored boycotts of German papers. Boy Scouts in Cleveland burned bundles of the German language newspaper *Wächter und Anzeiger,* and sauerkraut was renamed "liberty cabbage."

At one time as many as one third of the pupils of Ohio and others states not only learned German in the American public schools, but gained all of their knowledge in German. Yet by the time the World War hysteria had abruptly interdicted this practice in public schools, the proportion of German schools was already dropping as a result of cultural assimilation. After World War I the use of German continued sporadically in a few communities in America. It received a second mortal wound, one which proved fatal, with the advent of the unpopular Hitler government during the Thirties.

Unfortunately many a fine German tradition adopted earlier for American life was also discarded along with the schools, the newspapers and the language. Others were better disguised, or so deeply imbedded in the hearts and homes of individuals that they persist in American daily life to this day.

ARTISTIC ACHIEVEMENT

ARTISTIC ACHIEVEMENT

FROM THE Renaissance through the eighteenth century, Germany played a leading role in the production of art. Then in the nineteenth century something seems to have gone wrong; scholars and art critics of today generally dismiss what came out of nineteenth century Germany. Too fragmented, they say. There were schools of Neoclassicism, Romanticism, Realism, Neoromanticism, etc., but no originality. In the twentieth century, on the other hand, Germany outgrew her century of stagnation so completely that she became the home of some of the world's most creative artistic geniuses.

In this respect, both Germany and the United States share a common artistic plight. In America before 1776 there was really no creative art at all. As Richard Muther, *The History of Modern Painting,* observes, "American people ate and drank, and built and reclaimed the land and multiplied. But a large bar of iron was of more value than the finest statue, and an ell of good cloth was prized more highly than the *Transfiguration of Raphael."* (See Faust, *The German Element,* II, p. 293). In the century following the Revolution, American artists either came from Europe or studied there. Indirectly there was considerable German influence on American art but since German painting during that century was not in the limelight, the ideas came more from other European sources.

There were of course a few German artists who left or fled Germany and settled in the United States. For instance, Emmanuel Leutze is famous for his *Washington Crossing the Delaware* completed in 1851 and for his *Emigration to the West* of 1862. The latter forms one of the panels in the Capitol staircase in Washington, D. C. Also well-known in America is Albert Bierstadt who gained world fame and a gold medal from the Berlin Academy in 1868 for his American landscapes; some of the best known works include *Storm in the Rockies, Domes of the Yosemite, Mt. Hood* and *In the Sierras* which won him the medal. His paintings of the West have been featured repeatedly in *American Heritage* and other magazines.

Like their American counterparts, it took until the end of the nineteenth century before the German artists enjoyed a place in the sun. Around 1900 Munich became the rival of Paris as a world art center. About the same time America was able to make a contribution to the Germans in the figure of Carl Marr, born of German descent in Milwaukee in 1858. Marr, "a worker, a born professor, whose talent is made up of the elements of will, work and study and patience" (Muther), became a professor of art at the Munich Academy.

By the turn of the century there were also many German-Americans gaining fame on the American art scene. To mention a few, there are Frederick Dielman, who was president of the New York Academy of Design, and creator of the mosaic panels "Law" and "History" in the Library of Congress, Robert Koehler, who became director of the Minneapolis School of Fine Arts, Charles Kurtz, director of the Buffalo Fine Arts Academy, and Professor Otto Fuchs who held the directorship of the Maryland Institute in Baltimore.

The American art institutions also grew favorably disposed toward German art. For example, back in 1903 Harvard University already had established the Germanic Museum to which the Kaiser made generous contribution. German-American friends helped out and the King of Saxony in conjunction with the City Council of Nuremburg donated thirteenth century Saxon pieces and sculptures by Adam Kraft of Nuremburg.

Harvard University is still in the foreground on matters of German art. In 1957, for instance, the Harvard Press published a catalog of its twentieth-century collection contained in several museums of the University. Entitled *German Expressionism and Abstract Art,* the book lists about 475 works from the Busch-Reisinger Museum (the original Germanic Museum), the Fogg Art Museum, the Harvard Graduate Center, and Houghton Library. In 1967 the Busch-Reisinger and Fogg Museums had acquired an additional 350 modern German works. Through the donations of Julia Feininger there is also the Lyonel Feininger Archive which is part of the Busch-Reisinger, and which contains unfinished oils, documents and nearly five thousand Feininger drawings.

Feininger is, to be sure, an interesting figure because he is a genuine German-American artist. Born in New York City of German parents in 1871, he returned to Germany to study at the Hamburg School for Applied Arts, and then at the Academy of Arts in Berlin. After his marriage to Julia Lilienfeld in 1905 he went to work as a caricaturist and illustrator for various weeklies in Germany and Paris before joining the Chicago Tribune's comic section. Once he gained recognition for his painting as well as his caricatures he was recruited by Walter Gropius to join the Bauhaus (1919 to 1932) which was founded at Weimar, but later moved to Dessau and finally Berlin. With the advent of the Nazis to power in 1933, he returned to the United States to teach at Mills College in California and at Black Mountain College in North Carolina. He died in New York City in 1956 and lies buried at Hastings-on-Hudson.

That there should even be such a thing as a Feininger Archive at Harvard is due to the wolfish attitude of Adolf Hitler toward modern art. In July, 1937, Hitler was on hand at Munich for the opening of his new museum, the new *Haus der Kunst* or House of Art. Packing the huge square on *Prinzregentenstrasse* (where today the beautiful American Consulate building competes for attention) were thirty thousand Nazis delighted to hear the former water-color artist, Hitler, shout: "Works of art that cannot be understood but need a swollen set of instructions to prove their right to exist and find their way only to neurotics . . . will no longer find the road open by which they can reach the German nation. If they really paint in this manner because they see things that way, then these unhappy persons should be dealt with in the department of the Ministry of the Interior, where sterilization of the insane is dealt with."

The *Führer's* ninety-minute tirade created a gentle irony. For weeks afterwards, throngs of youths paid fifty pfennigs to parade through the *Haus der Kunst* and view what the conventional Nazi painters were offering in the way of "Strength Through Joy." Yet, for every one who paid to see what the *Führer* liked, more than three visitors walked on down the street to the Old National Gallery where they viewed free what the *Führer* despised. There, on specific orders from the dictator, the German Ministry of Education arranged an exhibition of *Entartete Kunst,* decadent or degenerate art. The objective was to instruct the people in "good" art by showing them what the Ministry of Education considered to be "bad" art.

The Nazis considered "degenerate" all painting which did not faithfully reproduce natural objects, or which treated with humor or revulsion such ideals as war or womanhood. The problem was that the huge bulk of German productivity in the twentieth century came into one of these categories. As Adolf Ziegler, professor at the Reich Chamber of Art put it, "Whole railroad trains would not have been enough to clear this rubbish out of the German museums. This has yet to be done and will be done very shortly." Of course it *was* trucked out—much of it finding its way eventually to museums in the United States.

German museums which suffered most from the Art Ministry's ruling were the Folkwang Museum in Essen, the Municipal Collection in Düsseldorf, and the Hamburg Kunsthalle, each losing nearly one thousand art works. The National Gallery in Berlin, the Berlin Print Cabinet, and the museums in Frankfurt and Breslau each lost between five and six hundred artifacts.

Sizeable collections were simply destroyed, but for some pieces the Nazis had more in mind than just "purification" of German culture. In May, 1938, a law bearing the authoritative signature of "Hitler" legalized the seizures and provided for their profitable disposal abroad. According to a follow-up report made by the Ministry for Propaganda, the sales netted some 45,000 dollars, 10,000 British pounds, and 8,000 Swiss francs. By far the major portion of the confiscated art was sold at a public auction held in the Theodor Fischer Gallery in Lucerne, Switzerland, on June 30, 1939. At this auction Germany lost virtually all her collection of French contemporary paintings as well as those of her own world-famous artists.

Other art works were bartered for such nineteenth century items as the Nazis liked and wanted for the Hitler

Museum at Linz, Austria. In one case, thirty expression-
istic paintings, along with nearly two hundred prints and
sculptures thrown in for good measure, were traded for a
single painting by an artist named Oehme. Whatever could
not be sold or bartered was burned by the Berlin Fire
Brigade in 1939. Exactly which missing paintings suffered
this fate, or were destroyed in the war, or vanished behind
the Iron Curtain no one will ever know for sure.

The place of honor at the "degenerate" exhibition in
Munich was held by George Grosz, who by 1937, how-
ever, was living safely and quietly on Long Island's Little
Neck Bay. Not on exhibition were Grosz's drawings of
Nazi Jew baitings and other Nazi bestialities which won
him both international fame and the vituperative hatred
of Hitler. Ranking nearly as "high" as Grosz was Otto
Dix for his skilled etchings of the brutal trench fighting of
World War I. In a section of the gallery dedicated to "The
Mocking of Christianity" was displayed Emil Nolde's
Christ and the Thieves. Also shown here were *A Peasant
Scene from a Jewish Point of View, The Manifestation of
the Soul of the Jewish Race* and a section devoted to "The
Derision of the German Women."

Mostly though, the viewers saw specimens of cubist, fu-
turist and surrealist schools. Many of these "degenerate"
works were by members of the three famous groups of
modern German painters: *Die Brücke* in Dresden, *der
blaue Reiter* in Munich and later the international gathering of the *Bauhaus.* The grotesque German dictator, whose
hatred of the Jews was almost equaled by his hatred of
the Communists, could see in the allegorical cloak of the
expressionists little more than zionists triumphant and Reds
waving their flags and capes.

Many paintings found their way into the United States,
some by direct purchase, some through the Lucerne auc-

tion, others for safe storage during the European upheaval. In 1947 in Washington, D. C., the National Gallery arranged an exhibition of these German masterpieces and it created a minor stir. General Lucius Clay in Germany insisted that these be returned immediately to Germany because he insisted that America must not stand accused by the German people for pilfering art. As the art became known the public clamored for exhibitions throughout the country, and even U. S. senators were drawn into the fray. Finally a settlement was reached allowing more fragile works to return immediately to Germany. Others were permitted first to make a tour of important museums in the United States and then be returned to their homeland. Following the announcement, distinguished directors of art galleries rushed to Washington to get their museums on the list. Thereafter, what did not belong to a private collection or had not been purchased in free negotiation was returned to Germany.

Today several excellent books on modern German art are available. One that can be recommended is entitled *German Art of the Twentieth Century,* edited by Andrew C. Ritchie and published by the Museum of Modern Art in New York, in cooperation with the City Art Museum of St. Louis. In addition to the text there are many colorful prints by the German expressionists, mostly those paintings that never found their way back to Germany. Some of the reproductions of course were loaned by museums in Germany or by private and public collectors in the United States. Municipal museums outside New York City and St. Louis where a number of the original Expressionist paintings are held include the Walker Art Center in Minneapolis, the Albright Art Gallery in Buffalo, the Art Institute of Chicago, the Philadelphia Museum of Art, the Portland Art Museum in Oregon, the Detroit Institute of

Arts, and others. In New York there are numerous paintings held also by private families. A sizeable number are
now in the Solomon R. Guggenheim Museum which concentrates on twentieth century paintings and sculpture.

The Guggenheim Museum, through its namesake and
patron, has deep roots which reach back into German soil.
Opened in 1959, the museum is the only building in New
York City designed by the late Frank Lloyd Wright. It
was built and operates by support of the Solomon R. Guggenheim Foundation established in 1937. Solomon was the
fourth son of Meyer Guggenheim who was born in Lang-
nau, Switzerland, and educated in German-speaking
schools. He came to Philadelphia in 1847. Beginning as an
importer of Swiss embroidery, the paterfamilias eventually
gained enormous wealth in the fields of mining and metal
processing in Colorado, Mexico and New Jersey. Throughout their lives all of the Guggenheims have retained interest and kept in contact with Germany and Switzerland.

The history of American architecture up to the twentieth century could be accurate without the mention of a
single German name. The Americans, it seems, have been
interested only in colonial styles inherited from British
sources or in the simple classical lines of antiquity. This
strain runs counter to a pioneering spirit which can best
be described as the American invention of the skyscraper.
In a real sense the latter development was possible only
because of America's technological prowess in the use of
steel, rather than relying on stone for strength in building.
Perhaps the greatest leader in this direction was Louis
Henry Sullivan with his Chicago School and its motto that
"form follows function." In his wake has followed Frank
Lloyd Wright, prominent member of the Chicago tradition, who made significant advances on his own. Whatever
influence in the field of architecture can be observed was

from America to Germany and the rest of the world, not the other way around.

One can of course mention a few nineteenth century Germans who penetrated the American realm of architecture. A German architectural firm, owned by the architects Smithmeyer and Pelz of New York designed and built the Library of Congress. Paul J. Pelz's father was a Forty-eighter in considerable demand as an architect throughout the nineteenth century. Actually, though, the architecture of these men was classical or Italian Renaissance in style with nothing distinctively German about it. There were others. G. L. Heins won a gold medal at the St. Louis Fair, Theodore Carl Link won a first prize for designing the railway terminal station at St. Louis. The Germans, William Schickel and I. E. Ditmars built many churches, hospitals and public buildings in New York. W. C. Zimmerman of Chicago was for years the state architect of Illinois.

More interesting from the nineteenth century, perhaps, are the few scattered structures that represent a genuine transplantation of German architecture into America. The large barns in the Pennsylvania Dutch area do resemble those in the Palatinate. The residential area of "German Village" in the heart of Columbus, Ohio, is distinctly North German in flavor. Still more intriguing are the smatterings of the half-timbered houses to be found on the highways and byways in Pennsylvania, Missouri and especially in Wisconsin and Texas. In the middle of Fredericksburg, Texas, one can stroll down West Schubert Street and see the actual *Fachwerk Häuser,* half-timber houses, common to any number of areas in Central Germany. There are others near New Braunfels and in Kendall County.

The Wisconsin structures are mostly in the southeastern portion of the state. Several are near Watertown in Dodge County and in the towns of Jackson, Kirchhayn and Freistadt in Washington County. In a few cases the half-timber construction was not limited to houses and barns but used also for churches and mills. The Trinity Evangelical Lutheran Church which formerly stood in Freistadt, Ozaukee County was built in 1844 in the half-timber style. While there were no pictures taken, it was described in detail by the German pastor Rev. L. F. E. Krause who maintained a daily record book in the German language during the entire period of its construction. In Freistadt there are other structures, such as the Hilgendorf House, which are excellent examples of the half-timber building technique.

In strict German terminology, constructing with half-timbers is known as *Fachwerkbau.* In the vernacular of southeastern Wisconsin it is called simply, *deutscher Verband,* German fastening. By this method, a frame is built of heavy logs hewn flat, mortised, tenoned, and finally pegged together. This furnishes a skeleton in the same way that a steel framework supports the bricks and mortar of a skyscraper. With this basic framework erected, whatever material is available can be adapted to fill in the spaces. Preferably used is baked brick, sometimes air-dried, mud blocks, field rocks, or just plain clay and straw plastered on wooden slats. If the latter is used, a thin coating of lime plaster is laid over the inner bulk to prevent crumbling.

The Langholff house near Watertown, Wisconsin, is one of the few structures in the United States which in a single structure incorporated both house and barn. Richard W. E. Perrin, *The Architecture of Wisconsin* (Madison, 1967, page 7), shows a picture of the Langholff house. Built in 1848, the half-timber structure also accommodated a vaulted smoke house for curing meat, known in Germany as the *Schwarze Küche,* or black kitchen. As in Germany, the barn section of the building included both a stable for the cattle and a hayloft with granary on the upper level.

Like their countrymen in Germany, these German-Americans displayed skill and high-quality workmanship. Not a single metal nail was ever used in the framework. Timbers were of oak, tamarack or pine, and pegs usually of white oak. Apparently the general layout was accomplished on the ground and a system of Roman numerals identified the place of each timber in the raised structure. Usually the rafters were slick poles of tamarack or cedar, but occasionally they were hewn and framed. Samples of old shingles indicate they were handsplit on small bench-sized lathes. A few houses may once have had roofs thatched with rye-straw.

In the twentieth century, of course, modern German architecture has largely set the pace for the rest of the western world. No one would deny that the German architects were eclectic throughout the late nineteenth century and even in the early part of the twentieth century, but by the 1920's the situation had changed radically. Predecessors of the triumph to come later were the Belgian Henry van de Velde and the movement known as the *Jugendstil,* or youthful style, and the Darmstadt colony of artists, especially Joseph M. Olbrich. Two other prominent figures were Peter Behrens and Otto Bartning. The real breakthrough came, however, with Walter Gropius who outstripped the other European pathfinders of modern architecture.

Founding his institute, the *Bauhaus,* in 1919 at Weimar, Gropius sought to bridge the gap between art and life. He also sought to expand horizons. To accomplish this he surrounded himself with an international entourage of the finest artists: architects, painters, designers, sculptors and work-shop artisans. Modern art, architecture, furniture and lamp design, even present day dinnerware and cooking utensils would be unthinkable without the influence of the *Bauhaus* school.

Significantly if not symbolically, the *Bauhaus* dispersed six months before the arrival of Hitler at the Chancellery in Berlin. In spite of their voluntary break-up, Hitler nevertheless moved quickly to scatter the men from the *Bauhaus,* to America's glorious benefit. Walter Gropius came to teach at Harvard and build buildings in the United States. Accompanying him to this country were Ludwig Mies van der Rohe, who among other duties became the director of architecture at the Illinois Institute of Technology. Eric Mendelsohn designed the Einstein Tower in Berlin, then in 1941 became professor of architecture at Berkeley where he designed a hospital and synagogues for St. Louis, St. Paul and Cleveland. Marcel Breuer was a partner of Gropius at the *Bauhaus* and remained with him as co-worker in their firm in Cambridge, Massachusetts, where both also taught architecture at Harvard. Most recently Breuer has gained fame for his imaginative campus and building designs at Collegeville, Minnesota. Ludwig Hilberseimer likewise followed Gropius, later gaining recognition for his master plan to decentralize Chicago. Richard Neutra came somewhat before his colleagues to study with Frank Lloyd Wright, after which he settled in Los Angeles in 1925 to carry out his plans for total community design—homes, shopping centers, schools, churches all in one unit of grand composite. Martin Wagner, also formerly with the *Bauhaus,* later became professor for city planning at Harvard University.

Perhaps we should mention a few other famous buildings these men contributed to their adopted country. Gropius produced the Harvard Graduate Center, the U.S. Embassy in Athens, Greece, and the Pan American Airways Building in New York City. Neutra came up with the Kaufmann "Desert House" near Palm Springs, California, the Lovell "Health House" of Los Angeles, the Ring Plan

School of Lemoore, California, the Mariner's Medical Arts Building of Newport Beach, California, and the Los Angeles County Hall of Records. Breuer enjoys world recognition for his design of the UNESCO Building in Paris, for the Research Center of the IBM company in La Gaude, France, and for the entire resort town of Fline, Haute Savoire, France.

If Americans were somewhat slow to develop their own architecture, in sculpture they were almost hopeless. And unlike in music, the German immigrants didn't have much to offer either. Seemingly the Puritan and Quaker prudishness put a stifling lid on all creativity regarding images and forms. One of the few German immigrant sculptors worthy of mention is Karl T. Bitter, Viennese-born, who became director of sculpture for the Columbian Exposition at Chicago in 1893 and the Pan American and Louisiana Purchase Expositions in 1904, as well as producing the Broad Street Station reliefs in Philadelphia. Another, Frederick W. Ruckstuhl, who was born at Breitenbach in Alsace, has examples of his works in St. Louis, the Congressional Library, in New York City and in Harrisburg, Pennsylvania.

German sculpture in the twentieth century, despite faint beginnings and heavy debts to sculptors in other nations, has forged its own cast without becoming too provincial. Works of the most important German representatives have been known in the United States for a long time. In fact, the artifacts of George Kolbe and Wilhelm Lehmbruck are probably better known in the United States than in any other country except Germany itself. Ernst Barlach remained in Germany after the rise of Hitler and was so harrassed by the Nazis that he eventually died there in 1938. In the meantime a large number of his sculptures had crossed the Atlantic. Likewise, the art of Wilhelm Lehmbruck is nowhere in the world so impressively represented as in the Museum of Modern Art in New York City. These works, like those of their successor Gerhard Marcks, have come to the United States principally through the efforts of an earlier immigrant from Germany, the art dealer Curt Valentin. At least one sculptor who remained in Germany during the Nazi period has, since the War, become well-known in the United States. He is Bernard Heiliger whose enormous abstract sculpture commemorates the American Airlift of 1948/1949 and now graces the entrance to Tempelhof Airport in West Berlin.

Significantly, after World War II there has been a constant interchange of the artistic spirit between the United States and Germany. Such programs as the Fulbright scholarship and the German Academic Exchange Service continue to foster it. Despite their own sophistication in taste, Germans at the grass roots are highly impressed with postwar American architecture, especially as they see it exemplified in the United States Consulates in Germany and in such highly acclaimed works as Hugh Stubbins' Kongresshalle in West Berlin. They also speak favorably of the America Houses. These are American information centers which, shortly after World War II, were prominently located and tastefully constructed in all the major cities of Germany. In them the United States continuously presents a wide spectrum of American creativity in the arts. One can only hope that the German and the American spirits of creativity will continue to interweave and cross-fertilize each other for many generations to come.

LIFE'S MILESTONES

LIFE'S MILESTONES

IN GERMANY as elsewhere the delicate process of bringing babies into the world is attributed to the stork, but there are local districts where other birds perform that function, such as the owl, the crow, or even, on the island of Rügen in the Baltic Sea, the swan. In Swabia, children who want to have a little brother or sister place lumps of sugar outside on window sills to attract the stork. In the Harz Mountains little ones are told that a turkey scratches babies out of the gatepost, while in Switzerland occasionally it is said that the midwife fishes babies out of the *Milchbrunnli,* the milk spring. More accurate biologically is the straightforward proverb which says, *"Was sich zweit, das dreit sich gern"* (what comes together in two likes to turn into threes).

Bearing children is a rather non-religious matter for most Germans and in many respects it is linked directly to pagan customs. Rocking an empty cradle is supposed to give birth to a sleepless baby. If the mother takes alcoholic beverages it tends to burn the unborn babe's heart out. For centuries pregnant women in Germany have kept their eyes on the zodiac hoping for a favorable sign at the birth of their child. The poet Goethe reports in *Dichtung and Wahrheit* that wise women neglected the stars in favor of signs gathered from the sun, moon, or clouds. Goethe notwithstanding, it is lucky to be born after midnight but not on the first of April, which, legend says, was the birthday of Judas.

A custom by no means yet abandoned is to plant a tree, the *Lebensbaum,* at the birth of a son. Lurking in back of his father's mind is the suspicion that the fate of this tree coincides with and determines the fate of the child in life. In Mecklenburg they even used to throw the placenta at the foot of the newly planted tree. Such practices indicate that the significance of the *Lebensbaum* lies swaddled deep in the German soul where it rests on the mystical, pagan beliefs concerning the forests—a topic that will be treated more specifically in the chapter on folklore and fairytales. In certain areas the baby's first bath was thought to have a purgatory value, hence some of the mother's milk was added to the water which was then poured around the tree as a harbinger of fertility and happiness.

To this day it is considered a good idea to leave a light burning for the sleeping child because the *Wichtelmänner,* the evil spirits who seize children from their cradles and leave changelings in their place, can see only in the dark. The mother is considered impure after the birth of a child until she has received the *Vorsegnung* or benediction in church about six weeks afterwards. Sometimes neighborly housewives drop in to bring her a *Weisat,* a token package of sugar, coffee, butter and eggs, and a *Schwatzei,* a gossip-egg, which they touch to the baby's mouth so he will learn to talk early.

Taufe, or baptism, takes place quite early, never more than three months after birth. Since some believe that the child will take after his *Pate* or *Gevatter,* the godfather is carefully selected. Godparents give handsome gifts at the christening, again at first communion, and generally on the child's birthday and even on holidays. At the baptism they contract a moral obligation to help and advise the child all his life. In the Bavarian town of Berchtesgaden, people still believe that if brothers and sisters are christened in the light of the same candle they will always love each other, so it is important to pick a heavy candle for the first offspring.

Naming is extremely variable but as a rule patron saints or Teutonic personages are favored for girls. Female appellatives are often long and are pronounced slowly: Hildegard, Elfriede, Margarete, Ursula, Johanna, Charlotte, Annemarie, Edeltraut, Irmgard, Brigitte, Liselotte. On the other hand, boys' names are frequently short and slightly harsh sounding: Kurt, Karl, Hans, Wolf, Fritz, Heinz, Gerd, Max, Lutz, Klaus, Georg, Ludwig. What are the most popular names? The city of Hamburg in 1968 studied the entries on its birth certificates and came up with a representative cross-section. The ten most popular boys' names were Michael, Andreas, Stefan, Thorsten, Thomas, Frank, Oliver, Dirk, Christian and Matthias. The most popular girls' names were Claudia, Anja, Susanne, Sabine, Andrea, Stefanie, Martina, Petra, Bettina and Nicole. Many German children celebrate their *Namenstag,* especially in the more religious families, and all of them enjoy the traditional cake with candles for their *Geburtstag,* birthday.

It is difficult, if not impossible, to separate the religious festival from the national holiday as we know it in the United States. Nevertheless certain religious feasts are better handled in this chapter and others will be treated later in a chapter on holidays and festivals.

Christi Himmelfahrt, Ascension Day, is a great occasion in southern Germany where in a few churches a figure of Christ is actually drawn up into the roof of the church accompanied by the blare of trumpets. Superstitions also surround the event, for example, that it would rain on Ascension Thursday when the heavens opened to let Christ through. In deference to the old god Thor it was wise not to work in the fields on any Thursday, and for that matter to take a bath either, particularly on Ascension Thursday.

Whitsun or *Pfingsten* rates next to Christmas as one of the greatest feasts in the calendar year. To celebrate this feast villagers in some districts go into the forest for green branches to make a *Laubmännchen,* a leaf man. In others, there is a parade of school children who later dance in the open air around a may pole. In Tyrol people tell how the Holy Ghost used to come through a round opening in the church roof. He appeared as a carved wooden dove that sat on a gilded wheel which circled down from the opening. Elsewhere young men today mount horses to compete at *Kranzstechen,* the medieval game of tilting at a wreath suspended from an arch. Afterwards the winner is crowned the *Pfingstkönig.* At Bad Homburg in Hesse, young men sometimes ride horseback to their girl friends' houses for gifts. Then they all come together for a gallop around a manure pile, in the belief that this will produce a bountiful harvest. More widespread is the *Räuberspiel.* A few fellows kidnap someone's fiancée and the others must find and liberate her. In the Rhineland children often build a trellis of twigs over a fountain, and decorate it with flowers and chains of eggshells. There are many similar practices but from these examples it is clear that Whitsun is a religious feast largely taken over from pagan custom, and not really separable from the spring rituals.

As a little boy living in a small German community in Wisconsin I could hardly wait for the yearly feast of Corpus Christi, *Fronleichnam.* On that day the women's groups of the church teamed up with their husbands to build three altars richly decorated with flowers and streamers at different locations in the town. Then the entire congregation and the priest with his ministers would march to each altar for a special benediction. The children in the confirmation class as well as those making their communion all paraded together in groups carrying floral bouquets and singing.

In southern Germany these traditions are even more elaborate. The streets are carpeted with freshly cut hay and trimmed with fragrant, fresh flowers. Grownups wear their local costumes and of course all stores and businesses are closed. Children wear garlands, white shirts and dresses, and sing the praises of the Lord. Door posts and windows are rimmed with crosses made of birch twigs, and often a red streamer of cloth is draped from the windows. The most interesting celebration of Corpus Christi takes place at the large lake in southern Bavaria, the *Chiemsee*. Here, instead of a regular parade, the local villagers elegantly decorate boats ranging in size from tiny canoes to large flats that haul over one hundred people. The procession in effect takes place when these boats move from altar to altar by water.

The word, *Fronleichnam,* is a translation of the Latin, *corpus christi,* body of Christ. *Fron* is an old word no longer in use which means *Herr,* lord or master. The feminine counterpart of this word is still used, *Frau,* lady or Mrs. As far as we can tell, the feast was first celebrated in 1246 in Lüttich. Thoroughly Catholic then as now, the ritual of the feast rests on pagan foundations. Once there existed the tribal custom of wandering through the fields performing certain rites to insure fertility of the soil. It is quite plain that the verdant grasses and fragrant flowers embellishing the processions for the Feast of the Body of Christ is essentially the same.

Courtship, betrothal and marriage are surrounded by a complex sequence of customs and religious ceremonies. In German-American communities as in Germany there is a principle for living that often shocked the more puritani-cally-oriented New Englanders. It underlies the student song:

> *Wer nicht liebt Wein, Weib und Gesang,*
> *Der bleibt ein Narr sein Lebenlang.*

> He who doesn't love wine, women and song,
> He remains a fool his whole life long.

The attitudes capsulized in this song apply to the use of alcoholic beverages, public celebrations and in a particular way to the matter of choosing a mate. Moderation, of course—but abnegation, that is another matter.

For no apparent good reason a German girl is a child until the age of fourteen years and seven months, when she becomes a *Backfisch,* literally translated a baked fish. Actually the term applies at any age when she knows the first stirrings of infatuation, *Schwärmerei,* for an idol or hero of the masculine sex. It takes years of course before *Liebe,* love, has a chance to unfold but once it begins all kinds of courting traditions can be practiced.

In Bavaria the prenuptial rite of *Fensterln* or "windowing" still happens. Accordingly a young man appears beneath the window of his beloved and serenades her. If he is particularly bold he takes a ladder and climbs to the window ledge where he serenades and engages his girlfriend in conversation, sometimes formalized as rhymed questions demanding a yes-or-no answer. If he is ardently persistent and she is sufficiently permissive, he gets to spend the night with her. The custom has rules such as no windowing on Tuesdays or Sundays, and anyone who is known to window at more than one house is soon not tolerated at any. However, society usually allows the same ladder to be seen repeatedly at the same house in spite of ecclesiastical disapproval.

Whenever these tactics can't bring a promise of marriage then perhaps magic can. Matronly aunts and mothers keep precepts, formulas and potions that supposedly excite love and one such book published in Leipzig, *Magic and Love,* saw its forty-sixth edition already before World War II. Anything seems to have the magical powers to ignite the fires of love: verses from the Bible, curses, love potions, snakes, fossils, blood, hair, four-leaf clovers, and all sorts of herbs. If magic helps, proverbs offer additional wisdom in choosing a beloved. A few examples of common ones are:

Es gibt mehr Tannen als Zedern. There are more evergreens than cedars.

Bei Nacht sind alle Katzen grau. During the night all cats look gray.

Andere Städtchen, Andere Mädchen. Other towns have other girls.

Eine schöne Blume steht nicht lang am Weg. A pretty flower is picked early.

More successful than magic or proverbs in the Germany of today is the widespread practice of placing newspaper or magazine advertisements for a suitable marriage partner. Both men and women do it, giving a brief description of themselves, offering a photograph and stating the qualifications he or she desires in the mate. According to reliable sources, the ads prove much more successful than our computer antics in resolving the mating game.

Assuming that either love, magic, or the newspapers have prevailed, there follows an engagement, *die Verlobung.* In older times the engagement was an official ceremony attended by all the relatives gathered in the church. The practice still survives in the Catholic Church's solemn engagement ceremony. The young man would present the girl with a ring and a pair of elegant slippers. The slipper tradition lives on in certain fairytales, notably *Aschenputtel* and *Cinderella.* Apparently wearing the slippers symbolized the young woman's subjection to her husband. Out of this practice grows the modern saying concerning the German wife who dominates her husband. In German one does not say she "wears the pants in the house" but she "has her husband under her slipper," *"unter dem Pantoffel stehen."* Nor is the man called a "hen-pecked husband" but a *Pantoffelheld,* ironically speaking, a slipper hero.

Recently I discovered that the old German custom of asking for the beloved's hand through a middleman is still alive in the rural German settlements in North Dakota, and perhaps elsewhere in the United States. As in Germany, the belief persists that the delicate mission of asking for a girl's hand in marriage belongs to a professional, a semi-broker, semi-diplomat who may but need not be a relative. Depending on the particular region he is known as a *Kuppler* (coupler), a *Schmuser* (twister), a *Freiwerber* (free applicant), or *Degensmann* (swordsman), the latter because the man wears a sword as a symbol of his "legal" and official capacity. Tested through the centuries, this system of messengers involves a refined process of communication. Consent or refusal is often given without words. Usually the delegated wooer brings a "codified" present of certain foods. If the agent is sent back to the waiting young man with a bottomless basket, it means the girl has refused. Even today one occasionally hears the expression, "to give a basket," when a girl rejects a lover's offer of marriage. If he receives other kinds of food and gifts, the young suitor is in business.

Engagement rings in Germany are the same rings as the wedding rings. No diamonds. During the period of engagement they are worn on the left hand, as is the case with the wedding ring in America. Thus, because I was married when I studied in Germany, fellow students often thought I was only engaged. After the couple has been officially married, they simply reverse the hands and wear the rings for the rest of their lives on the right ring fingers. Frequently the name of the spouse is engraved inside the ring. If an engagement is broken, a rare occurrence, all gifts and rings are returned by both parties. It is common to find an older woman wearing two wedding rings on the ring finger of her right hand. This shows simply that she is a widow, the second ring being that of her husband. Unlike Puritanical America, trial engagements have been tolerated in Germany much as bundling was long a custom among the Pennsylvania Germans and others in America. Writers working for the WPA in Schuylkill County in 1940 report that among these German-Americans both bundling and all-night courting were commonplace occurrences in past generations. Bundling is a fancy word for what happens when an unmarried man and woman sleep in the same bed with an object between. The WPA reporters state that while bundling was explicitly practiced only to keep warm, it was implicitly a kind of trial engagement. The girl's parents permitted it and usually made such superficial arrangements as requiring the girl to sleep underneath the top cover while the boy slept one layer down, or placing a board down the middle of the bed, or wrapping the boy in a pullstring bundling bag that covered him from waist to toes. One elderly man interviewed by the WPA stated simply, "Nothing more was thought about it than if the 'sweethearts' had been doing their courting in the kitchen; since kitchen or bedroom it would have had to be, as practically no house could boast of a living room."

Wedding invitations today are frequently mailed but in smaller villages, even here in the United States, a man called the *Hochzeitslader,* the wedding inviter, goes from house to house reciting a poem specially composed for the occasion. The following example gives us a taste of such a poem:

Guten Tag auch Kinder und Leute.
Ich komme geritten
Und nicht geschritten,
Ich bin ausgesandt
Von Hartje Goy, der ist euch bekannt,
Und seiner Braut, Jungfer Ulmke Tormälen,
Die taten mich als Hochzeitsbitter erwählen.
Ihr möchtet sie besuchen an ihrem Ehrentag,
Dann sollt ihr finden Hühnersuppe, eine tüchtige Portion,
Dazu gebratenen Schinken, und auch etwas zu trinken,
Tonnen Bier soviel wie ihr mögt,
Auch Flaschen Wein, wenn das euch erfreut,
Pfeifen und Tabak,
Ein jeder nach seinem Geschmack.
Und es soll getanzet werden, bis an den hellichten Morgen,
Für Stiefel und Schuhe müsst ihr selber sorgen.
Die wollen meine Leute nicht bezahlen,
Die muss der Schuster besohlen.
Und nun lasset mich wissen von ungefähr,
Ob ihr ihnen geben wollet die Ehr.

                                                August Hinrichs

Greetings to both children and grown-ups.
I have come riding my horse
And not walking on foot
From Hartje Goy, who is well known to you,
And from his bride the young woman Ulmke Tormälen.
They have chosen me as their wedding inviter.
You are invited to visit them on their wedding day,
At that time you will find chicken soup, a generous portion,
In addition baked ham, and also something to drink,
Pitchers of beer, as many as you like,
Also bottles of wine, if that be your pleasure,
Pipes and tobacco,

Each according to his taste.
And there'll be dancing, until the light of dawn,
As for boots and shoes, you'll have to provide them
  yourself.
My people do not care to pay for them,
Your shoemaker will have to sole them.
And now, let me hear from you your opinion,
Whether you will be there to give them your honor.

Before moving on, the inviter usually gets a glass of schnapps. Generally he wears a long coat with high hat, white gloves and high boots, and carries a ribboned cane, sword or possibly an umbrella.

In addition to a *Hochzeitslader*, the North Dakota German communities still continue the practice of a *Polterabend* the night before the marriage. Literally an "evening of uproar," the intention of the evening celebration is to drive off any evil spirits and guarantee a happily married life. Young men get together to make hideous noises by firecrackers, shotgun blasts, whip cracking, banging pans, and breaking crockery. In Germany today there are no pre-nuptial showers, but gifts are frequently delivered on the *Polterabend*. In a diary entry made January 7, 1855, the poet Longfellow gives an account of a German wedding near Boston: "R. comes to dinner, and gives us an account of a German wedding—a romantic and poetic wedding in Cambridge—and of the *Polter-Abend*, or evening before the wedding, when the bridal guests are presented. The Germans have so much poetry in their natures, and in their life! This was the marriage of a musician and a gardener's daughter; and guests came in various costumes—housekeeper with keys, ballad-singers with songs, girls with flowers, etc., each presenting a gift and reciting an appropriate verse."

The *Hochzeit* (wedding) is a full-blown affair. In cities, Saturdays are preferred but rural weddings are traditionally held on Tuesdays or Thursdays. For some families the zodiacal signs are observed in picking a day and for certain couples the moon has to be on the wane. In a few sections of the country the ceremony must take place exactly at noon and even if there should be a delay, the clock is stopped to assure the magical midday time.

The matter of bridal gowns and practices of dressing the bride vary so widely that nearly every family is different. The kind of material for the gown also differs greatly from region to region, and as everywhere else in the world, wedding gowns are subject to the pressures of fashion. Black Forest folk costumes for the bride consist of heavy silk with a brilliantly embroidered apron and bodice and a white ruffle around the neck. On her head she wears a tinseled cage covered with glass ornaments and gay colored flowers. Beautiful as the costume is, today's bride prefers wearing the store-bought white dress to the folk wedding gown.

Today, once again, brides much prefer to forsake the motorized limousine in favor of a horse-drawn carriage for the ride to and from church. If she can have a carriage, the horses should be black and choosing them is the prerogative of the bride. On the way, meeting another wedding carriage is a bad omen, passing a streetsweeper or chimneysweep is a good one. Nobody in the procession should ever look back and when possible the team of horses should trot at a good clip. To assure this, it is even a good idea to give the horses a little schnapps.

Unlike in the United States where the church officials can legally marry couples holding a state-issued marriage license, in Germany couples must be legally wed before the proper state official at the *Standesamt* in the city hall. The church ceremony, therefore, is only ceremonial, having

no legality. Most couples nevertheless have a church wedding after the civil marriage and even consider themselves
unmarried until they have appeared before a minister or
priest. In German and German-American churches alike,
there is a custom of roping the newly wedded couple. Long
red ribbons or a garland of flowers is held across the exit
by friends of the couple or ministers of the ceremony. The
bridegroom must buy the couple's ransom by offering
money, or more frequently by promising a wine or beer
party a few weeks after the wedding.

In older times and occasionally today the bride is taken
immediately after the church service to her new home by
cart. Piled on it is her dowry, in some cases the wedding
gifts, some smaller items of furniture, and a carved, oaken
hope chest on top of which sits the bride. I recall attending
a wedding in a small village in the *Schwarzwald* where the
wedding banquet was held in a local inn but during the day
every guest was expected to go to the bride's future home
to view the gifts and inspect all of her furniture. During
this lengthy ordeal the bridegroom welcomed everyone at
the door and saw to it that each received a shot of schnapps,
perhaps intended to dim overly snoopy eyes.

Germans no longer invite whole villages to week-long
weddings but the invited blood relationship can be extremely large. In America too, those three-day weddings are now
a thing of the past, but despite a less extravagant scale,
German wedding hosts still put on a sumptuous banquet.
At some weddings I have attended in Bavaria and in the
Schwarzwald, each guest, before departing at the end of
the evening, marches over to a cashier's desk where he pays
for all of his food and drink. You pay for whatever you
have had in more formal affairs, or a flat fee for all refresh-
ments in less stringently organized situations.

At most German weddings even in the large cities, the

couple is offered bread and salt during the banquet as a
good omen. I am told that "bread and salt" is a customary
gift also when a new couple moves into their home, particularly in families with Yiddish traditions. In Hessen a guest
will sometimes watch for his chance to pin the end of a roll
of red ribbon to the stocking of the dancing bride. At midnight the bride is blindfolded and her wreath removed from
her hair which is then covered with a bonnet, the symbol
that she no longer belongs to the single state. Still blindfolded, she must catch one of the bridesmaids who in turn
will be the first to marry. In northern Germany there is
often a *Kehraus* dance to top off the evening, a sweep-out,
danced by guests as they beat time with cooking utensils,
march out the door, and head home.

If the wedding couple plans to spend their first night
locally, they will probably find their bed has been molested.
But this is acceptable because the bed will usually contain
three pieces of bread and three lumps of coal, good protection against evil spirits and a sign that the marriage will be
blessed. In a few areas the couple is escorted to their house
by the band, a practice called *Heimblasen,* but most frequent now is for the couple to quietly slip away on their
Flitterwoche, or honeymoon, a term which literally means
"week of the sequins," the small gold spangles ornament-
ing the dress of a young girl. For centuries the word *flitter*
has also taken on a figurative connotation synonymous with
affection and love making.

Sometimes marriages end in divorce and for those unfor-
tunate ones there is the admonishing proverb, *"Scheiden
bringt Leiden"* (divorce brings sorrow). Germans have traditionally built strong family ties and even the Roman
writer Tacitus in his descriptive book on Germany praised
the morals of German women. "German women live in a
chastity that is impregnable, uncorrupted by the tempta-

tions of public shows or the excitement of banquets. Clandestine love letters are unknown to men and women alike.
Adultery in that populous nation is rare in the extreme. . . .
No one in Germany finds vice amusing or calls it 'up to
date' to debauch and be debauched."

Without commenting on how applicable Tacitus would
be for today's German women, his pronouncement that
German families were tightly united by their love and joy
in children still prevails. The attention Germans shower on
their children is well known. No other nation has so great
a history in toy-making, for example, as the Germans. In
fact, Germany's export of *Spielwaren,* toys, contributes
heavily to her foreign-trade balance. Whole museums honor
and document the history of German toys, and entire
worlds of the imagination have been given animated reality
by perfectionist German clock builders.

Throughout the world death occasions great sadness, and
yet, whether in the German communities of North Dakota,
Wisconsin, Pennsylvania, or Germany itself, a funeral is
also a time when friends and family can socialize. At the
home of a German family in North Dakota recently, the
wife whipped out her funeral photo album and showed me
a collection that, except for the ubiquitous caskets, resembled a family wedding album.

Pursuing funeral attitudes a little further I came across
a graphic account of German-American funeral customs
written by Mittelberger, *Journey in Pennsylvania,* and reported by Faust, *The German Element in America,* Vol. II,
page 389: "When someone has died, where people live far
from one another, the time appointed for the funeral is always indicated only to the four nearest neighbors; each of
these in his turn notifies his own nearest neighbor. In this
manner such an invitation to a funeral is made known more
than fifty English miles around in twenty-four hours. If pos-

sible, one or more persons from each house appear on horseback at the appointed time to attend the funeral. While the people are coming in, good cake, cut into pieces, is handed around on a large tin platter to those present; each person then receives in a goblet a hot West India rum punch, into which lemon, sugar, and juniper berries are put, which gives it a delicious taste. After this, hot and sweetened cider is served. This custom at the funeral assemblies is just the same as that at the wedding gatherings in Europe. The assembled people number from one hundred to five hundred persons on horseback. They ride behind in silence accompanying the dead body to the general burial place, or, where that is too far away, the deceased is buried in his own field." Likewise astonishing to view are the small, semi-abandoned, family-sized cemeteries scattered across the prairies of German North Dakota.

Many German proverbs seem also to reveal a lighter outlook on death. *"Auch der Tod ist nicht umsonst, er kostet das Leben"* (even death isn't free of charge, it costs us our life). *"Tod und Leben sind über einen Leisten geschlagen* (dying is as natural as living). *"Im Grab ist Ruh"* (in the grave one can at least rest). In a similar vein, I once asked the leader of a large university fraternity on what occasions they still wore their colorful costumes in public and he answered, "In *vollen Wichs* (in full ceremonial dress) we don't turn up just any and everywhere. But we do for weddings and for funerals. We might wear our less formal *Couleur* for going to church or even at street demonstrations." In some inexplicable way German weddings and funerals are closely related to each other.

Even in death the German affirms his "joy in living" and sociologists are in agreement that Germans have bequeathed to America their zest for harmless pleasure, clearing our eyes of jaundiced Puritanism. Few Americans realize for example that the Germans in the United States initiated "The Opera House," not however because they gave so many operas, but because they wanted to avoid the stigma Puritanism had attached to the word "theater," implying some kind of sinful enjoyment.

On another plane, death seems to have fascinated the German mind. German literature and painting manifest countless variations on the theme of death. Everyone has seen German pictures in which a skull is perched on a bookshelf, or where a skeleton stands erect with men as in Dürer's *Ritter, Tod und Teufel*. Also there is the Romantic painter Arnold Böcklin's *Insel der Toten* (Isle of the Dead). In the military too, the concept of death is enhanced by an honorable longing for the sacrificial *Heldentod,* heroic death.

In the traditional German countryside, if a man is dying he will be kept in a room with the windows open to permit exit of his soul, and with his feet toward the door apparently also to expedite the soul's departure. Strict rules forbid weeping or laments at the deathbed because this would disturb his spirit. In former times when the man stopped breathing he was clothed in a *Totenhemd,* or dead man's shirt. According to popular belief this garment goes back to the seamless robe worn by Christ before being crucified. The shirt had to be sewn without knots. Funerals in large towns have become routine, but in rural areas it still happens that a man is dressed in his elegant festival folk costume for burial. Unmarried girls are buried with a bridal veil and the traditional crown of crystals to signify a life of virginity.

Many superstitions have come from rural Germany to rural America. For instance, I have heard in Wisconsin that the dead remain in the houses where they lived for forty days and that women who die in childbirth come every midnight for six weeks to suckle their babies. Not infrequently, a dining place is set for a recently deceased relative at a family wedding or funeral banquet. The corpse is always carried out of a room feet first, and all mirrors in the house are covered so the image of the dead will not remain imprisoned there. Formerly the sad news of death was passed by a *Leichenbitter* who moved from door to door with a black stick to announce the death.

In Germany the matter of mourning for the dead is particularly intricate and rigid. Women wear black dresses with black stockings and often a black chiffon veil over their faces for all public appearances. Depending on the degree of kinship, the length of time for official mourning varies from a few weeks to a year but in rural Germany it is possible to find elderly women who are perpetually mourning for somebody or other.

In a few isolated sections there once were customs of putting something in the coffin with the corpse, a coin in the hand or under the tongue. This tradition goes back to the ancients who placed money next to the deceased so he could pay for his ferry ride to the distant shore. It has also been reported that some put a lemon under the chin or in the hand of the dead person. Cloves are pushed into the lemon in the form of a cross. In other areas, those present throw lemons into the grave after the lowering of the *Sarg* (coffin) before it is covered with earth. Apparently this is an old practice because we read that in the seventeenth century and for years thereafter, criminals on their way to the gallows usually carried a lemon in their hands. At German-American burials it is common to see the benediction followed by relatives each throwing a clump of earth on the coffin pronouncing a special prayer as they perform this symbolic ritual.

Funeral ceremonies do not end here. As mentioned

above, there seems to be an inexplicable kinship between weddings and funerals. Thus, after the burial, relatives and friends gather for the *Totenmahl,* banquet of the dead. In many instances we find also the *Leichenbier,* or beer of the dead, in place of or in addition to the meal. It could be that relatives drown their sorrow in alcohol, but more likely there is the sound philosophy behind it that, after all, life is to be enjoyed even in the face of death. Indeed it is not rare to learn that the dead man has left money in his will for the drinking party of his relatives and companions. Once when I showed up at such a party by chance and without an invitation I wanted to withdraw politely. But before I could do so gracefully, a middle-aged man approached me with an ultimatum, the proverb: *"Sauf oder Lauf,"* (drink up, fellow, or begone). Needless to say, I stayed.

EDUCATION AND LEARNING

EDUCATION AND LEARNING

THE OLD SAYING goes, *"Es lernt neimand aus, bis das
Grab ist unser Haus."* Literally, this means no one is
through learning until the grave is his home. By hook or
by crook mothers see to it that their children start to learn
early. The moment an infant can handle solids he gets
alphabet biscuits with his milk and alphabet soup before
his meal. Some mothers are naive enough to think that it
benefits the child if he sleeps with a book under his pillow.

Just the other day some friends in Munich sent me a
picture of their youngest son, taken on his first day of
school. He was holding a huge colored cone about three
feet long, a *Zuckertüte,* which looked something like the
horn of plenty. There is an old belief that the first day of
school is a highly significant pivot in life because it marks
the beginning of a life of duty and responsibility. To sweet-
en this bitter nut, the parents begin as much as a year in
advance to fill the horn with candy. It stands plainly visible in the living room on a buffet or table, constantly re-
minding the boy of what is to come. On the day he returns
from his first day at school he gets the whole bag of goodies.

The duty of learning is serious business and from the
start children imbibe this German devotion: *"Erfülle deine
Pflicht, um alles Andere kümmere dich nicht"* (do your
duty and don't worry about anything else). Despite the
criticism often leveled at the Germans by foreigners for

this disciplined approach to duty, the schools in Germany are really teaching character and life-long responsibility. If a child learns early that *"Muss ist eine harte Nuss,"* (what must be is a tough nut) then tomorrow's man has the stability to meet the challenges of life.

In all the states except Bavaria the German school year ends and begins at Easter time. Although plans have been made to put the whole country on the September cycle, at present only Bavaria operates on the United States school year. The German summer vacation is short, only six weeks free and another week for Pentecost, amounting to some compensation for the shortened summer. In a few areas the children still get *Kartoffelferien,* time to help with the potato harvest. This vacation is not unlike areas for example in Iowa where students until recently received a "corn huskers' vacation."

Schulpflicht, mandatory schooling, has existed in Germany for well over one hundred years. Children start school at the age of six, although they may attend a kindergarten a year before that. The first four years are spent in the *Volkschule,* sometimes called *Grundschule,* elementary school. Many pupils remain for nine years in the *Volkschule;* others shift after the fourth year into either the *Mittelschule* or the *Oberschule.* Still more academically oriented than these latter schools is the so-called *Gymnasium.* In many respects the *Gymnasium* is comparable to our high school except that it is far more selective and therefore academic. Subjects like Latin and at least one or two foreign languages are required. By the time a student finishes the *Gymnasium* he has, generally speaking, learned as much as an American student after about two years of college. Attendance at the university requires passing a tough final examination after being graduated from the *Gymnasium.* This exam, called the *Abitur,* is given in all subjects over a period of several months, sometimes over a year's time.

Without trying to describe the complicated process, it should be pointed out that virtually any pupil with talent can move up from a more technical school to a more academically oriented one. Nevertheless from the fourth year on, the individual already is delegated on the basis of a battery of tests either for academics and the professions, for routine business and clerical jobs, or for a mechanical-technical occupation. The apprentice system is highly developed in Germany; a seven-year trade school allows the student to spend up to four days a week on the job earning while learning, and two more days in school taking academic subjects as well as theory about the job he is already performing.

A word about some fundamental differences between German and American lower education: American schools have always been under local control. The school board is in charge and its members are elected by the people in the district. In Germany a state ministry of education stipulates how the school system will run the German education. Rudolf Haas, in an article entitled "German and American Education" appearing in the newspaper, *Bridge,* February, 1966, points out that the Americans have a working system of tests and measurements coupled with guidance and counseling. The Germans, he believes, would do well to improve this aspect of their education. Likewise, Haas feels that we in America are doing a better job of teaching the pupils social consciousness and democracy at an early age.

Haas points out furthermore that the two countries differ with respect to the mobility or flexibility afforded students in electing their education. Thus the American child has many choices open to him as he moves through junior and senior high school, and even earlier in the grades. But the German student has considerably more mobility at the college level than the American student. The German student "can drive at will and at the speed he likes best. In America, after the 'Huckleberry Finn' period of the open road in the high schools, the student has to face an elaborate system of signals, switches and ticket collecting at the end of each university and college semester." Then too, in America there is more social mobility within the educational system. European education still has a rather rigid set of professional values and archaic social scales which are not easily overcome. Says Haas, "Education for the masses as it prevails in the States may be defined as a tremendous utilitarian attempt to grant the greatest social mobility to the greatest number, to send people out into life well equipped for a broad range of different jobs."

The German university in many respects is comparable to our graduate schools. In fact, the very concept of a graduate school in the United States is founded directly on the German university system. The epoch of graduate education in America began in 1876 with the founding of Johns Hopkins University. Until a much later date, this institution had no undergraduate section and demanded a college degree for admission to all of its schools, including the medical school, which was the first medical college to set such standards. All of the founding faculty of Johns Hopkins were either German or held doctorates from German universities. Enunciating the principle that the best teachers are the diligent researchers and vice versa, the founding fathers of Johns Hopkins securely planted the German university system in American soil. So bountiful were the fruits that Germany soon recognized Johns Hopkins as one of its sister institutions.

More significant for the whole American graduate school system was the fact that the Johns Hopkins plan was adopted throughout the United States. At the 25th anniversary celebration for Johns Hopkins, President Eliot of Harvard gave an address in which he paid tribute: "Your first achievement . . . has been . . . the creation of a school of graduate studies, which not only has been in itself a strong and potent school, but which has lifted every other university in the country in its departments of arts and sciences. I want to testify that the graduate school of Harvard University, started feebly in 1870 and 1871, did not thrive until the example of Johns Hopkins forced our faculty to put their strength into the development of our instruction for graduates. And what was true of Harvard was true of every other university in the land which aspired to create an advanced school of arts and sciences." In another instance, in 1904 the University of Chicago dedicated its Fiftieth Convocation to the "Recognition of the Indebtedness of American Universities to the Ideals of German Scholarship." To this day the University of Chicago operates on a very German-oriented system of higher education.

It is no secret that before the American universities were able to prove their mettle, the exodus of American students to German universities had been large throughout most of the nineteenth century. Learning German, therefore, became a cardinal rule for all advanced degrees. This principle of education, enunciated by the President of Johns Hopkins, may have slipped in importance but in great part it still applies: "As Latin was the language of the scholar during the Middle Ages, so the knowledge of German is now indispensable for anyone who claims the name of a student and scholar."

In passing it ought to be pointed out that the University of Hamburg was a kind of Johns Hopkins in reverse, a German institution of higher education founded squarely on the American idea of a college. Establishing the university in 1919, the founders sought to develop leaders for German commerce, manufacture, transportation and politics. Today, although the University inevitably parallels her sister institutions in the Federal Republic more than her parent models in the United States, Hamburg University still has a distinct program while continuing to rank with the best of universities in the world.

Student life at the German university was, and still is, sometimes hard — poor food, bad housing, inadequate spending money, and much hard work. Nevertheless there is another side which more than makes up for the troubles. Ask any German established in his profession what were the happiest days of his life and he will invariably reply by singing a song learned in his student days at one of the universities. Entire "hymnals" filled with German university songs can be repeated by the students from memory. *"Ich hab mein Herz in Heidelberg verloren"* (I lost my heart in Heidelberg) and *"O alte Burschenherrlichkeit wohin bist du entschwunden"* (O wonderful student days, where have you escaped to) are the first lines of just two popular songs of the graduated set.

Until the last generation and in some respects even today, the time in life spent as a university student was an escape, a nostalgic period of development for the mind and the heart. In the university towns the professors were ostensibly in control but the students really ran the show. Though outwardly concerned, the citizenry tacitly indulged the deeds and misdeeds of carousing students. Hundreds of legends and songs tell of drinking, rousing elders from their beds, playing ingenious jokes on fellow students or officials, and staging colorful, costumed street riots. Each university had its own code to deal with students and even its own prison, a *Kerker,* for disciplining rowdy conduct.

One phenomenon of German student life that over the

years has caused much concern abroad is the activity of the student organizations known as *die Burschenschaften.* Broadly speaking these are fraternities. Each one has its own costume, regulations, colors, ceremonies and rituals. Unlike the United States, the *Burschenschaften* have been traditionally active in politics, frequently in a tragic sort of way. Loyalty among the members often became so strong that one could not get a position in certain government circles or industrial posts unless he belonged to the right fraternity at the university. In effect, a fraternity exercised a kind of monopoly in the social, civil, and economic life of the country.

Formerly attendance at the university was far more common for the male population than the female. Since World War II, however, increasing numbers of young women are also showing up for classes. Gone forever is the *Kinder, Kirche, Küche* (children, church, kitchen) trinity that the young German maid was once supposed to worship. Certain professions in Germany, notably medicine and dentistry, attract far more women proportionally than in the United States.

But co-eds have not been able to participate in one of the old traditions of student life in Germany, and that is the matter of dueling. The duel is part and parcel of the code of honor, and among students, has always been practiced within the *Burschenschaften.* Many a young man has lost both his heart and his smooth, unscarred face back in Heidelberg. After a temporary moratorium on dueling immediately following World War II, the sport, including occasional blood-letting, is once again common practice.

The art of fencing came to Germany from the Italian schools in the seventeenth century. After the practice became a refined sport, the poet Goethe advised it for developing actors and athletes alike. Once, though, fencing amounted to bloody encounters with daggers, sabers, poles and sticks. As chivalry gradually declined, military arts became more and more the responsibility of the burghers. Skills in using the swords had to be developed by the local citizens while artisans had to develop their skills at making them.

Out of these necessities there developed the swordmaker's guilds. For example in 1775 in Frankfurt the independent society of swordsmen organized a fraternity whose token of recognition was a costume with hats pierced by a long feather. Hence there arose such expressions as *Federfuscher,* a quill driver, or *Federheld,* a feather hero or paper tiger.

In Franconia there stands today a renovated castle, the Veste Coburg, which has become a magnetic attraction to over 70,000 visitors a year. Its appeal is an exhibit entitled "The Art of Fencing from 1500 to 1900." Using knight's armor, swords, pointed staves, tournament pennants, rapiers and swords as well as thousands of copperplate engravings, the museum tells the story in its romantic bastions and towers of the development of an art that evolved from the sporting life of knights, to the deadly serious mechanics of war, to the more playful practice of dueling.

A complex ritual surrounds the duel. Often the pretext of a duel is a point of honor but the purpose seems to be more a demonstration of superior courage. The gymnasium or hall where a duel takes place is equipped with medical staff and surgical utensils in case of serious injury. In attendance is a large audience of fraternity brothers dressed in their society's costumes, and possibly a few guests. Today the participants wear padded jackets to prevent bodily injury and their hands and eyes are covered with iron baskets so that the thrusts of the saber are exclusively to the face. The only apparent consolation for a cut in the cheek is being able to wear the "trophy" for the rest of one's life.

Virtually all fraternities once required their members to engage in a series of *Mensuren* (duels) on the *Paukboden,* or fencing floor. A student who joined as a freshman could not be promoted to full membership until he had fought a duel. Some societies pledged themselves to perform a fixed number of encounters each semester. In the old days the medical students who attended to aid the wounded developed a lore about their abilities; they could gather up nose ends and ear tips and replace them so skillfully that not even a scar would betray the facts. If a fellow was not particularly handsome, his whole countenance could be given a face lifting by the enterprising young meds.

The rationale for dueling lies deep within the military code of honor. In the Prussian military court of honor and to a lesser degree in the Bavarian, dueling remained the accepted way of settling questions of honor up to and during World War I. As late as 1900 an officer who declined a duel and resorted to due process instead was expelled from the officers' corps. Kaiser Wilhelm I declared around 1890, "I will no more tolerate in my army an officer who is capable of wantonly wounding the honor of a comrade than one who does not know how to vindicate his own honor." In theory, the duel was once a way of forcing God to intervene and pronounce judgment on the spot as to who had offended honor. This life-or-death approach to justice is an extension of the medieval recourse to a *Feuerprobe.* Accordingly, if a young woman should be accused of adultery she could request a *Feuerprobe* (trial by fire). Under the eyes of ecclesiastical and civil authorities an iron poker was then heated red hot in a fire. The woman was forced to grab its glowing end and hold it for a time with both hands. If her flesh did not sear the Church pronounced her innocent. In short, to prove the woman innocent of adultery,

God had to intervene with a miracle on her behalf.

Usually a duel, whether between officers or civilians, was fought according to specific rules. The pistol duel required fifteen paces. The combatants faced each other with their pistols pointed backward over the shoulder and advanced as the umpire counted from one to five, a step at each number. Either man could fire after the first step, or they might choose to wait until they were closer together, but if one fired and missed he had to wait and stand his ground until the other had his turn. The saber duel was more savage because once it began, time was not called until one man lay mortally wounded.

On first thought it may seem a little mysterious why the practice of dueling did not accompany the German immigrants to the United States. As anyone who has ever heard of Alexander Hamilton and Aaron Burr knows, however, the duel was occasionally a way of settling affairs even here in our country. The reason why German dueling never took root in America is no doubt because it is firmly embedded in a tradition of honor and social class. Originally a duel was staged to settle questions involving one's honor. Of course such absolute views of honor were possible only among the leisure classes, among the aristocracy or by extension, the upper levels of the bourgeoisie, in general among those who had no occasion to leave Germany. The vast majority of the immigrants were non-professionals who had never even seen the inside of a university. In contrast, the members of the professions in Germany and to a large extent, all the educated were also the members of upper middle class. One might say there was a business and professional aristocracy; each profession and each rung on the business ladder had its fraternity at the university. To these leaders, dueling and its continuation in the universities was simply another way of displaying their traditional upper-class heritage. To them dueling was a mark of high civility whereas to the American it has generally been considered a symbol of barbarism.

Much more agreeable in the university *Burschenschaften* is their ancient tradition of the drinking party. Drinking with the fraternity boys has always been a complicated and highly ritualistic ceremony. The writer Arthur Koestler devotes chapter ten of his popular book *Arrow in the Blue* to his days in the *Burschenschaft* at the University of Vienna.

The drinking party is called a *Kneipe,* formerly the word for an inn or tavern, and the verb *kneipen* has come to mean "boozing it up." The program of a *Kneipe* is half in Latin, half in German. First a fixed number of songs are sung while everyone stands at attention around a long, narrow table. On command all sit, laying their swords before them on the table. Trophies of duels and competitive bouts as well as emblems decorate the walls of the hall.

Toasts to absent members, dead or alive, are drunk while standing at attention and clicking the heels. The full glass must be raised with military precision, emptied and ordered back to the table much like going through the right-shoulder-arms drill. Any misconduct during the ceremony is punishable by ordering the *Fuchs,* a fox or junior member, to "dive into his glass." This is done either *ad diagonalem,* that is, until the liquid in the tilted glass touches the upper end of its base, or *ex,* draining it to the last drop. Anyone can express sympathy for the offender by jumping up, clicking heels and also drinking *ad diagonalem* or *ex.* With permission sick members may visit a lavatory to vomit or to douse their heads in water. Returning, they are cheered like wounded soldiers rejoining their regiment.

The book by Koestler describes other student diversions in the city of Vienna, such as *Das süsse Wiener Mädl.* The sweet Vienna girl "was a shopgirl or typist or a dress-maker's employee. Unlike her French equivalent, the *midinette,* who became extinct early in the century, the sweet Vienna girl was still a most comforting reality in the 1920's. Her tastes were modest; she loved for love's sake; to be occasionally taken to the movies or to a *Weinstube* for dinner was regarded by her as the peak of generosity. She was pretty, flirtatious and extremely well-behaved; and she was treated by her student friends with great consideration and courtesy. Thanks to her existence, the Viennese fraternities were free of homosexuality and of the neurotic quarrels and entanglements so frequent in other youth clubs."

German fraternities, though temporarily blighted after World War II, have by no means died out. When the German association of fraternities met at Landau in 1968 there were 126 *Burschenschaften* represented. Nearly all of them were founded during the nineteenth century, still wear the colorful costumes to distinguish identity, and still practice dueling. Once the *Burschenschaften* were radical, anti-Semitic, anti-French and bore names from the legendary past: Germania, Armenia, Teutonia. Active members in the fraternities today are more congenial to out-groups. They still number over 5,400 and there are more than five times that many former students maintaining their inactive membership. The business duties of the association are managed each year by a different local. The national association takes a stand on political issues ranging from reform of the university system to protest marching against such *status quo* targets as Germany's coalition government.

Nor is the fencing duel by any means dead. Says a student at the University in Berlin, "Whoever doesn't take part in fencing shows no solidarity with our causes." *Kneipen* is also a tradition still in good health, as is the *Salamander,* the ritual toast drunk when a chief gives the cue for all to stand, rub the bottoms of their glasses three times on the tabletop and with group synchronization, empty their mugs in a single gulp. If a member breaks a rule he is *"in den Schwarz- wald geschickt,"* literally, exiled to the Black Forest. This means in reality that he is ostracized from his brothers who will not eat or drink with him for a prescribed period of time. Furthermore he has to be in every evening at nine o'clock.

Germany's highly respected weekly news magazine, *Der Spiegel* (June 17, 1968), carried a lengthy article on the fraternities in Germany.

The American graduate school was not the only institution strongly influenced by the German educational system. In 1843 the great American educator Horace Mann crossed the Atlantic to scout European education in hopes of adopting what he found to be valuable for America. Returning he wrote that of all the schools he had visited, he would rank schools in Prussia first, in Saxony second, in Southern Germany third, in Holland fourth, etc. Horace Mann was not the only admirer of the German school system. The legislature of the state of Ohio sent Calvin E. Stowe abroad also to study foreign school systems. He returned with a similarly favorable report on German schools which was subsequently read by schoolmen all over the United States.

Germany was the first country to adopt on a national scale the techniques of the Swiss educator Johann H. Pestalozzi, in the 1830's. Shortly thereafter the German educator, Friedrich Fröbel, came to the United States and introduced the system of the *kindergarten,* today a household word in every American family. Soon the Fröbel technique was adopted in the American schools for all the grades. The third German figure to influence American education was Johann F. Herbart who was responsible especially for the integration of subjects into an educational whole.

According to some scholars the first kindergarten in the United States was the one founded in 1855 at Watertown, Wisconsin. This one was established by the wife of Carl Schurz, nee Margarethe Meyer, and called the Fröbel Kindergarten. There is evidence that such a kindergarten may have been established in Columbus, Ohio, as early as 1838 by Caroline L. Frankenburg. (See the author's "The Columbus Germans" in *Report 33, SHGM* 1968, p. 25.) Close on the heels of Mrs. Schurz was the German immigrant Carl D. Douai who started a kindergarten in Boston in 1859 and thereafter in Hoboken, Newark, and New York. Soon the cause was taken up by Miss Elizabeth Peabody who first studied Fröbel's models in Germany, then returned to found the American Fröbel Union in 1867. During the 1880's the kindergarten concept grew rapidly. Both public and private ones were successful. What began with a couple hundred kindergartens in the 1880's grew to over five thousand in 1900. Today, of course, the kindergarten is part of every school system in the nation.

One other area in which German education had at least an indirect influence on the American system was through the parochial schools. As such, there are no parochial schools in Germany but there are many which are designated as Catholic or Evangelical while belonging to the overall public school system. In the United States a principle recognizing the separation of church and state prevented such an arrangement. Thus, on their own the Lutherans and Catholics established their private schools adjoined to each parish church.

Around 1900 the Lutheran synods in the United States boasted some 2,100 parochial schools. In them were close to 3,000 teachers and nearly 100,000 pupils. It cannot be maintained that these institutions were modeled on German schools nor that they were schools where German was the exclusive vehicle of instruction. In most, however, the German language held a prominent place.

The Catholic parochial schools in this country were founded as a result of the First Plenary Council of Baltimore held in 1829 which directed that Catholics should provide their own schools for the religious training of their children. The first German Catholic schools did not begin, however, until about 1840 when the influx of immigrants from Germany became sizeable. Quite a number of communities in Ohio, Pennsylvania, and Maryland had no schools at all until the Catholic priest opened a parochial one. In such cases it was common for Catholics and Protestants alike to attend the Catholic school because it was the only one around. The German parishes had an advantage because the unrest in Germany forced many teachers from the religious orders to seek a new existence in America. Both to give these people employment and to upgrade their religious training programs in the parish, pastors in German communities founded elementary schools.

Being private, these schools were answerable only to the pastor, or by extension to the parishioners of a given church. As such there was no problem with maintaining the use of German as the language of instruction for generations. Most of those I have investigated in Ohio, Wisconsin and Minnesota retained German until 1917 when the United States entered World War I against Germany. Although the subsequent generations discontinued the use of German, the schools have thrived. They have in fact remained so dominant that I know several communities today where there are still no public schools. The few non-Catholic families who happen to move into the areas apparently do not object to sending their children to the parochial schools.

Taking the year 1900 as a basis for our statistics we find

that there were roughly five thousand Catholic schools in the country and that they enrolled about 1,200,000 pupils per year. Furthermore, we know that the use of German as the language of instruction began to decline after 1900 but estimates of how many Catholic schools still used German at that time run as high as 50 percent. In tribute to the zealous German pastors who strove for quality in education I quote briefly from the decrees of the Provincial Council of bishops held at Cincinnati. Referring to the general status of the Catholic schools at the time, the bishops decreed: "Our excellent German congregations leave us nothing to desire on this subject. . . . We have nothing more at heart than that the pupils of our English schools should imitate these examples."

In summary, one might say that the extremes of our educational system, the kindergarten and the graduate school are totally fashioned on German models. The secondary schools are native to the United States but were developed by men who took suggestions from European schools, particularly the Prussian ones. The American undergraduate college however is patterned on the English system. Germany, on the other hand, consciously borrowed from the United States in setting up her University of Hamburg in the early part of the twentieth century. In the increasingly technological society of America it might be wise to restructure the vocational and manual arts centers more directly on the pattern of the German apprenticeship program.

Once the German is educated well enough to take a job he gets a title. If in the course of a social evening you need to call him by name a hundred times, then give him his full title a hundred times. Virtually all titles begin with *Herr, Frau* or *Fräulein* followed by the title and/or family name. It may sound ridiculous but a South German newspaper

in a death announcement referred to a surviving wife as
Früchtegrosshändlerswitwe, that is, a wholesale fruit dealer's widow. Frequently grave stones carry a man's name
plus a title of the job he had held. I have even seen stones
on which the survivors could write no more than "Herr
So-and-so, *Hausbesitzer"* (house owner).

Take a poll of what profession enjoys the highest status
in the United States and the medical profession will invariably be on top. Repeat the poll fifty times in Germany and
everytime the university professor will head the list. He is
Herr Professor, never simply *Herr Doktor,* since the higher
of several titles is used exclusively. The head of a university is always a professor who has been elected by his colleagues and is then addressed as*"Magnifizenz."* Clergy are
Herr Pfarrer or *Herr Pastor, Ehrwürdiger Bruder* for a
monk, *Herr Landesbischof* or *Herr Oberkirchenrat* for a
higher ecclesiatic. In government it is *Herr Minister, Herr
Staatssekretär, Herr Bundeskanzler,* etc. A cultivated German never uses his title when introducing or identifying
himself, but it is proper to call a man by his title if you
know it in advance.

A woman who holds a doctoral degree can be addressed
Frau Doktor but she is not properly addressed with her husband's title, for instance as *Frau Direktor.* In general it is
always safe when dealing with women in social situations to
use *Gnädige Frau,* which means "madam." The little prep-
osition *von* denotes that a person formerly belonged or still
belongs to the ranks of nobility and it should be used as
part of the official name. Thus the correct form would be
Herr Wernher von Braun.

The business of titles is tricky. If two gentlemen know
each other only slightly and meet by accident they might
say, *"Wie geht's Ihrer Gattin?"* (How is your wife?) More
polite and formal would be, *"Wie geht es Ihrer Frau Gem-*

ahlin?" If they know each other well they would say, *"Wie geht's Ihrer Frau?"* Nevertheless, no matter how formal the occasion, ladies would never refer to their husbands by using the words *"mein Gatte"* or *"mein Gemahl."* Nor can a wife refer to her husband as *"Herr* Schmidt." For women the matter is quite simple; they merely say, *"mein Mann."*

The matter of education in Germany can aptly be concluded with a couple of proverbs. *"Lehre bildet Geister, doch Übung macht den Meister"* (teaching develops minds but practice makes the master). The saying is particularly appropriate in a country where the philosophy of Kant is taught, but where one must learn his trade according to the principle "practice makes perfect" that is so excellently applied by the apprenticeship program. Also to be kept in mind: *"Wer sein eigner Lehrmeister sein will, hat einen Narren zum Schüler"* (he that teaches himself has a fool for his master).

LEGEND, FOLKLORE, FOLK WISDOM

LEGEND, FOLKLORE, FOLK WISDOM

THE RHEINGOLD was the accursed treasure of the Nibe-
lungs which no one could retain without destroying his soul.
When Hagen, killer of the heroic Siegfried, cast the horde
into the Rhine it was swallowed in the throat of Germany's
bowels and still lies hidden in the twilight of her soul. Siegfried carried a sword which was forged by elves working
fiery smithies in the caverns of mountains, and tempered by
the blood of dragons. All of this and much more is reported
in the *Nibelungenlied,* Germany's greatest epic. Siegfried,
the supreme hero of German saga, came to life in the nineteenth century through the music of Richard Wagner's
Ring of the Nibelung. He was again immortalized when
the German High Command under Hitler ordered a massive
defense wall built along the German-French border and
called it the "Siegfried Line."

For all her epic heroes, Germany has produced so many
flesh-and-blood demigods that she would not even need the
purely legendary ones. Take the colorful Hermann the
Cherusker, famous defender of Germany in the *Teutoburgerwald,* mentioned in the first chapter. When Hermann
savagely fell upon the Roman legions led by Varus, the
Romans died—as Romans have always done—almost to a
man. The few survivors received nothing from life but a
wicker cage and volatile straw which torches ignited as a
sacrificial offering to the gods of the forest.

The sacred eagles, emblems of the seventeenth, eighteenth, and nineteenth Legions, all were captured. When Augustus Caesar heard of the disaster he wept for days crying aloud like a child, "O Varus, Varus, give me back my legions." Six years later Hermann climbed a tall pine tree along the Weser River to watch another battle with the Romans, this time out in the open with no shelter from the sacred forests. Then suddenly, as a flock of eagles swooped down over the field, the Romans regained their spirit at the good omen and were inspired to take back their own "eagles." Murdered with the daggers of his own chieftains, Hermann left his young wife, far along in pregnancy, to be dragged in chains through the streets of Rome.

As if in revenge, the Huns eventually took the Roman Empire into a calloused fist and wrung forth her life's blood. One deep thrust and a dark curtain was thrown over European history. Then, like a conflagration in the night, came the almost barbaric revival of Christian faith and the resultant crusades. In place of the Roman Empire, the Holy Roman Empire was born and grew to adolescence. Commanding this loose confederation in 1189 was the German Emperor Frederich Barbarossa who set out with his fierce army to free the Holy Land. One day, sweaty from the heat of battle he plunged into the cool River Calycadnus to refresh himself and suffered a cardiac arrest. Thus ended Barbarossa, a member of the Hohenstaufen family from Swabia, who in a few years had created a German imperial grandeur that dazzled all of western Christendom.

Less than eighty years later in 1268, Konradin, the last of the Hohenstaufens mounted a scaffold in the market place of Naples and was put to death. At the age of fifteen he had crossed the Alps to try to restore the greatness of the imperial family. Two years later when he ended in ignominy he was not yet seventeen. Nevertheless, the German armies retreating from Naples in World War II carefully removed and took with them to Germany the sarcophagus containing the remains of this, the last of their Hohenstaufens.

The army had good reason in legend for its decision. Ever since that great Hohenstaufen, Barbarossa, died leading his crusaders, Germans have been fascinated with his power. It has been eight hundred years now since his death but legend keeps him alive, portraying him asleep deep inside the womb of a mountain, either the Untersberg near Salzburg or the Kyffhäuser in Thuringia. In slumber he is thought to be waiting for his country to need him. There remains alive among Germans a very old belief that if ever Germany should need a savior, Barbarossa would be reawakened by ravens encircling his mountain top. He would then arise and wrench his homeland from defeat and bear her to the glory of a new golden age. In history this has come to be known as the Kyffhäuser legend.

If ever the Fatherland was in need of the *heimliche Kaiser* (the hidden savior) it was during World War II! Bound by the spell of this and other legends, the German people have sometimes lost sight of political realities, and with sinister cleverness the Nazi rulership played insidiously on the German people's wistful dreams and fondness for legends. It is no secret that Germans rallied around Hitler who in his appeal to folk myths did indeed look like the *heimliche Kaiser* risen from the depths in Germany's direst hour. Likewise, in the most awesome and catastrophic of all Hitler's undertakings, the invasion of Russia and the proposed establishment of his vast *Reich,* it is no accident that the code name he prescribed for the entire operation was *Unternehmen Barbarossa.* Catastrophically, Hitler, promising a second thousand year *Reich* like the first Holy Roman

Empire, ended with unprecedented disaster in just twelve years.

The great Swiss historian and diplomat Carl J. Burckhardt reports that in 1925 he spoke with a young man doing his Ph.D. at the University of Göttingen. The man foretold the return of the *heimliche Kaiser* whose task it would be to remove all vestiges of western civilization and bring *Gesundung* (health) to the German people. What he foresaw, the student explained, was the *"Entfesselung mythischer Urkraft gegen civilisatorische Tücke"* (the unfettering of mythical primeval folk-powers against treachery of western civilization). Commenting on the prophecy, Burckhardt writes that myths have always been intoxicating for the Germans. Beyond their apparent simplicity as harmless allegories, the legends are invitations to *Schicksal* (fate) and *Verhängnis* (doom).

Between the South-German Hohenstaufen family and Hohenzollern family of Prussia, which provided the North German hegemony for Germany in modern times, there is a curious linkage. When Barbarossa died unheroically, the remnants of his army—knights, priests and lay brothers—bound by a vow of chastity and a military oath, decided to forsake their crusade for the Holy Land in favor of another crusade. The knights remounted their worldly steeds and rode off to found a new religious order, calling it the Teutonic Knights. With missionary zeal they threaded their way back northward to found a home and to build their immense brick fortress, the Marienburg of the Knights, in the savage heathen country of East Prussia.

Severely damaged during World War II, that huge gothic structure is now slowly being restored by the Polish government. Here in the cool mews the knights bred their famous black falcons which were once sought after by every king and nobleman in Europe. Here, too, they made their forays into the wilderness to convert and to civilize with the waters of baptism or if that didn't work, with swords and cannons —whatever the situation demanded. Here they kept their monastic discipline by bestowing upon recalcitrant knights a "year's penance" in which a man was kept alive on bread and water in a primitive cell and flogged at least once every eight days.

Before the onslaught of the Teutonic Knights, Prussia had been ruled by tribes of warlike Borussi or Prussi—a medieval Latin term which gives us the word "Prussia"— for over a millennium. The Vikings raided them several times and the Poles tried to convert them. When they failed, Poland welcomed the Teutonic Knights, who either promptly converted them or, for the most part, annihilated them. Between 1231 and 1287 the knights attacked and conquered all the territory of East Prussia and built fortified towns to serve as bastions against possible returning Slavs. The German language was forced on the Borussi and christianized German peasants were brought in to farm the large tracts of land. Later under the Kaisers and under Hitler we would hear the phrase often, but in every sense of the word, this was truly the first German *Drang nach Osten,* a German penetration toward the east.

For the next hundred years the knights expanded into Lithuania and up the Baltic coast consolidating their gains and inserting German culture and Christian civilization into the pagan, slavic territory. Given this bit of history, it is no coincidence that in the middle of World War II, Hitler moved his headquarters from Berlin to the East Prussian town of Rastenburg, formerly one of the mighty knightly bastions of the East. Both in public declarations and in private assemblies Hitler rated himself as the messiah sent to save Europe and civilization from the Communistic "Slavic hordes from the East." Egotistically identifying himself with the sleeping *Kaiser,* Barbarossa, Hitler considered it imperative that he "move in with" the Teutonic Knights while directing "Operation Barbarossa," his campaign against Russia.

At first invincible, the sternness and ardor of Teutonic Knights gradually became flabby. In 1410, dragging with them the largest cannon ever forged in Germany until then, the knights rode against the Poles at Tannenberg. There the iron monster proved inflexible and unable to drown out the Poles who attacked viciously, singing their hymns of faith. By the end of the day all fifty-one of the Teutonic Order's standards had been captured. Clad in cumbersome mail that was the latest in fashion when the Crusaders were young, the brave "monks" were overwhelmed by the newer tides of war which left heaps of armored knights to rot in the marshy lowlands. The Order managed to survive however, and in 1511 the south German Prince Albert of the Hohenzollern family became its Grand Master. Turning the Order into a secularized dukedom, the family eventually married into the territory of Brandenburg, thus forming not only the core of the future Kingdom of Prussia, but also the future family of the Kaisers. These eastern provinces remained German for more than eight hundred years. The irony remains—in 1945 they were once again brutally overrun by the onrushing Slavs from the East, the Red Armies. To intercept them was more than the SS Divisions could muster despite their proud titles of legendary origin, like Viking, Nibelungen, and Hohenstaufen.

In this chapter I do not want to present history. I only want to demonstrate the compelling force which myth, legend, and folklore has worked on the German nation. Side by side with today's German miracle also lies today's German mystery. To plumb this fascinating mystery one should sift the Lüneburg heathland, stroll above the barge-peppered Rhine, wander through rural Hesse, tarry in the Harz thickets, brood with nature in the *Schwarzwald* and quaff the *Gemütlichkeit* of Bavaria. That being impossible in a verbal tour, let us take a broad look at German *Volksglaube* (folk belief) and *Volksbrauch* (folk practice), or in short, folklore.

When Jacob and Wilhelm Grimm set out to collect all the German fairy tales in the first half of the nineteenth century, they went into the highways and byways to actually record what they heard. Tom Thumb, Little Red Riding Hood, Hansel and Gretel, Snow White, the Seven Dwarfs, the Frog King, the Bremen Musicians, and thousands of other characters today belong to the intimate dreams of children throughout the world. Only the Bible has been as frequently translated into other languages. The brothers Grimm didn't invent these tales; they only collected and edited them. The creators of this marvelous segment of literature were fanciful German people. Take any fairy tale and it may sound silly, yet the child never misses the fundamental message about good and evil, the supernatural, beauty, wisdom, or, briefly, its profound significance for humanity.

In their fascination for the tales, few people realize how frequently the forest serves as a narrative background. In the voluminous dictionary of the German language compiled also by the Grimm brothers, the meaning of the Teutonic word for "temple" is akin to the word for forest. Among the primitive speakers of German, a *Wald,* the word for a religious sanctuary, was simply a sheltered place in nature, a *Wald* or forest. Almost fanatic in their worship of trees, these people meted out penalties to anyone who stripped off a tree's bark. Using an absolute justice unthinkable today, the tribes punished an offender by skinning him alive and wrapping his hide around the wounded tree. Tit for tat, the life of a man equals the life of a tree. Earlier it was mentioned that the *Lebensbaum* is planted when a child is born, a custom not unrelated to the ancient equation of a tree with a man.

The epic *Nibelungenlied* likewise exalts the forests, for example the glorious Spessart (formerly *Spechteshart,* meaning *Spechtswald,* Wood-pecker forest). And Siegfried is murdered as he drinks from a fountain in the dark *Odenwald.* The Minnesingers, Germany's troubadour singers, meandered through the *Thüringerwald.* The Harz forests are the scene of the bewitching festival of the *Walpurgisnacht,* and in all the forests the pagan gods still seem to lurk silently. As one German puts it, "Forests are to us what the sea is to the English and what the Wild West is to the Americans; it's *our* epic."

The Druids venerated the oak. Early German tribes worshipped Donar, the god of Thunder, in the oak, and Wotan was adored everywhere through the tabernacle of the oak tree. Our own superstitious fascination for mistletoe seems to stem from the Germanic belief in its magic. Because it was a parasite on the oak, mistletoe was thought to be the spirit of the oak since it remained green even in winter.

The *Lindenbaum* also enjoys a semi-religious place among the German folk. Frequently there is a *Dorflinde,* a village linden in the main square, which has functioned as the official center of town life. Apparently the city council once sat under this linden and we even have documents and proclamations which begin, *Gegeben unter der Linde,* issued under the linden tree. Yearly, festivals call for dances around the linden and the tree is revered in hundreds of German songs in which the tree witnesses the meeting or parting of lovers. Many a hotel or inn bears the title *"Zur Linde,"* at the linden tree. Berlin formerly called its grand boulevard *"Unter den Linden,"* under the linden trees. Prussia had a cloistered church called *Heiligelinde,* the holy linden, and near Fürstenfeldbruck there is a thousand year old linden which is honored because in its limbs a saint is supposed to have spent all of her adult life.

Originally the Grimms titled their immortal volume, *Kinder-und Hausmärchen.* However, when the fairytales engrossed the learned as much as, if not more than, the tot they regretted including the *Kinder* in their title. The introduction clearly indicates their broader purpose in collecting the tales, as "a great treasure of antiquity indispensable for research." Particularly, the collection was to delve into the subterranean narrative literature of the unlettered peasant. As far as possible it was to open a window for the scholar into the submerged riches of an outwardly barren environment. *Märchen* and *Sagen* were the *Naturpoesie,* the natural, indigenous literature of an area, blending with the forests and meadows of the total countryside. When complete, their work grew to five volumes of fairy tales for which they are best known today. Equally significant for scholars, however, are their studies in myth, legend, and language, *Deutsche Sagen, Deutsche Mythologie, Deutsche Rechtsaltertümer* and *Grimmsches Wörterbuch.*

It is impossible to distinguish between festivals that are more religiously oriented and those that are best grouped with pagan mythology and folklore. Nevertheless, as the more religious feasts were considered in the previous chapter, let us now look at a few myth-oriented celebrations. Surely these would include the *Walpurgisnacht,* the May Day, and the harvest festival or *Oktoberfest.*

Since the *Walpurgisnacht* is mentioned in the chapter on the German landscape, I shall be brief here. From the practices once common to the festival it becomes obvious that the night from the thirtieth of April to the first of May had to do with the conclusion of winter and its horrors. On this night, it was thought, witches rubbed themselves with ointments of fat, opium and hemlock after which they went into a trance. Roaming across all of Germany throughout the winter, they would come together for a yearly rendez-vous on the top of the Brocken mountain in the Harz. The witches of course, were associated with evil or the devil. One belief is that the witches would gnaw off a piece of each church-bell they passed before landing on the Brocken to dance away the snow. As they thundered in for their landing, it would lighten. Throughout the night the devil directed proceedings until the first cock crowed.

Sometimes a witch betrayed herself by letting a little red mouse scamper out of her mouth. Her hooked nose, bushy eyebrows and hump back were known to everyone through fairytales. If a visitor at the Brocken heard one of them give the password he could gain entrance for the orgy, which is what Mephistopheles did for his client, Faust. Churning clouds ring the summit and a huge bonfire burns crazily; the devil himself mounts the pulpit and preaches a sermon, which is followed by a banquet and *Zaubertränke,* mind-expanding potions, after which the *Reigen* or circular dance continues until morning.

With witches meandering all over the landscape, peasants devised ways of protecting themselves against their magical wiles. Noise was the best—shots, firecrackers, horns and whip-cracking. A special ceremony of whip-lashing is re-enacted today in Munich on the *Königsplatz* where up to three hundred men take part. However, this ritual may be held earlier in the year than on *Walpurgisnacht.* A fire was always thought to be a good method to stave off evil, and it is even more effective if a straw doll representing the witch herself is burned.

The death of winter and the rebirth of summer is an

occasion for some celebration in every country north of the Alps, particularly in the Scandinavian trio but certainly also in Germany. German winters may not be as severe as in Scandinavia, but particularly noticeable are the long nights and the short days. Remember, almost all of Germany lies north of the Canadian border with the United States. The winter-turning-to-summer ritual is enacted differently in each region. In the town of Effeltrich, for example, young men gaily clad in white regional costumes represent summer. Their suits are richly embroidered and they wear flowers and streaming red and black ribbons. Other young men clothed in drab and ragged black costumes imitate winter. The forces of summer then fight a contest with the sovereign powers of winter, the former of course always winning.

May Day is no invention of the Communist world. Traditionally the first of May signifies the arrival of spring and villagers throughout Europe celebrate with a *Maibaum* (May tree). Not really a tree, the *Baum* is a pole hoisted into the air, adorned on top by a huge wreath of green branches and flowers. Long ribbons of many colors flood down and out from the wreath, forming a kind of inverted cone. Special dances are then performed around the pole and sometimes the wreath has little presents imbedded in it, which were once given to young boys if they could climb the pole with their bare feet.

On May Day a young man may put a birch tree under the window of his beloved to tell her he loves her, or a shrivelled shrub if he wants to tell her it is over. If she finds a cherry sprig it means she is pretty. Oak is for constancy and thorn twigs are for deceit, while a beech branch means her lover has left her for another girl friend.

In a few areas green wreaths or bunches of twigs are hung on the barn door and Westphalian farmers even put them on manure piles, with a thought to fertility. Related to the principle of fecundity is the Bavarian custom of putting green sprigs on the doors of newlyweds. Surely the pre-Christian German worship of trees explains the symbolic significance of the maypole signifying spring, rebirth, and its connection to the tree of life.

Here mention must be made of the *Richtfest,* or Topping-out festival. When the last roof timber goes up on a new house the workmen will fasten a little fir tree, decorated with tinsel like a Christmas tree, to the peak rafter. Occasionally the tree is supplanted by a pine wreath tied with colored ribbons. The ceremonies vary, some thank God the great builder, others merely the masons and carpenters. Mostly, though, after fastening the tree or wreath the owner simply buys plenty of beer for the workmen, who sometimes drink it on the roof and ceremoniously throw their glasses to smash on the ground. Some go to a tavern to drink where journeymen carpenters, wearing their bell-bottom corduroy pants, vest and jacket, pearl buttons and floppy-brimmed hat serve the master carpenters. In older days neighbors brought donated items for the house at this time: a carved beam, a painted window glass, colorful emblem or painted motto. Generally the little tree is allowed to stand for weeks until the house is virtually completed.

For May ceremonies in a few places, young boys bring an oak sapling to town and plant it in the public park. Then a kind of spell-down is conducted in which many historical questions are asked. The boy standing the longest is decorated with birch branches or birch bark and called the *Maikönig* (King of the May). Accompanied by friends he can go from house to house and collect candy, sausage and eggs which are later eaten by the whole group. Occasionally the King is wrapped in straw and sometimes he carries a straw scarecrow. Frequently he chooses a *Maikönigin* (May Queen) who, adorned with flowers, personifies summer. Often at the end of the day the King of the May goes through a mock execution, the belief being that he represents the spirit of vegetation which must be killed if it is to be reborn fresh and strong next year.

Similar to the basket socials once common to youth clubs of the American churches is the *Mailehen,* a kind of auction in which not the girl's food basket, but the girl herself is sold. Usually the auctioneer describes her in terms of a real lumber auction—an older girl as a "good chopping block," a younger one as a "flowering apple tree," an ill-tempered one as "knotty wood." What the boy gets if he buys the girl is the right to date her for a year. After the auction he sends her the tribute of a birch bough and a bottle of wine flavored with cinnamon, and she responds by giving candy. If the "engagement" does not lead to marriage by the next year, the boy may burn a straw dummy of her at next year's auction and naturally look for some other "piece of timber."

The spring festival is widely celebrated to be sure, but in scope it does not compare with the harvest festival in fall. Spring is filled with promise of growth and fertility for the year, but the harvest is the proof of fulfillment—a more solid and secure feeling somehow, and one that demands thanks. As with our Thanksgiving, religious sentiment combines with ancient custom. In Germany the harvest celebrations include much pagan belief, perhaps the strongest being that one must kill the spirit of the grain. In the mysterious germination process ancient peoples thought the "mother of grain" bequeathed life to the seeds. Thus, as sickles narrow the fields of standing grain, the spirit is thought to retreat until the last plant falls, in which case she withdraws into the last sheaf of grain. Called the Old Mother, peasants formerly brought this bundle into the village, fashioned it into a human shape and often mocked or burned it so the spirit would leave to reinspire the fields next year.

With literally thousands of harvest festivals, let us look at just two types, a *Weinfest* and later the world-famous Munich *Oktoberfest*. Since the former implies fountains of wine and the later rivers of beer, we ought to begin with a proverb:

> *Wein auf Bier, das rat' ich dir,*
> *Bier auf Wein, das lass sein.*
>
> Wine on beer, I recommend to you
> Beer on wine, let that be.

The *Weinfest* is mostly confined to the Rhine-Mosel river area of Germany but it can also extend south in Baden-Württemberg to the *Bodensee*. Some wine festivals take place as early as June but the season really begins in September when the grape harvest is in progress. At today's wine festivals the village square is saturated with merry-go-rounds and carnival machinery but old traditions are also continued. Church doors are covered with evergreen branches and the faithful often donate samples of their fruits to be delivered later to the poor. In certain towns the farmers march in processions carrying their tools of harvests or driving their modern tractors.

At Winningen along the Mosel, folk dances are held around the old village fountain which is topped by a stone carving of the wine witch. Then comes the post-pageantry revelry when the fountain's flow of water is reversed to make its spigot deliver wine. There is no shortage of guests hustling to partake of this "fountain of life." Of course every festival has its wine king and queen as well as its parade.

The largest *Weinfest* is at Bad Dürkheim. Called the *Wurstmarkt* or sausage fair, it began in 1442 and now draws a half million visitors every year. As one visitor put it, "The Sausage Fair is a festival where you meet lots of friends you have never seen before." A few years ago the seven-day festival consumed fifty thousand gallons of wine, seven hundred eighty three pigs, sixty calves and one hundred and five cattle in addition to more than fifty thousand roasted chickens.

Check the August ads in the national weeklies and one will find the airlines offering tourist flights to Munich's *Oktoberfest*. Likewise, September ads in Milwaukee, Chicago and Minneapolis include invitations issued by the City of La Crosse, Wisconsin, luring guests to its *Oktoberfest*. The name notwithstanding, Munich's festival takes place in September although the sixteen-day affair does run until the first Sunday of October. After several successive years of bad weather in October, the Munich authorities decided in 1880 to bring the celebration forward into September. In actual fact, the celebration is a Bavarian national festival and hence the festival emphasizes beer, not wine.

Incredible quantities of *Wiesenbier* (meadow beer), a strong beer made especially for the festival, are consumed together with tons and tons of sausages and roasted chickens, not to mention oxen on the spit and fish broiled on sticks. Seven or eight of the giant Munich breweries each fits out a big-top tent with a seating capacity of up to five thousand persons per tent. Plenty of beer and up to three bands that play continuously keep customers happy and drinking. In a given year there may be six million visitors who will drink four million quarts of beer. In 1968, visitors devoured 355,000 chickens, 677,000 sausages and thirty-one oxen roasted whole on a spit. With garish sideshows and a full-sized circus, plus the usual rides combined with screaming loudspeakers and dazzling lights, the atmosphere is one of buoyant frenzy.

The festival began as a wedding in 1810 when the Princess Therese of Saxe-Hildburghausen was married to the Bavarian Crown Prince Ludwig who became Ludwig I. As part of the wedding ceremonial a horse race was staged for enthusiasts from all over Bavaria while forty thousand looked on. Such was the success of the party given afterwards that the meadow was named the *Theresienwiese* in honor of the Princess. Even now the meadow retains its name and is kept as a large open clearing within the heart of a city grown far around it.

Today the folk festival comes alive at noon on opening day when, as the clock on St. Paul's Church in Munich strikes twelve noon, the Bürgermeister enters one of the beer tents and, to a twelve-cannon salute, taps the first cask and quaffs the first stein. On the following day is the *Trachtenfest* parade, one in which thousands of participants from all over Germany dress in their *Trachten,* native costumes. Bands, floats and decorated beer wagons drawn by the beautiful big brewery horses wind their way through the downtown streets and out to the *Wies'n,* short for the festival grounds.

The *Volkstracht* is one article of clothing still proudly worn in Europe that never really caught on in America. The reason for abandoning it in America may well be that it was for a long time associated with social class. In the Middle Ages the ruling classes circulated in fine velvet, silk and gold. As in everything else the lower classes copied the extravagancies of the higher, though necessarily made of rougher cloth and imitation materials. In Saxony there was even an ordinance dividing the population into five classes, *Stände,* and prescribing what the women in each class could wear. Thus, clothes identified the people, occasioning also the proverb, *"Kleider machen Leute,"* or clothes make the man.

Then came the French Revolution along with romantic

philosophies preaching back-to-nature and illusions about the beautiful simplicity of country living. On the one hand class differentiation diminished, and on the other people of high fashion now sought out the virtues of the peasant class. Simultaneously, patriotism encouraged a love for what was local and native with the result that Germans revived their regional dress and the rules for wearing it. Once each village had a local costume that never changed in style. Everywhere married women wore bonnets while unmarried girls wore wreaths—a custom still alive in the German wedding ceremony. As time went on and pride in the region grew, the headdress became more elaborate. Women wore crowns instead of babushkas. Young girls embellished their headpieces with flowers, embroidery and jewelry too complex to describe here. A hasty perusal of the German *Brockhaus* Encyclopedia under the heading *Trachten* will reveal the many ornate models of the folk finery still worn today.

The one *Tracht* that has won wide acceptance in all of Germany and even abroad is the Bavarian *Dirndl*. It is a cotton dress made up of a gathered full skirt in colorful flowery print, and a light-colored blouse with tightly fitting short sleeves. A white or light-colored apron from the waist down is a must. The well-known *Lederhosen* are also native to Bavaria but they were unknown there until 1800 when they arrived from the Tyrol in Western Austria. These leather shorts are held up by suspenders joined by an ornamental breastband on the chest. With the *Lederhosen* men usually wear a light-colored shirt and knee-high stockings. Formerly a rural costume only, the *Lederhosen* are now commonly worn in the streets and at work, and are frequently seen even in the United States. In cooler weather the *Lederhosen* reach below the knee and are either tied (Tyrolean) or buckled (Bavarian) over the stockings. If it is raining or cold, the thick, woolen, tightly-woven Loden cape is worn also.

Otherwise the *Volkstracht* is not worn for everyday. Church festivals, or in the Black Forest villages any Sunday of the year, will bring out the older women in their costumes and headgear. A carnival or *Fest* of any kind is occasion to wear the traditional garb. Last but not least, those intensely personal, familiar affairs, weddings and funerals, can still bring forth women in their costumes. A visit to Germany should include a tour of at least one local costume museum. In the best toy shops—lately even gift shops—one can buy *Trachten-Puppen,* dolls dressed in regional costumes. A representative set would be one each from Berchtesgaden, the Black Forest, Hesse, Swabia, Westphalia and perhaps Schleswig-Holstein.

In the course of the summer, literally hundreds of local festivals take place in every village and town. Everywhere there is a *Volksfest* of one kind or another sometime during the year. There are also specialized festivals, such as the Pied Piper of Hamlin, the re-enactment of the *Meistertrunk* at Rothenburg, the *Stabenfest* at Nördlingen, the Marriage of the Prince at Landshut, the *Schafflertanz* or Wild Dance of the Coopers at Munich, Nürnberg and other cities, the midsummer festival of *Johannistag,* the Race of the Shepherds at Markgröningen, and many, many others. As a German friend put it, "With a little bit of planning you can go the whole year celebrating."

Folklore the world over is replete with medicinal-magical cures for the sick. At any German university one can still take regular courses in *Heilkunde,* the art of healing, not that the students practice it but from an anthropological point of view they learn about it. Since the bulk of the German immigrants to America were from the peasant classes, it is not surprising to find that many of their charms and sayings, in short their *Bräuche,* were transported with them. Below are a few of these as collected by Richard M. Dorson, *Buying the Wind, Regional Folklore in the United States* (Chicago, 1964). Because of the erratic German-American dialect, all are given here in English.

—Bloody milk indicates a bewitched cow. Thrust a red-hot iron into the bewitched milk.

—Plowing down snow with a plow is as good for a field as manure and lime.

—Plant peas and potatoes when the moon is on the increase.

—Eggs laid on Good Friday should be preserved as charms.

To deal directly with the sick person one must be a *Braucher,* a woman who has learned the highly secret art from her mother; it dare not be passed on to the next generation until the mother is on her deathbed. Mostly these practices consist of special biblical quotations spoken while making certain signs over the sick person.

Much folk wisdom is disguised in the stories about Till Eulenspiegel, and whether recounted in Germany or in German-America they have remained constant for hundreds of years. The following sample of a very common story is also taken from Dorson, *Buying the Wind.*

Eileschpijjel went with a two-horse team for wood. As he threw piece after piece on the wagon, he said, "If the horses can pull this piece, they can pull the next one." Reasoning thus, he kept on loading until the wagon was completely filled. Then he found that the horses were unable to pull the load. He proceeded to unload, saying as he threw off piece after piece, "If they can't pull this piece, they can't pull the next one." Reasoning thus, he kept on unloading until the wagon was empty. Then he drove home with an empty wagon.

Customs, traditions and peculiarities die out in large cities usually because the people there have such different backgrounds that the cohesiveness necessary to continue a tradition is simply lacking. One must go to the rural villages and visit the farm houses to feel the vibrancy of *Sitten* (customs). In Germany this is actually very simple. Few Americans realize, for instance, that German farmers do not live out on the land. They live together in villages of about one thousand people and drive their horses or tractors out to the fields each day. It is even possible that through inheritance a farmer will have one field a mile or two out of town in one direction, and another field the same distance in the opposite direction. This is inconvenient, to be sure, but when the Federal Government recently tried to promote equalized exchanging of such fields, great difficulties, mostly sentimental in nature, were encountered. On the one hand families who have held a piece of land for a long time grow desperately attached to it. On the other hand, of course, the fertility and productivity of scattered acres under diverse management can vary greatly.

Today as formerly the village itself owns the forest lands where many villagers find work in the winter and buy what wood they need at reduced prices. To a lesser extent the village also owns common pastureland, and thanks to such holdings a village council can often reduce property taxes or even occasionally eliminate them altogether.

It is fascinating to be a guest in a *Bauernhaus,* an old fashioned German farmhouse. There is a saying in the

Schwarzwald that a farmer's house is built according to the formula, *"ein Drittel Herz, ein Drittel Hand, ein Drittel Verstand"* (one-third heart, one-third hands, one-third understanding). In Northern Germany where strong winds are a problem, the *Bauernhaus* is lower and made of stone, brick, or plaster and beams, the so-called *Fachwerkhäuser.* Farther south they use more wood and build three-story structures with steep shingled roofs. In Bavaria the custom is a flatter roof covered with red tile. Throughout Germany the rule is—house and barn are all one building. Men and animals inhabit a common dwelling. The American method of separate buildings scattered on the landscape is Scandinavian and English in origin.

In a typical *Bauernhaus* the family living quarters take up one end of the structure, usually all the way to the roof. In some houses, however, the bedrooms are over the cattle, or on the contrary, hay may be stored above the living rooms. A *Diele* or hallway is the only separation between the living quarters and the barn and inevitably smells shift back and forth. Generally the walls in this entry are of rough stone which has been plastered over and painted with shiny enamel—identical to the interiors of the sod houses built and still used by numerous German households in North Dakota.

The first room to be entered is the kitchen, the center of living in every *Bauernhaus.* Usually several rooms open off the kitchen: bedrooms, pantry, and the living room called simply the *Stube,* rarely *Wohnzimmer,* as in the city. In other cases the living room is but an extension of a large kitchen. Joining the two rooms in many homes is a *Kachelofen,* a large stove made of stone and covered with glazed tiles which are frequently ornamented either with religious figures or geometric designs. When the housewife cooks and bakes from the kitchen side the living room side and remainder of the house is heated. So convenient is the *Kachelofen* that to bake bread in the summer you simply build a good fire early in the morning, insert the bread in the oven and forget about it. By the time the heat of the day increases, the fire has long since gone out and the bread slowly bakes on the hot stone. It is removed at night or even a day or two later.

Invariably a wooden table stands kitty-corner across the room from the stove. Along the walls around the table wooden benches have been built into the wall, substituting for chairs. Mounted on the wall above the table is a devotional shrine, maybe a crucifix, or a statue of the Virgin. The old folk belief is that in life one must be constantly reminded of the two alternatives for eternity—either heaven, as represented by the shrine, or hell, as modeled by the stove across the room.

With luck, one may find a richly painted *Bauernschrank* in one of the bedrooms. These are tall cabinets with two full-length, center-opening doors for hanging clothes. In a *Bauernhaus* there are no built-in closets. Recent years have brought a heavy demand for these antique cabinets because art collectors everywhere recognize their value. Ceilings are either covered with boards, carved and decoratively painted, or they may be the simple wooden beams painted brown. Sometimes the owner of a *Bauernhaus* exhibits his faith by having biblical sayings carved in the wooden beams, either on the outside or inside. More amusing is the doggerel written by the farmers themselves, partly folk wisdom, partly entertainment. On the ceiling of the kitchen may be:

> *"Dreitägiger Gast ist eine Last"*
> After three days a guest becomes a burden.

"Gebratene Tauben fliegen keinem ins Maul"
Roasted doves don't simply fly into your mouth—
meaning, nobody gets something for nothing.

"Es wird überall nur mit Wasser gekocht"
They cook everywhere with water—
meaning, we are just as good as the next man.

Examples of pious verses:
Des Hauses Schmuck ist Reinlichkeit
The House's jewelry is cleanliness.

Des Hauses Glück Zufriedenheit
The House's fortune is contentedness.

Des Hauses Segen Frömmigkeit
The House's blessing is piety.

A placard over the kitchen door may read:
Wir bauen alle fest, und sind doch fremde Gäste,
und wo wir sollen ewig sein, da bauen wir gar
wenig ein.
We all build well but we are foreign guests
here, and where we are to be forever, thereunto
we build very little.

Over the door leading outside:
Herr, in deinem Namen geh ich aus,
Bewahr allzeit das ganze Haus,
Meine Hausfrau und auch die Kinder mein
Lass dir, O Gott, befohlen sein.

Lord I go out in your name,
Preserve always my whole house,
My housewife and also my children
May they be commended to you.

Near New Braunfels, Texas, a nineteenth century German immigrant had inscribed over the entrance to his house:

> *Der Herr ist mein Hirte*
> *Mir wird nichts mangeln.*
> The Lord is my shepherd
> I shall not want.

The following are in a more secular vein:
> *Das Bauen ist eine schöne Lust*
> *Dass es soviel kost't hab' ich nicht gewusst.*
> *Gott behüt uns all' Zeit*
> *Vor Maurer und Zimmerleut.*
> Building is a delightful pleasure
> But I didn't know it would cost so much.
> May God shelter us always
> Against masons and carpenters.

> *Eigner Herd*
> *Ist Goldes wert,*
> *Ist er schon arm*
> *Ist er doch warm.*
> One's own stove
> Is worth gold;
> If it is poor,
> It is yet warm.

Over the door to the hallway in one house are the words:
> *Das schönste Wappen in der Welt,*
> *Das ist der Pflug im Ackerfeld.*
> The most beautiful coat of arms in the world
> is the plow out in the fields.

Whatever one might say of him, the German peasant still takes pride in his breed and in his earth. Honest, industrious and pious, he is at the mercy of the weather, the economy, politics—in short, the threat of catastrophe—and this has left its mark on him. In a great many ways he embodies the soul of the German. He patiently bears a chorus of the berating city folks who "with their light-weighted hearts are uncouth barbarians." Failing to comprehend they can only laugh and sneer. Convinced all the more of his destiny, the *Bauer* merely clenches his teeth and continues some of the finest traditions of the German, nay, of all mankind.

CHRISTMAS AND OTHER HOLIDAYS

CHRISTMAS AND OTHER HOLIDAYS

IN GERMANY, Christmas is more a season than a holiday. The Christmas season there runs from December 1 to January 6, when the German calendar looks like a checkerboard of religious and secular festivals. Traditions, celebrations, and rituals live on, although today's families seldom realize their full implications. Many of these customs involve superstitions but others are simply entrenched practices once prevalent throughout all of Germany. Today certain celebrations have either lessened or disappeared altogether as a result of the political events of recent years. However, there are still remote villages where there seems little danger that too many of these charming old customs will ever become obsolete.

The German Christmas season begins with Advent and grows in a symphonic crescendo to its climax on Christmas eve. Then the season remains at a peak of festivity for two more days, and gradually levels off to its conclusion with Epiphany on the sixth of January. Perhaps only a native or one who has lived in Germany for a long time can fully appreciate what Christmas means to the German. Christmas is a time to be at home with one's immediate family. Christmas is lighted candles, good food, exchanging gifts, intimacy, and inner warmth. It is the emotional impact of enkindled hope, light, and grace. A German Christmas is a very special celebration; it is a happy blend of pagan ritual and Christian sanctification.

Advent is the time of expectation for all of this. Hardly a church or home in Germany begins the period of Advent without an *Adventskranz* (Advent wreath). Woven from boughs of fir, the wreath is bound with red, gold, or purple ribbons. Strictly of Christian origin, the time of Advent is a four-week period spent in commemoration of our waiting for the birth of Christ. Symbolizing the four thousand-year wait of the Jewish people for their Messiah, the four weeks are marked off by four candles mounted on the wreath. Each Sunday another candle is lighted until all four burn during the last week of the period. Usually the family gathers around the wreath each evening before eating, sings a hymn, and looks on while the head of the family lights the appropriate number of candles for that week, which then burn throughout the meal.

In some sections of Germany, especially the Palatinate and Hesse, fathers build their children an *Adventshaus*. Such a house has four little "stained-glass" windows, behind each of which stands a candle. Every Sunday of Advent a new window is opened and an additional candle lit. These housed candles take the place of the Advent wreath. It is also common for school children to make an *Advents-kalendar,* that is, twenty-five shutter-like windows mounted on poster paper and hung on the wall. Each day the next little window is opened revealing a different picture with the next date. Also during Advent there are numerous presentations by school and community, mostly tableaux and pageants celebrating the mystery of the Nativity.

Unknown to many Americans is the fact that in Germany, Santa Claus day is not the same as Christmas. Most Americans do know though, that Santa Claus is a shortened form of Saint Nicholas whose feast is celebrated on December 6. In Germany, St. Nicholas arrives in person on his feast day to bring candy and nuts for the children but he never shows up on Christmas eve. He has been visiting homes with children ever since the fifteenth century. In bishop's garb and with a long beard, St. Nicholas usually wears a miter and carries a crozier. His namesake, the original St. Nicholas of Bari, is surrounded by legend; his specialty was saving sailors in tempests and school girls whose virginity was in peril. In the course of time enough lore has built up to make him the patron saint of entire nations (Russia and Greece), classes of people, and occupations. After a student in Paris first masqueraded as the saint bringing gifts to poor children in the late 1400's, his spirit quickly migrated to Germany. Today St. Nicholas is usually accompanied by his mentor, Ruprecht, who is dressed in black and carries a stick to paddle errant children. The American version of the name Santa Claus reflects the spirit of the Paris student, but the name no doubt is a corruption of the spoken Dutch title which is written *Sinterklaas.*

Even before the feast of St. Nicholas certain German towns, notably Nuremburg, open the Christmas season before December 6 by an official pageant accompanying the start of the Christmas fair. Known as the *Christkindes-markt* (Christ Child's mart), Nuremburg's market-fair is the oldest and largest Christmas fair in Germany. Legend says that about three hundred years ago a dollmaker by the name of Hauser had a beautiful little daughter who had died shortly before Christmas. So distraught were the parents that one day after wandering aimlessly through the streets, Hauser returned home to find his wife ill with grief. When she finally fell asleep Hauser went to work making an angel which he placed on the bed next to his resting wife. So perfect was the product that when his wife awakened she thought she found her sleeping little daughter in bed beside her. When neighbors heard about this accomplishment, they beseeched Hauser to make a doll for them. To this day Germans arrive at the Nuremburg fair from far and wide to buy the little golden angels made by the local people.

The fair opens December 4, St. Barbara's day, when a figure of the Christ child, usually a young boy or girl robed in white and accompanied by two tinsel angels, appears on the balcony of the *Frauenkirche,* the Church of Our Lady. In rhymed verse she narrates a formal invitation to fair visitors. Trumpets blare out, bells ring, and carolers sing. Finally when the pageant concludes about eight in the evening, canvases draping the booths are rolled back and business begins with a boom. All sorts of candy, bread, nuts, sausages, schnapps and toys are available. But the most popular as well as the most traditional are the *Zwetschgenmännle and Zwetschgenfrauen,* little figures of men and women about ten inches tall which are made of dried fruits and nuts and dressed in crepe paper or hand-made cotton clothing. During the remainder of the Christmas season school children return often to the square below the Church of Our Lady to sing and reenact the Christmas story.

Most spectacular of these returns is the one on December 12 or 13 when the school children stage the *Lichterzug.* This is a lantern procession representing the climax of the season for the school children. Many of them fabricate their own lanterns from a wooden or wire skeleton around which an elaborate design of a star, snowflake, sunburst or other intricate pattern is built and decoratively painted. On the night of the procession the children march ten abreast from the *Fleischbrücke* (butcher's bridge) passing the *Christkindlesmarkt* en route to their destination at the castle grounds on the hill. There the festivities conclude with a series of five tableaux depicting the Christmas story.

Neither the *Lichterzug* nor the market is by any means exclusively a Nuremburg event. Munich, Stuttgart, Frankfurt, Berlin and other cities also have their *Christkindlesmarkt* and other towns in Bavaria celebrate the feast of St. Lucia on December 13 when school children stage a lantern parade. In Fürstenfeldbruck for example, instead of carrying their self-designed lanterns on high poles, the children build models of their own houses and other buildings in their community. After attending an evening Mass they march through the streets carrying their lighted houses until they reach the central bridge spanning the Amper River. Townspeople, gathering on or near the bridge square, watch as their children deposit lighted "dollhouses" in the swift current. The houses bob precariously as they float under the bridge and charge downstream. Here and there the weaker structures capsize and sink swiftly; others nod to and fro in the whirling eddies, duck around fallen trees and roots, and then peacefully the lights disappear around the distant bend.

Some authorities believe the lantern procession originated with the Swedes when they occupied Germany during the Thirty Years' War. After all, the December 13 feast of St. Lucia is the day of lights which actually opens the Swedish Christmas season. Lucia is a name that stems from the Latin word *lux* which means light. In Roman times Lucia was a fairly common name for girls. In the Christian tradition, however, the name Lucia has come to signify a certain kindly girl from Sicily who married a Roman nobleman. When Lucia turned out to be so generous that she gave away family valuables, her husband objected. When it went so far that she gave away her wedding gifts, the nobleman was furious. Eventually he turned her over to the Roman prefect who had Lucia tortured by gouging out her eyes. But so strong was Lucia's faith that her eyesight was miraculously restored. Just as miraculously the tradition of celebrating the feast of light on St. Lucia's day seems to have been born.

The connection between a festival of light and the feast of Christmas goes back as far as the old Germanic tribes with their gods of nature. Winter is at its darkest from December 21 to 23. After the winter solstice, or about December 24, the sun's light begins to grow again. On this date in the Germanic era, whole tribes once gathered on tops of mountains to celebrate the rebirth of the sun. Often huge wheels were stuffed with straw, which was then ignited. The great flaming wheel symbolizing the brilliant sun rolled and tumbled down the side of the mountain with a spinning display of light. However, this festival of lights has generally disappeared from the Germany of Christian time, but it is this pagan feast from which Christmas was adapted in Germany by the Christian missionaries. In effect the Christian festival of Our Savior's birth displaced the pagan ritual observing the "rebirth" of the sun. It is because of this pre-existing feast that Christ's birth has come to be celebrated on December 25. In reality we have no idea as to precisely when Christ was born.

Pagan beliefs lie at the very roots of the German word for Christmas, *Weihnachten*. This word always appears in the plural and means "during the holy nights." Actually the Germanic peoples had a total of twelve nights in which their gods wandered on the earth before entering the Walhalla, home of their gods. The wandering period began with the winter solstice, the shortest day of the year. It continued for twelve succeeding nights when the most severe storms of winter were supposed to take place. Surprisingly the traditional twelve days of Christmas are still observed and celebrated in the world today.

Returning to the more biblical Christmas customs, Germans, like Americans, today give gifts gaily wrapped in paper displaying Christmas scenes and tied with bright-colored ribbon. On *Heiligabend* (Christmas eve) a ritual ceremony takes place. In a parlor room known as the Christmas room, a tree has been erected but rarely is it completely decorated beforehand. Trimming the tree is a part of the Christmas eve ceremony. Balls of glass, gingerbread cookies, and strips of tinfoil adorn the fir tree, while the top is almost always capped with a star or an angel symbolizing the Annunciation of the Angel Gabriel to Mary. Under or near the tree is a manger scene. Most astonishing to the American visitor is that there are no electric lights on the tree. No German would think of putting colored sets of light bulbs on a Christmas tree; in fact, a traditional-minded German will settle for nothing less than white candles. By means of special clips these candles are mounted to the branches of the tree and are never lighted until Christmas eve when Christ, biblically referred to as the light of the world, arrives.

During the entire pre-Christmas season, the parlor room is assiduously guarded and locked. The children never catch a glimpse of it until the *Gabenbringer* (gift bringer) has come and gone. Usually this mysterious guest is taken to be the *Christkind* although to a few regions an angel or the *Weihnachtsmann* performs the duties of the *Gabenbringer,* the German version of our Santa Claus. Before that, however, families often have a Christmas Eve meal consisting of fish as the main food. Finally when the solemn moment of Christmas arrives, the door to the room is opened, the candles are lighted, and the entire household gathers around the tree to sing *Stille Nacht/Heilige Nacht* as well as a few other Christmas hymns, perhaps *O Tan-*

nenbaum. Then comes the *Bescherung* or distribution of gifts to the great delight of the children, and to the warm, joyous feelings of all adults. Slowly the evening tapers off and, depending on religious affiliations, older members usually attend church services at midnight. Then church bells peal out through the peaceful night, ringing into the minds of all an unforgettable Christmas experience. In a few areas the Christmas meal is eaten only after the midnight worship service.

Traditional foods for the Christmas season include especially *Pfefferkuchen,* spicy gingerbread cookies in the forms of stars, hearts, or rings. Often whole dollhouses are made from slabs of gingerbread. Skilled hands of mothers and children intricately decorate them with frosting and often there are fairytale figures inside. Perhaps best of all is the Christmas *Stollen.* This is a type of coffee cake about the size of a loaf of bread. The dough is folded over, forming one large crease through the center of the loaf, which creates that delectable appearance. Inside are chopped dried fruits and raisins; outside the *Stollen* is decked with powdered sugar. These cakes are available at every bakery in Germany during the Christmas season.

Who first started decorating the *Tannenbaum?* It has been determined that the Christmas tree had its birth in Germany. Scholars write about how the Christmas tree came to America during the Revolutionary War via the Hessian soldiers who were serving here as mercenaries for the British. The first known use of the fir tree as a Christmas ornament is found in a description written by a German traveler visiting Strassbourg, Province of Alsace, in 1605. He tells of trees being planted in rooms and he notes that they were ornamented with roses of colored paper, apples, tinsel, sugar, and cookies.

A few authorities believe it could have been Martin Luther who started the Christmas tree idea. The story goes that Luther tried to recall an emotional experience one night when on his way home he viewed stars shining through the branches of pine forests. Later at home he tried to reproduce this beautiful feeling by placing candles on a fir tree.

Whatever the true source of the German Christmas tree one thing must be remembered: to the Germanic tribes, many trees have been considered sacred and holy ever since primitive times. Not only was the oak a symbol of their pagan deities, but if we analyze the role of the tree for gods and men, it will be seen that even the Bible uses the metaphor of a tree to speak of good and evil. Thus the tree, as a fundamental mediator between God and man, has at least two homes: one in the pagan ritual, one in the Christian metaphor.

Mistletoe is common in Germany too, but its purpose is not to trigger a kiss but to head off diseases and old age. In former times this parasite of the oak tree was hung in stables to ward off evil spirits. Other practices in a few of the northern provinces deal with such things as burning the Christmas tree after the holidays. The charred trunk is then kept until spring when, having dried out, it is burned again and the ashes are ceremoniously spread over the fields to fertilize them.

There are many other rather superstitious traditions connected with Christmas in Germany. In the northern regions the winter is truly a dark period in the year. After all, the northern area of Germany rests on the parallel which runs through Hudson Bay in Canada. Hence it is quite understandable that much is made of the spirits of darkness. Although these spirits are of pagan origin, to this day there are beliefs that invisible dark personages accompany the *Gabenbringer* on Christmas eve. These spirits have differing names and appear under several guises but the names and guises always suggest a belief in the constant threat of the devil himself.

A traditional fairy tale usually told or reenacted during the Christmas season is that of *Frau Holle*. When she goes out to shake the pillows and make it snow she also symbolizes even in her name the spooky *Höllenfahrt,* the trip of the witches. Ever since the Middle Ages Germans have also spoken about the *Wasserhollen,* or water sprite. In the Schleswig-Holstein area of extreme northern Germany, the *Schimmelreiter,* knight on a white horse, is another ghostly personality who still rides on Christmas eve accompanied sometimes by the *Christmann*. In these same provinces, the twenty-fourth of December witnesses a solemn ritual of stomach gorging. Incredible quantities of herring, poppy, carp, breads, sweet rolls, *Baumkuchen* and other delicacies are stuffed down to dispel attacks of the nocturnal demons.

A German Christmas is literally a three-day affair for both December 25 and 26 are legal holidays. Often factories and business operations simply close from December 23 to January 2. The New Year, likewise, is a salubrious three-day event lasting from New Year's eve to January 3. Throughout most of Germany December 31 is known as *Sylvestertag* because that is the feast day of St. Sylvester. As *Sylvester,* New Year's eve, approaches, the local bakeries and delicatessens exhibit new pastries. Most notable are the miniature chimney sweeps and vast quantities of little pigs made of candy or cake. The pig, of course, is known to bring good luck. This belief is probably linked also to our own custom of the piggy bank. As in America, New Year's eve brings carousing beer parties and rowdy celebrations. Then, towards midnight, the New Year is heralded by a thundering barrage of firecrackers. This custom supposedly brings good luck by frightening off old witches.

In Berlin it is a tradition to eat carp on New Year's day and to keep one of its scales in one's coin purse. The conviction is that such an amulet will keep the purse from ever getting empty. It is also important to encounter the right person when stepping out of the house first thing in the morning on New Year's day. If a young man passes by, that is a good sign. Should it be an old woman, one will probably suffer misfortune during the coming year.

The German Christmas festivities finally twinkle out on January 6, the feast of Epiphany, a full month after their initiation. The feast of Epiphany brings out one of the loveliest of all German customs. As soon as it gets dark a man carrying a tall pole appears on the streets. On top of the pole is a lantern with the shape of a star. Behind him follow the children of the village, called the Star Singers, who symbolize the wise men from the east. Each carries his own lighted star and, at each square or corner, the troupe stops to sing a few carols. Clear voices ring out in the crisp air as the stars twinkle through the night. Often these *Sternsinger* wear crowns and wigs and dress in long white gowns. In a few areas can be found the *Sterngucker,* star gazers or troupes who come outdoors to sing Germany's ancient and hymnic *Lieder.*

The night before Epiphany Germans must eat well but they never forget to leave something to be eaten by the spirits. In some areas the salt of the Magi is thrown into the soup and butter to protect the household against evil spells for that year. Since Germans in southern areas have traditionally thrived on Christmas drama, they still stage medieval pageants of the Magi. In some towns the Magi receive a welcome of gunshots, firecrackers and the ringing of bells. In a few communities parishioners try to walk to the next village to attend church in commemoration of the long trek of the first Magi.

Finally on the night of Epiphany, the Christmas tree's candles are lighted for the last time. By every way of reckoning, the twelfth day has come and the Christmas festivities abruptly end. The Christmas tree, that rallying symbol for the entire season, is disposed of immediately.

Hardly have the children settled down from the excitement when the grownups are off to the balls—this time to celebrate *Fasching* in one continuous festival lasting from the end of the Christmas season until Ash Wednesday. *Fasching* is a time for the rigorous pursuit of fun and frolic. As long ago as the fifteenth century a respected churchman wrote, "A wine barrel that is not tapped will surely burst." Today it might be more appropriate to say a "beer barrel" but the principle has not changed. Every German city has some sort of pre-Lenten celebration, but three cities consistently would take first prizes for their intensity: Munich where the festival is known as *Fasching,* and Cologne and Mainz where is is called *Karneval.*

The key words in any *Fasching* celebration are the masked ball and the costume parade. It all begins officially on the eleventh day of the eleventh month of the year at the eleventh hour in the evening, hence at 11 p.m. on November 11, when cities choose a *Fasching* king and queen. After only a few insignificant sputters the season then dies down until about January 10 when things open with a bang, picking up a faster and faster pace reaching full speed just before Ash Wednesday. The royal *Fasching* couple must attend three and four balls per night. Back in 1958 in the city of Würzburg a young lady from Ogden, Utah happened to be in town teaching grade school children of American servicemen, and was chosen *Fasching* queen. Night after night she led the singing and dancing, made ceremonial speeches in German, danced with all comers, always stayed until the end, frequently 5 a.m., and lost over ten pounds. Whatever other losses she suffered, the event was unusual enough to get her picture on the cover of *Life*.

Three or four times weekly the earnest partygoers attend a *Fasching* or *Karneval* ball. In Munich alone there will be seven thousand public or semi-public parties held during the season. It is not unusual for a couple to go deep in debt and even visit the pawnbroker to have enough cash for a good time at *Fasching*. On *Rosenmontag*, the Monday before Ash Wednesday, and of course on *Faschingsdienstag*, Shrove Tuesday, all businesses and schools close to allow everyone to take part in the revelry. On both days there is eating and drinking together with every imaginable means of merriment in the beer halls and on the streets, which by evening are literally covered with confetti and paper debris. In the Rhineland there is the *Karneval* parade on *Rosenmontag*, but in Munich the parade is usually held on the Sunday before. On Tuesday at midnight everything comes to an immediate halt after the traditional *Kehraus Ball*, the clean-out dance.

Ash Wednesday is a somber ordeal, though not really without its festival. In the town of Wolfach in the *Schwarzwald* men do a kind of penitential "service" carrying empty purses hanging from poles or broom sticks. Dressed completely in black and wearing black top hats they march dolorously first to their local tax bureau where they perform a "wailing wall" lament, then to the main square where they cleanse their purses with tears and water from the central fountain. In Munich it is the same story where the "mourning" gentlemen parade to wash out their pocketbooks in the *Fischbrunnen* on the *Marienplatz*.

For most, however, there is little to do but go skiing and drink beer. In southern Germany, at least, most factories allow workers to take a one or two-week skiing vacation, usually with pay, after the *Fasching* time. A week or two before St. Joseph's Day on March 19, the Holy Father Beer, once known as *Sankt Vater-Bier* but since corrupted to *Salvator* flows abundantly. The *Salvator* period begins when some official of the Bavarian government or the mayor of the city tastes the first barrel during the morning and a pilgrimage of the general populace arrives promptly at 2 p.m. to commence the long celebration on the *Nockerberg* in Munich.

Now there is no choice but to wait for the solemnities of the Easter season. As for Christians all over the world, Easter for the Germans is a commemoration of the triumph of life and light over death and darkness. It comes conveniently toward the end of winter and the beginning of spring with its new life. At this time, as around the Christmas season, there are Easter bonfires and "Easter wheels," the straw-stuffed wooden wheels which are ignited at night and rolled from a hill crest to the valley below. Actually farmers once gathered the ashes from the burnt out wheel to scatter on their fields, partly for fertilizer, partly for the blessing it was thought to provide.

The religious observation of Easter begins with Palm Sunday as in the United States. First among the rites is the blessing of palms, especially in the predominantly Catholic regions of the Rhineland and Bavaria. Actually, in my own days in Germany palms were at a minimum and the faithful carried instead branches of pussy willows or even hazel and holly. Some people put pine or box elder in the living room or at the head of the bed. In the town of Berchtesgaden children bring pussy willows to church for a special blessing after which they distribute the sprigs among houses or plant them in the fields. Occasionally one reads about the fir tree on Palm Sunday, an obvious parallel to the Christmas tree. It is closely trimmed, however, and the bark is removed in a spiral around the trunk. Set up in the church near the altar, the tree is adorned with juniper, apples, empty egg shells, etc., blessed, and carried in procession to a stable where it is kept for years as protection from the elements. On Palm Sunday in some towns the villagers come to church carrying sticks or poles decorated with large pretzels and egg shells in gratitude for the return of spring and in petition for blessing on themselves and their property.

Next comes *Gründonnerstag,* Holy Thursday (literally "green Thursday," so called because people liked to eat lots of vegetables in preparation for the all day fast of Good Friday). Formerly on this day the Bavarian king used to wash the feet of twelve poor people who were invited to the palace for the ceremony, a banquet and a gift of money. In a few towns children go from door to door singing Easter songs and collecting gifts of eggs and candy in anticipation of the Resurrection of Christ.

Karfreitag literally means "lament Friday." In Catholic and Protestant Germany this is the most solemn religious feast of the year and it is marked by general retirement and sorrow. Most businesses are closed and every church holds services. This tapers off on *stiller Samstag,* quiet Saturday, and blossoms into rejoicing and *Osterlachen,* Easter laughing, on *Ostern.*

Easter customs abound and vary greatly from region to region. All of them still revolve around the egg, and many include the *Osterhase,* Easter rabbit. Like Santa Claus, the Easter bunny brings the eggs, while the stores fill their shelves and windows with cascades of chocolate bunnies, marzipan, and candy eggs. Children play many games with the eggs, one of which was brought to the United States from Germany by my parents; as children we found and gathered up our hard-boiled, colored eggs and hurried to start the "battle of the eggs." As competitors we would bump the eggs together, first the tips then the round ends. To get an even, fair crunch we often had to get Dad to referee. The prize for the winner was to pocket the dented eggs and swap them for his brother's chocolate bunnies. In Germany there are a few areas where this custom is still practiced even by adults. As on our White House lawn plenty of German towns have Easter egg rolls for the children.

Since pagan times eggs have been considered symbols of fertility and therefore appropriate to a festival commemorating the Resurrection or new birth of life. Far and wide the eggs are colored and painted, occasionally with exquisite artistry, and offered to the Lord to ask His blessing on crops. In Oldenburg the water used to boil the eggs is thrown against the walls of the stable to rid the cows of infection. Everywhere eggs are given as presents. Lovers often exchange eggs painted with coded pledges of love and faithfulness. In older times a girl could give just one egg and that meant the courtship was on the rocks, or she could present six eggs which indicated to her lover that it was time to be getting married.

In rural Germany there are other ceremonies of purification, such as sprinkling each other with water. Washing hands to the sound of bells on Holy Saturday was once thought to be a preventative against disease. Drawing water at midnight from a local brook and sprinkling the animals is said to be beneficial, while the dew on Easter morning is a general panacea for all difficulties. People even say that one should roll naked in this dew before the sun rises if he wants to be healthy all year.

No less superstitious is the custom of the fire. If the villagers do not use the burning wheel, they will probably light a bonfire from wood gathered by young people wandering from house to house and begging for sticks of kindling. The rubbish is heaped on a nearby hill so that it will shine for all to see. Villages even compete, with good reason, to see which will have the highest fire; the bonfire is believed to have special power to prevent disasters from striking all the property on which its light shines. To incorporate the symbol of evil, villagers sometimes build a straw dummy, label him "Judas" and throw the figure into the fire while the peasants and farmers dance triumphantly around the holocaust.

As with the ritual fire used in the Catholic Easter Vigil Mass, this bonfire, too, must be started by natural techniques, either with flint stone or preferably by rubbing sticks together. In a very few Catholic communities, all the lights in the homes are extinguished and rekindled again from this ceremonial bonfire. Likewise, during the Easter Vigil the lights in the church are turned out so all members of the religious community may light their candles from the sacred fire of Easter. It takes little imagination to figure out that the new fire symbolizes the risen life of Christ reentering the souls and homes of the people on Easter Sunday.

Soon the solemnity of Easter recedes into the more secular feasts of *Walpurgisnacht* and the *Maibock* beer time. Nevertheless, these are still interlaced with the sanctifying rituals of Ascension and Pentecost, not to mention *Fronleichnam* or *Corpus Christi,* all described elsewhere in this book. The months of summer come and fade into fall while every week there is one festival or another continually in progress. Many are local, being the commemoration of some historical event or the heroic feats of a local

SPORTS

SPORTS: PATHS TO GLORY

COMPANIONSHIP often becomes boring without some competition. The competitive spirit is manifested amicably in the many festivals, of course, but it comes to the fore much more sharply in the various sports. There are the *Schützenfeste* (competitive shooting festivals), track meets, swimming contests and many others, but the teams are more often than not representatives of a certain town or district, rarely from a grade school, high school or college. In fact the universities derive none of their competitiveness from anything other than academics. Sports are simply not dignified by the ivory tower of academia.

Sports in Germany are more zealously pursued than in many other countries. For the German, sports are an activity worthy of the same enthusiasm which characterized the early Christian missionaries. It is almost a religion for the German. Whether it's a local soccer game, competitive skiing, or flying glider airplanes, the Germans don't go at their games half-heartedly. Soccer is without question the most popular sport in Germany but that's not so unusual since it's the favorite all over Europe and South America.

A sport that is not common all over Europe, is unknown in South America and almost as rare in the United States is the sport of flying glider airplanes. Gliders of course are a relatively new phenomenon in our world, having been developed in the 1930's. That the Germans are still glider enthusiasts is due to a quirk of history, namely, the Versailles Treaty. Since that agreement forbade the Germans to make more than a very few self-propelled airplanes on their own, they gently circumvented the law by building gliders. Needless to say, pilots trained themselves for tricky maneuvers and effective use in transporting men and supplies by glider. Later when the war broke out they were able to use these silent air buses with distinction in many a night attack almost anywhere in Europe or North Africa.

To be sure, gliders need to be towed by another plane to get off the ground and theoretically the unpowered vehicle should glide to the ground quickly after being unhitched from its draft plane. But this is where the sport comes in. With a proper breeze and a skilled glider pilot, the motorless aircraft can stay in the air for hours and travel for miles and miles before being forced to land. The sportsman competes against the elements in a uniquely daring way, but he also competes against himself testing whether a faint breeze plus his skill of operation can carry him to distant ports.

Skiing is so widely practiced in Germany, particularly in the south, that many offices and factories as well as most schools grant skiing vacations of a week or longer to permit everyone the opportunity to ply the slopes and traverse the mountains. Tobogganing, bobsledding and ice skating are common though probably no more so than in the United States. One sport that has now declined but was once popular in many parts of America is curling, or as the Germans say, *Eisschiessen.* Many an ice rink in South Germany bears daily witness to games of curling played frequently but not exclusively by older folks. The game isn't very strenuous and compares in general to our game of shuffle board.

The younger men are often drawn to a more reckless if not severely strenuous sport and that is car racing. Some older gentlemen contend that driving around the race track in sports cars is taking your life into your own hands, but other older gentlemen would affirm that it's just as risky to drive down the sleek, speed-limitless autobahns which extend all over Germany. Be it a Mercedes, an Opel or a Porsche, on the autobahn you tend to drive at one speed only and that is top speed. If you're heading out on the race track where you have no choice but to race—your best bet will probably be a car built by Porsche. Any sports car fan in any country knows that one of the very best vehicles for auto racing is still the Porsche, pronounced *porsha*. With all its streamlined sportiness, the little Porsche is a beloved car in America also.

Racing and gliding may not generate much zealous patriotism but there have been periods in German history when certain sports have been directly linked to love of country. You think of hiking in the fields and forests, and you hit upon the philosophy that one can't love and cherish what he doesn't know much about. Thus the entire country of Germany is peppered with Youth Hostels, called *Jugendherberge,* which have been built to provide overnight accommodations for the youthful hikers out to get a first-hand look at their country. In certain periods, this concept of hiking has been used to proselytize the young people and to foster a solid faith in their Fatherland. The youths of Germany were organized on several occasions into corps of gymnasts who hiked for their health and who became physically fit for the health of their nation.

Athletic prowess has long been linked to nationalism as is proved by the international Olympic games. Here we have nations legitimately "fighting" other nations through their representatives in the athletic arena. But even the

Olympic games became tainted with the smell of propaganda when in 1936 Adolf Hitler tried to turn the Berlin Games into an elaborate showcase for Nazism and Aryan supremacy. Luckily, as he and his 110,000 spectators looked on, an American Negro named Jesse Owens played havoc with Nazi doctrine. Turning in perhaps the greatest performance in Olympic history, the black Owens left white Aryan supremacy in something of a shambles. He equaled the record for the 100-meter dash, set a new world record for the 200 meters, almost single-handedly helped set the record for the 400-meter relay, and left a record lasting twenty-four years by his broad jump leap of over twenty-six feet. Hitler fumed and spewed. Adding insult to injury nine other American Negroes on the sixty-six-man American track team excelled in one way or another. In all, American Negroes won eight gold medals, three silver and two bronze medals.

Since their beginning in 1896, the Germans have hosted the summer Olympics only once, at Berlin in 1936, but they will be held in the city of Munich in 1972. The United States has hosted the summer Olympics but once also, at St. Louis in 1904. As for the winter Olympics, they have been held in the German-speaking countries of Switzerland (St. Moritz 1928 and 1948), Germany (Garmisch-Partenkirchen 1936), and Austria (Innsbruck 1964). The United States held the honor twice, at Lake Placid, New York in 1932 and at Squaw Valley, California in 1960.

On the subject of German sports we ought to say a word about the German gymnastic societies known as *Turnvereine*. An excellent source of information about them is contained in A. E. Zucker, *The Forty-Eighters* (New York, 1950) in which Chapter Four, written by Augustus J. Prahl, concerns "The Turner."

The founder of the *Turner* movement was Friedrich Jahn who, during the period of Napoleonic occupation of Germany, initiated a program combining physical exercise with the ideals of free citizenship. Wrote Jahn, "The education of the people aims to realize the ideal of an all-around human being, citizen, and member of society in each individual; gymnastics are one means toward a complete education of the people." These lofty goals took speedy root while Napoleon was around but once Prussia was cleared of the dictator, the Metternich regime saw the *Turner* ideals as conflicting with its own and suppressed the societies of 1819.

Americans who had been in Germany before that fatal date had become rather enamored of the *Turner* and a good many of the political refugees of the 1848 revolutions had been members of the societies in their student days and thereafter. Prior to the Karlsbad decrees banning the existence of the *Turners,* many had composed songs, written poems, or contributed slogans that were to breathe life into the movement for decades, perhaps even centuries to come.

Thus, when the *Turners* were suppressed in Germany it was logical that they would immediately be transplanted to the United States. Carl Follen, expelled from Germany for political reasons, was called to teach German literature at Harvard University in 1826. There he organized a gymnasium modeled on the principles of Jahn. Shortly thereafter Dr. J. C. Warren, a professor of medicine at Harvard, established the Tremont Gymnasium in Boston and intended to call *Turnvater* Jahn to be its director. But when he couldn't raise the funds, he turned instead to Dr. Francis Lieber, later to become famous as an encyclopedist and active political scientist. Another political refugee from Germany became a teacher of Latin in Round Hill School, where he also began a gymnasium and in spare time translated Jahn's *Deutsche Turnkunst*. Now the idea of a *Turnverein* was diffused into the American atmosphere.

Actually no American society was officially organized until the popular hero of the Baden Revolution, Friedrich Hecker, came to Cincinnati in the fall of 1848. Greeted on his arrival by an enthusiastic mob of countrymen marching in a torchlight procession, Hecker found a fertile seed bed for his new society. The local Germans, many of them victims of the reactionary forces in their homeland, automatically subscribed to the principles of Jahn as propounded by Hecker. One year later they dedicated their new gymnasium, one wall of which bore the slogan *Turner: Frisch, fromm, froh, frei,* (Turner: Fresh, pious, happy, free).

In less than ten years there were Turner societies in every United States city where there was a distinct German population. Frequently their boisterous parades and beer parties aroused the suspicions of the nativist Americans resulting in street brawls and violence in Covington, Kentucky and Columbus, Ohio. In Hoboken, Baltimore, and other cities the Turner were sometimes attacked by the Know-Nothings but these incidents of barbarism soon vanished in the rising crisis of imminent Civil War.

Perhaps the most interesting story of local Turner history is the founding of New Ulm, Minnesota, the result of efforts undertaken by the Forty-eighter, Wilhelm Pfaender. Born in 1826 at Heilbronn in Württemberg, Pfaender had such poor health that he practiced his gymnastics just to grow strong enough to survive in the world. In 1845 he moved to the city of Ulm where he became active in Turner groups. Thus in 1848 when the repressive armies moved against all the liberals, they were particularly thorough in rubbing out the Turner circles including those at

Ulm on the Danube. With Hecker, Pfaender became a founding member of the Cincinnati *Turnverein*.

After a few years he conceived the idea of a settlement of workers and freethinkers somewhere in the Northwest where they could find adequate soils and lumber supplies to support a socialistic society in which public ownership would prevail. With financial support from the Turner Society of Cincinnati, Pfaender went out to search for a site. Eventually he compromised by agreeing to join a society of German working men from Chicago who had already made a small settlement on the Minnesota River. They quickly merged the two projects.

With three thousand dollars from the Cincinnati society and eight hundred shares of stock sold at fifteen dollars per share the colony grew rapidly. Pfaender subsequently entered the army, distinguishing himself in Civil War battles. Later he served in the Minnesota legislature, as state treasurer, and mayor of New Ulm.

Established originally as a utopia with communal ownership of property, New Ulm almost immediately went the way of all other such experiments in America. After only three years of existence, the Settlement Association was dissolved in 1859. The shareholders lost their money, free enterprise became the rule, and the community-owned mills were sold to private citizens. The *New Ulm Pionier* newspaper was to be owned by the city while remaining "independent of everybody, neutral on no point" and bearing the slogan, "free soil, free men, free labor, free press." This ended when the editors bought the newspaper from the community in 1859. Likewise, a school committee transferred its undertakings to the public school district of New Ulm. By selling some of their land, they set up an endowment fund for teachers' salaries and textbooks for the public school. There was one condition: there could be no religious education offered in the school. Before dispensing all the public property the founders set aside plots of land for a hospital, fire department, and public recreation facilities. Streets were laid out on a spacious basis.

From the very beginning the principles of the Turners prevailed at New Ulm. Know-Nothings, nativists and their Blue Laws were without influence in this community whose population was more than 80 percent German. While Americanization occurred gradually, the Turner background never faded. The schools used German and practiced their gymnastics as part of the regular curriculum. The *Turnhalle* was not just a gymnasium for athletics, but a community center for social activities, musical and theatrical performances, and public lectures sponsored by liberals and freethinkers. The public library received support from Germans in New York, and two German papers thrived for a long time with Forty-eighters as editors.

Gradually both Protestants and Catholics moved in to swell the population but never with opposition from the freethinkers. According to Hildegard B. Johnson, "Adjustment to the United States" Chapter Three in *The Forty-Eighters,* a church in New Ulm was once partially destroyed by a storm. No worry, a New Ulm brewer, despite religious differences, simply offered one of his structures for Catholic worship. All classes and all religious groups could always meet and discuss their points of view over a cool glass of beer served at the *Turnhalle.* The unwritten rule also prevailed that on the six-member school board there had to be two freethinkers, two Catholics and two Protestants.

Recently an interesting study of the sociological composition of the New Ulm community was completed. (See

Noel Iverson, *Germania, U.S.A., Social Change in New Ulm, Minnesota,* Minneapolis, 1966.) According to the finding, New Ulm today remains largely in the hands of the Turners. In business as in the professions, by far the bulk of activity belongs to Turners. The Turners enjoy status and they remain fairly cohesive. Families of course still own large establishments and they retain their members in key positions or they hire other Turners. Holding an elite status, many shelter each other and monopolies are permitted to continue. Gradually as outside industry crops up in the society, New Ulm may cease to be controlled by the Turner in-group. Yet the economic pressures when linked with the social will tend to perpetuate this community, unique in all of ethnic America.

At New Ulm's annual celebration of Polka Days, the most elaborate float is still likely to be that of the Turners. Young men with sinewy muscles exercise on the vehicle and demonstrate the results of a hundred years of physical training inherited from their immigrant forefathers. By their disciplined play the citizens continue to learn the rigid tenacity necessary for success in their work.

The German hikers, the track stars, the skiers and the swimmers have their ideals from the Turners of the nineteenth century. In this movement which reached its zenith in the last century almost at the same time in the United States as in its parent country of Germany, we find an interesting association between physical fitness, mental toughness and patriotic devotion to one's country.

The same William Pfaender who founded New Ulm spoke at the dedication of the first *Turnplatz* or exercise grounds for the Cincinnati *Turnverein* on New Years Day, 1850. In the speech he elucidated many principles that have governed German sports enthusiasts from the beginning of the Turners until today. ". . . Gymnastics were practiced zealously by the Greeks and Romans primarily as a means to achieve excellent body coordination. If we go back to our ancestors, we see that training and discipline of the body have always occasioned the highest pinnacles of achievement not only in physical fitness but in culture and intellectual prowess as well. Indeed with the gradual disappearance of *Turnen* or gymnastic exercises the medieval world witnessed the inevitable decay of knighthood and courtly conduct."

It might be pointed out here that the practice of chivalry was ceremoniously nowhere more in evidence than through the pageantry of the tournament. The word "tournament" is still alive in the German word for athletic exercise, *Turnen*. Pfaender went on to elaborate that after this high courtly period of the Middle Ages, "it took a long time before either the high-mindedness or the physical culture of the Turners was again reawakened. It took a crisis of civilization itself to do it, namely, the advent on the European continent of the dictator Napoleon. Under the yoke of Napoleon people suddenly realized that through physical exercise they could do something to cast the hated foreigner out of their Fatherland. Through physical conditioning and the mental conditioning that goes with it, they distinguished themselves famously in the campaigns to oust Napoleon from their homes. . . . Thus too . . . we Americans should now strive vigorously by means of body exercise to awake and fortify in our very being a harmonious balance consisting of physical and mental strength. Thereby we will create a superior generation of men, intellectually strong and ingenious, willing to speak out in support of freedom and able if necessary to take up weapons to defend it . . ." (William Pfaender, in *Jahrbücher der deutsch-amerikanischen Turnerei,* Vol. I, New York, 1890, 38-39, translated by the author.)

In twentieth-century Germany the hiking groups continued the zealous ideals of the Turners while the traditional Turners in Germany and in America took on more of a middle-aged steadiness. School-age youths were the chief component of the new breed of hikers. Known as *Wandervögel,* the hikers were very active during the 1920's, then receded for a time only to be resurrected as the Hitler *Jugend* (Youth) in the 1930's. Once again tinged by a semi-religious strain, the hikers were more heavily indoctrinated than any Turner captain ever imagined possible in the nineteenth century. Often they would meet on Sunday mornings allegedly because that was a free day from school and a whole day was needed for a vigorous hike, but in reality because the Nazi leaders knew that the popular group dynamics would be welcome among teenagers not enthusiastic about going to church. The effect was to break down loyalty to parents and clergy while instilling in the group a devotion for another leader in place of priests and parents. Aided by the complimentary uniforms, the music, the songs and the games that accompanied the activities, the program met with astounding success.

Long before the twentieth-century victories of Jesse Owens and his fellow black men, American athletes of German descent met their native German competitors in the homeland. In the year 1880 the New World Germans were astoundingly successful when they met the Old Worlders at Frankfurt on the Main. Despite their small team of only nine men, the Americans walked off with seven of the twenty-two trophies being offered the participants from the various nations.

A proud and ubiquitous organization all over the United States, the Turners of America printed their own national newspaper, *Die amerikanische Turnzeitung,* at the *Frei-*

denker or Freethinker Publishing Company in Milwaukee, Wisconsin. Almost every American city with a sizeable German population had, besides its German singing society, its German gymnastic society. In most cases the Turners of Duluth, St. Louis, Chicago, Seattle, Boston, Cleveland, New York, etc., had their own local Turner paper to supplement the national publication. In 1890 they also began a semi-scholarly publication, the *Jahrbücher der deutsch-amerikanischen Turnerei,* which was edited and printed in New York. In nature and scope the organ was partly historical, partly for biography but also partly for the dissemination of free-thinking ideas. It did not enjoy a long life. After three years of four issues a year the editor closed publication in 1894 with an entry extolling the achievements of the Turners and of his own semi-scholarly endeavor. With the same *esprit de corps* that characterized the group from its cradle to its grave he proudly penned a closing salutation not with "sincerely," or "cordially," but with the glorious motto, *"Bahn frei,"* and his signature, H. Metzner, December, 1894.

As mentioned earlier in this chapter, one of the singular achievements of any specific group of Turners was the founding of the city of New Ulm, Minnesota. Today that city is one of the few, if not the only place in the United States, where a *Turnverein* has survived. Once it seemed that the gymnastic society had become as American as the Volkswagen automobile is today but unlike the swarm of beetles, the gymnasts have faded from the American scene in a way that reminds one of the physical conditioning they stood for—silently, imperceptibly, but organically, exactly like growing old.

THE SWEETNESS OF WORK

THE SWEETNESS OF WORK

A FEW YEARS AGO the popular film, "The Mouse that Roared," cleverly illustrated how a tiny country could conquer the United States super-power simply because we would be so clumsily weighted with weapons that we couldn't wage war. A similar theme underlies the current joke that the way for any small country to get ahead in the world is to lose a war with the United States. The imaginary state president simply announces, "We declare war on the U.S., we lose the war, and then the Americans will spend millions on us." Consternation quiets the cheering populace only when some die-hard pipes up, "But what if we beat America?"

True, the Marshall Plan was highly significant in Germany's recovery after World War II. A donation of a few hundred million dollars could not hurt any country. But vastly larger sums have been donated to other countries without preventing their economic disaster. Usually missing from these other nations is the insatiable hunger of the Germans for work, which is what really performed the economic miracles. Frenchmen, Englishmen and Italians look forward to retirement with expectation and gusto; the Germans dread it. For a Frenchman life begins when the working day ends; for the German when work ends, life ends.

Today if one should go to Munich, for example, and

stroll along the Isar River he would eventually climb a hill where children play and women drive baby carriages. As the German explains, "When World War II ended half of Munich was in ruins. Before we could rebuild we had to get rid of the rubble. So we constructed a railway through town and everybody was expected to clear his property by loading the rubble onto the cars as they moved by. As the wagons were emptied here the hill grew. Later we spread on some topsoil and—look!—what a nice park." There is also a Bavarian joke which commands, "go to the park if you want to stand on old Munich." Go to "new" Munich today and you will find a gleaming city, but not without its building still in progress. As the city girds herself for the 1972 Olympics she is constructing a network of subways to handle the traffic and presently half of Munich looks nearly as torn up as in 1945.

The point is that war or natural catastrophe can turn buildings into wreckage but it takes much more than that to destroy the skills in workmen's fingers, or the indomitable will of the workers to accomplish their jobs. Thus the willingness to work and the skill and knowledge of her people must be recognized as Germany's true capital which enabled her to rise from the ashes and become a powerful western ally in Europe.

Hard work is still a precious commodity no machine can replace, and Germans do love it. Concerning no other topic are there as many German proverbs as for working. One of them runs, *"Die Arbeit macht das Leben süss,"* work makes life sweet. Another states, *"Ohne Fleiss, kein Preis,"* without industriousness, there is no reward. Still others are: *"Sich regen bringt Segen,"* to get a move on brings blessings; *"Erst die Last, dann die Rast,"* first the burden, then a rest; and *"Morgenstund hat Gold im Mund,"* up at an early hour puts money in your mouth—or in a more familiar version, the early bird gets the worm.

Though the country is highly industrialized, craftsmen in Germany have not yet been fully replaced by machines. A blacksmith in the northern part of Germany hammering out cutlery explains that a good chef's knife simply cannot be made by machines. "Machines can do well enough, but the best steel still comes from a man's hand. The size and type of blade requires that each piece be forged differently and carefully tapered."

German sagas and fairytales from ancient times tell of industrious little elves and dwarfs practicing their handicraft. Long ago when the cities first blossomed, artisanworkers were the first to organize into guilds and unions. At that time there was no distinction between a worker and an artist. Even the best-known artists of the German Renaissance, for example, Albrecht Dürer (1471-1528) and Hans Holbein (1497-1543) were considered no more and no less than regular handiworkers.

It was the German guilds who pioneered a system in which young men learned a trade. They insisted that on-the-job training alone made the "master." Eventually every young man who wanted to become a full-fledged member of those powerful organizations had to study the trade diligently and work ardently for years before being commissioned a *Meister*. Many an old *Meister* subsequently became known to history as a great artist. Even today, the young boy begins as a *Lehrling,* or apprentice, matriculates as a *Geselle* or journeyman and only after years of work is graduated as a *Meister* of his trade. In our universities the Master's degree is not unrelated to this medieval pattern of training.

Formerly it was customary for a learning youth to move from town to town, even from country to country studying for a time with each great master of his particular trade.

This tradition of moving about is still common for German university students. When the young man eventually returned to his hometown he could not simply settle down and open his shop. First he had to prove his industry and creativity through an original *Meisterstück,* not exactly a Master's thesis, but any piece of work which the local masters of that guild then judged either worthy or unworthy for admission of the young journeyman into the guild.

There is also an old saying that *"Handwerk hat goldenen Boden,"* literally handiwork has a golden soil. In Germany the saying is applicable even in the age of the atom and the computer. Numerically only a few of the worker-professions have declined in the past decade, the greatest decline being among the tailors followed by a slight decline in the number of shoemakers. Otherwise such fields as bakers, metalsmiths, masons, butchers, etc., have been increasing at a faster rate than the population generally.

To this day each of the professions has its own seal or coat of arms, which usually displays the tools of the trade: carpenters, surveyors, painters, waiters, chefs, auto mechanics, etc. Instead of producing some art work at the end of his training period, today's journeyman must pass his *Meisterprüfung,* his Master's test, known as the Grosser *Befähigungsnachweis,* his major proof of capability.

The apprenticeship system is organized on a national basis and broken down for each county and city. As an organized group, these vestiges of the medieval guilds maintain the *Handwerksinstitut* in Munich for the development of scientific methods and techniques for their professions. Likewise in Munich there is a yearly international *Handwerksmesse,* a handiworker's fair, which not only displays the wares of the workers but also serves as a market for their products.

Anyone who thinks the United States is full of working wives should visit Germany. No other country in the world has as high a proportion of wage-earning women. Every second woman has a job. There are many reasons for this situation, major among them being that Germany's industry is booming at such a heady pace that the employers literally cannot import enough workers to get the jobs done. Just as significantly, the loss of males during World War II has left present-day Germany with a surplus of two million women (four million more women than men in the over thirty-five age group). Thus a standard joke is that the typical German is a woman, and working is the most important thing in her life because it is the only way she can earn a living.

Working women alone fall drastically short of providing the labor force necessary for the dynamic German industries. Riding the trains leading from Rome, Athens or Istanbul one will invariably meet workers bound for Germany as *Gastarbeiter,* guest workers. Millions of young men and women who want a solid start in life or those who need to meet a new financial crisis will take off for a year or two to earn good wages in Germany. Radio, television and newspapers have lately adapted to this situation by offering short programs in the different languages of the "guest workers."

Employment agents are known to fan out into the streets and to frequent the bars in hopes of talking the local workers into switching jobs. Yet, according to a recent article in the *Wall Street Journal,* the German government is almost embarrassed because the German work force is so stable and strike-free that there is fear the German product will gain almost too favorable a position in

international trade. The next day an American corporation president wrote to the editor wishing that the United
States would have a similar "problem."

Social laws and federal laws for the protection of the
workers in Germany are much older and certainly more
comprehensive than in the United States. Such New Deal
inventions as Social Security and unemployment compensation became the law in Germany around 1885 when
Bismarck found it to his advantage to provide broad insurance coverage for his nation's workers. Curiously
enough, the model plans for Germany's social legislation
were drawn up by one woman, Bertha Krupp, wife of
Gustav Krupp whose munitions makers had for generations honed the swords of war on their family anvils in the
Ruhr Valley. Actually the Krupp family dealt in military
hardware only because it was good business. In search of
a superior product, the nations of the whole world flocked
to Krupp's doors. Since war has always been popular,
Krupps have always been prosperous.

As members of one great family, the over 200,000
Kruppianer who worked in the factories always enjoyed
the best conditions at the factory and in the home. The
management furnished medical care, housing, seaside rest
havens and pensions. What the privately owned Krupp
firm did for their workers the Federal Republic does now.
Today the insurances are compulsory and inclusive.

America's bill providing medicare for citizens over
sixty-five strikes German folks as something of a joke, for
they have enjoyed the fruits of the *Krankenkasse,* the national plan for health insurance, for over seventy-five
years. Under their plan all medical costs are free and only
a tiny charge is made for prescriptions. Unlike the Scandinavian countries and England, however, foreigners may
not simply walk in and take advantage of the medical of-

ferings. As with any other insurance plan, you must be covered by prior affiliation with some organization in Germany.

Some make the charge that Germany is oversocialized, but this would be hard to substantiate, for the tendency has been away from federal control rather than toward it. For instance, the Volkswagen firm, nationally owned from its origin in the 1930's, has been turned over to the stockholders by a series of steps beginning in 1960. Lufthansa Airlines, although the only airline in Germany, is nevertheless a privately managed corporation. On the whole, German industry is no more subject to federal regulation than in the United States, certainly less so than in England and in most other European countries.

However, the *Bundesbahn,* the system of federal railways, is a nationally owned government corporation just as it has always been since its inception. As in America, German postal services comprise a federal agency but in Germany the functions of the Post Office are more extensive. Covering the entire German nation is the postal bus system, essentially a regularly scheduled network of bus lines which haul the mails. Because busses are used instead of trucks, passengers have the opportunity to ride as well. Moreover, the Post Office provides such services as telegraph and telegram, as well as the *Postsparkasse.* This is a savings account in the Post Office which enables the saver to withdraw funds at any post office in the country, thereby providing a traveler's check supply for the man away from home. Not least, the Post Office directly operates the telephone communication's network for the entire nation. A note in passing: Germany's postal authorities pioneered the *Postleitzahl,* the postal direction number, which almost immediately became the pattern for the zip code system in the United States.

As in most countries the German highways are state projects and there are no German turnpikes subsidized by tolls. In the 1930's Germany had already pioneered the four-lane freeway system called the *Autobahn* (note that *Bahn* means "way or road," hence we say *Eisenbahn* for the railroad and *Autobahn* for highways limited to motor vehicles). In part these highways were constructed to relieve the unemployment problem, much as our conservation corps operated during the thirties in America. The point is sometimes made that the *Autobahn* was built primarily for the rapid movement of troops and supplies in preparation for World War II, but concrete proof of this is scanty. More interesting to Americans may be the fact that when our first major four-lane highway was constructed, the Pennsylvania Turnpike, it was modeled after the German *Autobahn*.

Like the highways, the major canals and harbors are also owned in common by the government. Although Germany's landscape is described in detail in an earlier chapter, it is worth being reminded here that through an intricate canal network the country is interwoven north-south and east-west with water transportation, as well as ample access to railroads and highways. It is this factor which enables Germany to remain a major exporting nation. Highly industrialized, she must import large quantities of food to feed her factory-oriented population, but her balance of payments nevertheless remains among the most favorable of all nations.

Finished products such as heavy machinery and automobiles rank high among the exports, so high in fact, that the phrase "Made in Germany" is famous throughout the world. Everyone has seen the ubiquitous Volkswagen beetle and if you pay attention in the dentist's chair or in the hospital, there is a fifty-fifty chance that the "machinery" you are staring at was made in Germany. For that matter, Bayer aspirin (Bayern means Bavaria), are made by the Bavarian Drug Company. Many of America's printing presses, the cigarette-making machines of the North Carolina tobacco firms, and a whole ship loading installation on Lake Erie were all made in Germany. The city of Schweinfurt recently exported an entire ball bearing factory to Joplin, Missouri. And in Chillicothe, Ohio the paper industry wanted to construct a huge smoke stack made of concrete. Since it required special techniques, among them continuous pouring, a German construction firm was called in to apply its skills learned in the Ruhr.

The most modern steel plant anywhere in South America, the installation at Campo Limbo, Brazil, is the work of the Krupp Firm of Essen, Germany. The Krupp complex, implicated for its role in gun trafficking and for slave labor during World War II, has discontinued the manufacture of all weaponry and concentrates instead on the export of heavy machinery and entire factories, including three to the Soviet Union and numerous others to iron-curtain countries.

Few Americans realize how great was the impact of German science and skill in the development of America. In his recent book, *They Came from Germany,* Dieter Cunz presents short biographies of just nine German immigrants whose skills were of great significance to the development of the United States. Everyone has probably read about General von Steuben who aided Washington in the Revolutionary War, and about Wernher von Braun, key figure in our interplanetary space program.

Less well-known but likewise significant were men like John A. Roebling, the German-born, Berlin-educated engineer who pioneered the suspension bridge. Having demonstrated the possibility of cable suspension in a bridge he built over the Monongahela River in Pittsburgh in 1845, Roebling had by 1855 accomplished the then incredible feat of a railroad bridge suspended over the roaring whirlpools of Niagara Falls. By 1866 he had again defied the impossible by a 1,057 foot span, then the longest in the world, across the Ohio River at Cincinnati. After years of haggling and dangers which eventually cost him his life, John A. Roebling designed and began work on the Brooklyn Bridge, a suspended span of 1,600 feet. On opening day in 1883 a million spectators turned out to see it, including the United States President Chester A. Arthur.

The political leader Carl Schurz is also relatively well-known, but Ottmar Mergenthaler is not. Printing, which had remained essentially in the same archaic form in which Gutenberg gave it to the world, was revolutionized in the late nineteenth century by the German immigrant to the United States, Ottmar Mergenthaler. Born in Hachtel, Germany in 1854, the boy gained some distinction in grade school when the old clock in the church tower refused to run and the village clockmaker could not repair it. When it began once again to resound the hours it was discovered that young Mergenthaler had secretly climbed up and fixed it.

True to accepted practice, the boy underwent an apprenticeship training program with Louis Hahl, a watchmaker in Bietigheim. Hahl's son, August, had emigrated to Washington, D. C. and eventually Ottmar joined him. Occupied for a time building models of ideas proposed by other inventors (a prerequisite of the U. S. Patent Office before registration was possible), Mergenthaler eventually set out to invent a streamlined way of setting print. It took him more than ten tedious years but in 1884 Baltimore witnessed the first demonstration of his finished machine.

What typesetters formerly accomplished by fishing individual letters out of compartments and mounting them on a block of line, was now done in fifteen seconds by an operator who tapped a lettered keyboard. Thus was born the Mergenthaler Linotype which made possible a revolution in the comprehensive newspaper coverage of events and the printing of books for the education of the masses. At its sesquicentennial celebration in 1940 the U. S. Patent Office listed Mergenthaler's machine among the nineteen most significant inventions.

A late beginner, Germany quickly developed the rugged sinews of an industrial titan. Wars could not destroy them nor the human resources that made them possible. Their chimneys flickering through the nights, German factories and research centers produce as never before a seemingly endless tide of new products. The researchers, by linking their arms with those of handicraftsmen and skilled artisans, together form the true raw materials of the German nation.

Perhaps the best symbol of German achievements in this respect is the *Deutsches Museum* in Munich. Here is an enormous edifice devoted to displaying technological achievements. Mines, steel mills, textile machinery, electrical devices and flying vehicles intrigue the visitor. Instruments for physics and astronomy, chemical laboratories, automobiles, bicycles, rockets and even musical instruments represent all the epochs of German development.

Founded in 1903 by the German engineer Oskar von Miller, the *Deutsches Museum* is the best of its kind in the world. In addition to comparing the displays and models in a study of the historic development of science and technology, one can also learn in its library of 500,000 volumes. It is also something of an honor for the *Deutsches*

Museum that the distinguished Museum of Science and Industry in Chicago was patterned after it.

The world-famous German architect Walter Gropius, who taught at the Massachusetts Institute of Technology until his death, once advised, "Architects, sculptors, painters, we must all turn back to craft. The artist is the craftsman in his highest form—he is the *Steigerung des Handwerkers,"* literally the intensification of the handicraftsman. In a sense, the *Deutsches Museum,* by its isolated position on an island in the Isar River, symbolizes the high status of craftsmanship in German society. Following this line of thought, the most characteristic feature of the *Deutsches Museum* is an exhibit in the section for musical instruments. As a splendid tribute to the teamwork of the artist and the artisan, talented musicians are hired to play each model in the display, thus demonstrating in one bold stroke the finest admixture of German genius.

GERMAN FOOD

taken into English without translation). Even though the
origin of "hamburger" sounds German too it is unknown
there, and seems to be of American birth. The word "hamburger" came into English by means of a process in word
formation which philologists call analogy. The ground
meat is named after the city of Hamburg just as those
sausages have the names of German cities, Frankfurt-er,
Wien-er, Regensburg-er, etc.

Perhaps the reader has also been in a delicatessen recently without realizing that this is a particular kind of
German store where fine foods are sold: *Delikat,* delicate,
and *Essen,* food. No American any longer thinks of Germany when eating sauerkraut, but during World War I
the word (though not the food) became so offensive to
"patriotic" Americans that the term "Liberty Cabbage"
was temporarily substituted. Munching on pretzels one seldom thinks of their origin as Germany, *Brezel* or *Pretze,* a
word which comes from Old High German, *brazzilla.*

What American has ever heard of *Hase im Topf,* a di-
vine brew of rabbit, or of *Perlhühner oder Fasan mit
Ananas,* a delicate dish of guinea hens or pheasant with
pineapple, or for that matter of *Gefüllte Käsepfannkuch-
en,* cheese filled pancakes? Some feature writers and even
members of the author's family affirm that the tradition
in German cooking is to balance the table by serving seven
sweets and seven sours but in actual fact this is more myth
than practice. It is true, though, that Germans like sours.
There are such things as *Sauerteig,* sour dough, *Sauerbraten,* meats soaked in vinegars or brines before cooking,
and of course there is plenty of *Sauerkraut* as well as many
sour dressings for salads. Even cakes, cookies and puddings have distinctly less sugar than their counterparts in
the United States. German frostings seem more like
creamy pudding than rich candy. It is a fact that Germans

use less powdered sugar and more shortenings for frostings than we do.

There are other fundamental characteristics about German food. In France and Belgium they cook with butter
and its substitutes; in Spain and Italy olive oil prevails; but
in Germany, no one goes to the kitchen without his lard.
Starch is plentiful too and do not expect to find anything
served without noodles or dumplings if it can possibly be
served with them. Salads are not exactly the national specialty and the whole vegetable kingdom is best represented by its king, the potato.

When in Germany, it is fun to eat in a little *Gasthaus,*
those little restaurant inns nestled in every town where
ceilings are low and beamed, and large round oak tables
are nicked and darkened with age, and the atmosphere is
cozy and *gemütlich.* Or, one may prefer the huge expand-
ing beerhalls, more noisy and less intimate, but where the
food is just as palatable.

Germans have their big meal at noon and survive at
night with open faced sandwiches, cold-cuts, sour pickles
and liver sausage served around eight in the evening.
Those who do not like the heavy lunch find a little *Bäck-
erei,* bakery, where they have small tables and serve coffee.
Or even pick out a *Mölkerei*—here one can have cheese
on hard biscuits and a glass of milk. At the latter store
many German women will be filling their cans and pails
for the day's supply of milk. This is a necessary daily
trip because there is no house-to-house milk delivery.

On the other hand every brewery has its delivery trucks
—in many places it is still an old wagon drawn by husky
draft horses. The beer wagon does not need to come by
every day (usually once a week) but if one chooses to
patronize all the breweries, he can probably have one drop
off a case each and every day but Sunday. In Germany

beer is simply part and parcel of the normal human be-ing's diet. For dinner and supper beer is as routine as drinking coffee in the United States. Only infants drink milk. Preschool children and their parents and grandpar-ents thrive on the many excellent beers. Coffee is for breakfast and the afternoon coffee break, not for other meals. German beer bottles are handy to take along on the job too, because they have snap-on rubber caps that permit the bottle to be resealed after opening. Outside my window in Munich the construction workers on the streets as well as those high on scaffolds all had their half empty beer bottles close at hand for that hourly transfusion of energy. (More on the different kinds of beer in the next chapter.)

First of all, here is a run-through of a German's eating day. Up early, the German's *Frühstück*, breakfast, usually consists of hard-crusted buns with butter (German butter is unsalted) and *Marmelade*, jam. A few Germans like cheese slices or sliced salami, more prefer a soft boiled egg. Breakfast tableware often includes little egg stands for the boiled eggs and even little jackets to keep them warm. Usually the egg is eaten with a small spoon, straight out of the shell. Coffee is coming to be the standard drink for breakfast although tea and cocoa still hold their own. Do not expect fruit juices, cereals and toast, although occa-sionally the latter is available under the English name, toast.

Work often begins very early in the morning and for such men it is still quite common to have a *zweites Früh-stück*, a snack taken at midmorning and consisting of a swig of beer and a sandwich often made of dark bread and bacon or sliced sausage. For those performing less strenuous labor this morning break is much like the now common American coffee break.

The *Mittagessen,* dinner, is the primary meal of the day and can be taken any time between noon and two in the afternoon.

The *Mittagessen* starts with soup, standard fare on the German table. There are lots of good ones, *Leberknödel-suppe,* liver dumpling, *Ochsenschwanzsuppe,* a wonderful oxtail variety, and *Hühnersuppe,* chicken soup. Two broad categories of soups are the *Kraftbrühe,* similar to our consommés or bouillons, and the *Rahmsuppe,* a cream soup which can include almost any base—peas, asparagus, etc. Likewise there are plenty of soups with a fish base as well as cheese, barley, and what have you, to make a different variety of soup for every day of the year.

It has become commonplace at family tables to follow the soup with a bowl of fried noodles, rice, or *Klösse,* dumplings, as a kind of filler before the meat course arrives. Then comes the platter of meat served usually with vegetables. Especially common are potatoes followed by such favorites as cauliflower, cabbage, asparagus, peas, onions and mushrooms. In restaurants one generally finds soup followed by a plate of meat garnished with one or two vegetables, including potatoes of course, bathed in various kinds of sauces.

Again without going into particulars, one should realize that Germans eat a lot more *Schwein,* pork, while Americans tend more toward *Rind,* beef. Similarly, German menus always include some choice of *Kalb,* veal, and no menu is complete without some cut of *Hammel,* mutton. Rare is the menu lacking a few game meats such as rabbit, venison and wild boar. Likewise, no menu is adequate without its offerings of *Geflügel,* be it wild or tame fowl, and of course its *Fischgerichte.* A great variety is available, from the sour meats to those marinated in wine, to the pickled pork and herring dishes. Smoked meats are popular and tasty too, as are the many cold or warm sauces to pour over meat concoctions. Brains, heart slices, tongue and kidneys are especially delectable while *Schaschlik, Kalbschnitzel,* and *Sauerbraten* are everyday essentials.

For dessert forget about cake or ice cream. Those American favorites simply do not belong to the German bill of fare. Think instead of the puddings and the many stewed fruits, the latter served under the title *Kompott.* For that matter, do not count out fresh fruit or even cheese, that French dessert which has happily found its way across Germany's western frontier. One should never expect to find pie as we Americans know it in Germany. It has never been made in Germany and it is even difficult to buy a round pie tin to make one's own.

Jello with fruit is now taking its place on the German table, but cookies, tortes, and layer cakes are still reserved for that ritualistic coffee pause taken in the middle of the afternoon when rich dark coffee whets the appetite for those tantalizing decorated layer cakes, fruit-filled tortes and cheese delicacies.

This afternoon snack is sometimes known as *Vesperbrot,* a word taken from monastic life where vespers are the prayers sung by the monks around three in the afternoon. Frequently workmen talk of the *Vesperschnitte,* that is, a sandwich eaten in the middle of the afternoon. The coffee break varies a great deal from one locality to another and from class to class of people and certainly its style is conditioned by the type of job one has.

One meal that almost never changes from one household to another is supper or *Abendbrot.* The most striking thing about this repast is that it is always served cold. Usually it is a matter of eating open-faced sandwiches— buttered slices of bread, *Butterbrot* or *Belegtes Brot,* covered with sliced salami, possibly ham, liver sausage, rare roastbeef, slices of hard-boiled eggs, cheese, and even mayonnaise or sliced pickles. In a family that likes both fowl and fish, be prepared for goose liver smeared on pumpernickel bread, slices of duck, chicken, patés of every consistency, and a spicy assortment of breads topped with herring, anchovies, raw salmon, smoked eel, shrimp and, to be sure, sardines. Those with other tastes may substitute vegetable and fruit sandwiches — chopped apples and onions, marinated asparagus, slices of orange with paprika or sliced tomatoes—very popular in the summer time.

Needless to add, the standard drink for the *Abendbrot* is beer, although women frequently prefer tea.

The *Abendbrot,* therefore, is just that: the evening bread. Having had a lunch in the afternoon the German usually postpones his supper until around eight o'clock or even later. Also, it is quite common at the opera or the theater to find the guests eating their *Abendbrot* after the first intermission. Due to these eating habits nearly all the major theaters and opera houses have lunch counters where, in addition to a full line of beverages, plates of cold sandwiches are available. Guests who have already eaten frequently have a glass of champagne or other hard liquor during the break.

Granted that the open sandwiches are tasty and the variety is intriguing, a steady diet of this kind eventually becomes monotonous. Perhaps luckily, the *Abendbrot* is one custom that our German forefathers left in the old country. Countless German staples from the *Mittagessen,* of course, have been absorbed into the muscle of American life. In magazines and bookstores everywhere one can clip and buy recipes attributed to the Pennsylvania Dutch, concoctions which in fact are translations of the rudimentary cooking patterns of the average German family.

There is an old student saying which runs, *"Lieber den Magen verrenken als dem Wirt einen Pfennig schenken,"* literally, it is better to strain your stomach than allow a morsel to remain for the restaurant owner. The proverb may reflect the days when students were even shorter on cash than they are today. It also says something about the German's attitude toward eating out. Since noon is the time for a hefty meal, dining out in Germany is less a special occasion than a daily necessity and this condition is somehow evident in the restaurant. Eating is like a duty and whether one is dining in a fancy establishment or in a warehouse-sized beer hall, chances are that other people will move in and fill up any extra space at the table. It is no trial to have company and certainly not bad manners to talk to the strangers at the table.

Whether dining out or eating at home, window shopping in Munich or Milwaukee, Cologne or Cleveland, one can see and smell that ubiquitous German staple, the sausage. Call it the Bratwurst, the Frankfurter, the Regensburger, the Weisswurst, Rindswurst or a hundred other names, it all adds up to sausage. Whole window showcases are stuffed with sausages, frequently with fifty or more different varieties, not to mention the familiar meat and bologna types. There are also such tantalizing servings as *Leberkäs,* a liver paste cooked in chunks and sold to be consumed while still hot, available at booths almost anywhere in Bavaria. *Münchner Weisswurst* is made of calves' brains and veal, and is supposed to be eaten as a snack anytime between midnight and noon.

In Germany, cities compete with one another as to which one can produce the best *Mettwurst* (Braunschweig and Göttingen are famous for their rivalry), the best *Cervelatwurst, Leberwurst,* etc. Citizens of every city readily enjoy *Gänseleberwurst,* goose liver sausage, *Milzwurst,* a spleen meat base, *Zungenwurst,* made from tongue, the *Thüringer,* sausage made mostly of salt pork, and of course the *Dauerwurst,* salami, and the infinite variety of cold cuts available especially for those bleak, cold suppers.

Bread counters in America show signs that the variety is increasing but to a great extent American bread is still rather uninteresting. This is partly the result of living in a land and climate suitable to the growing of good wheat for white bread. For centuries in Germany, bread meant rye bread because no wheat was rugged enough to withstand the German winters. Working under these handicaps the Germans became good bakers and their people developed unshakable preferences for dark bread. Still undiminished is the popularity of pumpernickel bread made of whole rye, an aromatic, sweetish, Westphalian bread that is almost black. Formerly it was produced by baking the dough for several days in outdoor, stone ovens. Today it is produced by essentially the same process, though speeded up to meet the world-wide demand.

Nevertheless, pumpernickel remains a sour dough made from unsifted rye flour. The kernels are cracked, thrown into a mixer, bran and all, and a little water is added along with some hard, stale pieces of old pumpernickel. These chunks of bread start the fermenting and replace the yeast as a leavening agent. It still bakes for twenty-four hours but at the low temperature of 212 degrees. After removing the loaves, they are too hard to eat so they must soften up by standing for about three days. Then they are sliced, wrapped in aluminum foil and heated once again for a brief period. This heating sterilizes the bread so it will not mold in storage.

Sometimes people ask the origin of the name "pumpernickel." Nobody knows for sure but there are some good theories. One holds that the name originated during a famine when flour had to be extended by whatever means available. Thus bakers added sawdust to the rations. The local bishop one day issued some pious propaganda by eating a piece of the bread publicly. After his first bite he smiled broadly and declared that this was *bonum panicolum,* that is, "good bread." Another story says a French soldier was fighting long ago in Germany and after eating the bread made a sour face and said *"bon pour Nicol"* which is, "good for my horse, Nicol." More likely, however, is the theory of scholars that the name came from the French province of Auvergne. There the same black bread was known as *pompou nigle,* which means in the local dialect, "black bread." This name probably turned up in Germany as "pumpernickel."

Regular *Schwarzbrot* is similar to pumpernickel though somewhat lighter in color, and is also baked for at least twenty-four hours. As a child I remember reading that the poor peasants of Europe had the full horror of poverty rubbed in by having to eat black bread. The implication was that the bakers and millers were not yet advanced enough to refine the dark color from their flour. In the United States, of course, we do that but in the process take out the vitamins as well. This is necessary so we can add them again artificially. The Germans concur with their proverb *"Salz und Brot macht die Backen rot,"* salt and bread make the cheeks red.

White breads are generally available in Germany but unpopular except in the form of the *Brötchen.* Breakfast, of course, calls for *Brötchen* which are sometimes called *Semmel,* depending on the geographic position. In restaurants do not expect to find sliced bread—*Brötchen* is the rule—served in baskets on every table and be prepared to pay a small fee for each one you eat. There are variations of this basic roll or bun. They can have names like

Knüppel, Schrippen, or *Hörnchen,* if they have shapes like a stick, oval, or the curve of a horn. *Kümmelbrötchen* have caraway seeds and *Mohnbrötchen* are sprinkled with poppy seeds, while other characteristics give rise to still other names. The rolls have to be hard, apparently for no really good reason. Recently there was some publicity given to a stunt by the East German bakers who planned to get up early enough to bake and deliver warm *Brötchen* in time for breakfast in West Germany. The idea seems to have merit because West Germans still adhere to an old Nazi curfew at night which prevents even bakers from being up and about getting the rolls in the ovens. One may assume that West Germans do not change that law because their tastes have not changed.

A market for German breads does exist in the United States. In a few cities, for example, New York, Cleveland, and Cincinnati, enterprising bakers have found such demand for the authentic *Schwarzbrot* and *Kommissbrot* that they have the yeasted dough flown over several times weekly to be baked in their local bakeries for distribution to lovers of German bread. He who craves Westphalian Pumpernickel and is not satisfied with local substitutes, should write to Swissrose Inc., 99 Hudson St., New York, N.Y. 10013. They import it and wrap it in triple foil to guarantee its original flavor on delivery.

The gamut of German cheeses is small even though the little town of Limburg in Hesse has gained great notoriety for the smell of Limburger. Such brands as Tilsiter, Mainzer, and Weisslacker are common. Many other cheeses are available, to be sure, but they frequently have French, Swiss, or Dutch names which are derived from their places of origin. Those with fancy German titles often are processed versions—smoked cheese, packaged in sausage skins, spiced with olives and herbs for colorful effect, or boxed in catchy tinfoil primarily to please the eye.

Let us leave the cheeses to Germany's neighbors and take a bow instead to that other German gastronomic delight, the herring. If you thought herring belonged to the hearty Scandinavians, you are only partially right: Germans consume herring in every imaginable form. In Emden (and elsewhere surely), one can have an entire meal on herring alone. Start with an hors d'oeuvre, move on to fresh fried herring, sometimes called "Green Herring," or perhaps sour pickled *Bratherring* served fried, or *Matjesherring,* presented with potatoes broiled in their skins and buttered. Have some herring salad, that is, Bismark herring spiced with sliced cucumbers. Or, if they are rolled up around pickles, cucumbers and onions, the Germans call them *Rollmops.*

Kiel sprats are also supposed to be good, and along the North and Baltic Seas every store has smoked or jellied eel. Canned cod liver is available any place, as are smoked flounder and German caviar, not to mention a wide selection of sardines. Atlantic salmon are know as *Lachs* when ground up with onions and served raw. In northern Germany and especially in Hamburg, no one should miss eating in one of the *Austernstuben,* the small restaurants which specialize in oysters but serve the whole shellfish line, lobsters and shrimps included. As a special treat try *Labskaus,* a stew prepared from pickled meat, potatoes and herring, sometimes garnished with a fried egg and sour pickles.

It would be impossible to give any meaningful treatment to the many regional specialties whose variety pepper German cookery. Leaving that to the cookbooks, let us turn instead to a brief presentation of German pastry. As a rule tarts and sweet rolls are sold in the *Konditorei,* shops where one can usually also get a cup of coffee or tea and eat at the tables provided. Such cafes are plentiful and throughout history have often been popular as meeting places. An interesting statistic is that although Germans have for centuries sung the praises of beer and wine, they nevertheless drink more coffee and tea than any other beverage. More than forty thousand confectioners make and serve the cheese cakes, apple tarts, plum breads and cream buns, primarily at the magic midafternoon hour of *Kaffee und Kuchen.* This snack time is also the hour for such regional specialties as *Schwarzwäldertorte,* a thinly-sliced chocolate cake heavily layered with cherries and whipped cream; or for *Küchle,* made of wild berries, hazelnuts and rose petals all rolled up in dough and then deep fried. Almond paste serves as the basis for many desserts, especially the Rhineland specialties *Spekulatius* and *Manzelmandelchen.*

While on the subject of desserts and cakes mention must be made of whipped cream. Over three hundred years ago a Viennese cook scooped cream off milk and whipped it, the result being *Schlagobers.* Ever since, whipped cream has been spread on more and more German palates and is referred to simply as *Schlag.* Today all of Austria and much of Germany is addicted to *Schlagobers.* They pile whipped cream on *Torten,* spoon it into their coffee and even order it in addition to their cake as a separate dish.

Quite a few *Konditorei* feature special baked goods for the different seasons of the year. In December Bavarian shops, for example, might feature fairytale landscapes surrounding chocolate mountain chalets hanging on marzipan glaciers and draped by sweet, creamy meadows. At New Year's, cake lowlands become the terrain of the

Glücksschwein, good fortune pigs, and candied streets are tread by tasty little chimney sweeps, also a New Year's good luck symbol. Naturally at Easter there are chocolate bunnies with candy eggs and baskets.

One seasonal specialty that deserves at least passing mention is the *Lebkuchen.* Literally meaning "cake of life," *Lebkuchen* is a cookie-type pastry made in autumn from dark dough sweetened with honey. Often the cookies are pressed from forms whose designs go back to medieval and even pagan traditions. *Lebkuchen,* therefore , can have the shapes of stars, hearts, rings, animals, soldiers, curvaceous females and even a knight riding on a rooster. Although *Lebkuchen* is common everywhere, Nürnberg generally claims to be the home of true *Lebkuchen.*

If there is one pastry now considered more German than the Germans, it is *Apfelstrudel.* The fact of the matter is, however, that *Strudel* is neither German nor Austrian. It is a Turkish delicacy known as *baklava* which entered the Austrian Empire through Hungary where apples predominated as the most desirable filling for the thin dough. It has been said that only Hungary's outstanding wheat could be milled into a flour so excellent that *Strudel* became a possibility in central Europe.

All of the many recipes for *Strudel* published in magazines and cookbooks in America usually emphasize that the dough must be rolled and pulled until it is very thin. Exactly how thin is left to the imagination. In Germany they are a little more specific, prescribing that the dough ought to be as thin as an onionskin or so thin that one can read a newspaper through it. In all seriousness, a good *Strudel* maker must be as skilled as a tightrope artist. One slip and everything is lost. Although in the German speaking countries apples are the most popular filling, other fruits, sweets, meats and even vegetables and cereals are sometimes substituted for *Strudel* filling.

The normal beverage served with the cakes is coffee. About this black brew we find no record in German annals prior to 1683 when the Turkish army besieged Vienna. As far as history is concerned the Turks lost but coffee won, for although the Turks receded from the European scene, coffee definitely took over and the coffeehouses grew and spread, eventually becoming a sort of Everyman's Club. Authors frequented them to write books and plays and politicians plotted deals that evolved the fates of empires while nobles and commoners alike simply read the papers and just sipped and sipped their coffee.

ABOUT DRINK

ABOUT DRINK

IT IS A FACT, the Belgians drink more beer, the French imbibe more wine and the British gulp more whiskey per capita than the Germans. Statistics show that since World War II the Germans have been drinking 50 percent more wine than before and still the non-German image persists that the Germans are the greatest, most remarkable beer drinkers in the world. Some even think that the word "German" is synonymous with beer. Germans do love to drink, of course, and even that earliest foreign observer, Tacitus, wrote of the Germans, "It is not considered shameful for any of them to pass the day and night drinking." Delineating the collective nature of German habitual intemperance, the austere Roman concludes that "if their tendency to drunkenness is favored by giving them as much as they want, they'll be conquered by this vice as easily as by arms."

The prediction of Tacitus may have turned out wrong but the fact remains that beer is emphatically the national beverage of the Germans while brewing the alcoholic beverages is a German proclivity. Beer for the German lies in the realm of staples. As mentioned in the previous chapter, beer is a food used at major meals. This attitude, differing fundamentally from the orthodox view of alcohol subscribed to in both England and the United States, is easily recognized in the disproportionate taxes levied on alcoholic beverages. By way of contrast, the English system has always regarded alcohol as a luxury and taxed it heavily. Having always taken the view that beer is food, many German states have for centuries placed no taxes at all on beer and wine. Eventually finance ministers made themselves intensely unpopular by instituting small beer taxes which even today are considerably lower than in other countries.

Because beer has always been allocated a place in the daily diet, inebriation in Germany has never become the problem that it has in the English speaking countries. Bismarck may have been at least half serious when he claimed that although beer was good for the body it made people stupid. Not even he complained, however, about it making them go to hell. In this vein, German immigrants to the United States often became the butt of stern condemnation from Anglo-Americans because native puritanical traditions conflicted with the German attitude toward alcoholic beverages. Nevertheless the Germans continued to cherish their beer and beer gardens, their Sunday picnics, dances, bowling, theatrical performances and concerts, none of which ever took place without its accompanying flood of beer.

In the nineteenth century, therefore, it is not surprising that Yankees and German-Americans were polarized into two camps, pro and con, concerning the laws of prohibition. In the fray certain leaders of the German immigration concluded that their own culture was superior to the native American fundamentalism. This attitude is quaintly expressed in a poem written by Karl Heinzen, journalist and revolutionary expellee from Germany who arrived in the United States in 1850:

Sich amerikanisieren
Heisst ganz sich verlieren;
Als Teutscher sich treu geblieben
Heisst Ehre und Bildung lieben;
Doch lieber indianisch
Als teutsch-amerikanisch.

To americanize oneself
Means to lose oneself;
As a German, to remain true to oneself
Means to love honor and good breeding;
But rather become an American Indian
Than a German-American.

In her book, *The Homes of the New World,* published in London in 1853, Frederika Bremer, after visiting the German sector of Milwaukee, left a charming description of a German-American immigrant and his idea of life's enjoyment. In Milwaukee she found German houses, German inscriptions on doors and signs, German newspapers, German music, dancing and the many other pleasures which "distinguish them from the Anglo-American people, who, particularly in the West, have no other pleasure than 'business'." In Cincinnati she found that the Germans "are *gemütlich,* drink beer, practice music, and still ponder world history." On Sunday evenings "they congregated with their pipes and their beer in the *Biergarten* to talk and argue, and to sing the songs of the fatherland." A visitor from the German university town of Göttingen, once remarked that where two Germans settled in America a third immediately opened up a tavern to furnish beer and a place for the pair to argue.

According to another foreigner's observation (See Allan Nevins, *American Social History, as Recorded by British Travellers,* New York, 1931, page 400), liquor was consumed in large quantities by the Germans living under the southern sun of Missouri. And in some of the theaters, the audiences smoked and drank beer served by German waitresses. In the public *Lustgärten* scattered about the town, German bands played nightly, and German families, including the children, sat for hours in continental fashion drinking beer and listening to the music. To be sure, as beer gardens crept toward the outskirts of cities they clashed with Sunday closing laws. We must conclude, however, that since there is little evidence to the contrary, the German beer gardens and *Weinstuben* were orderly places where drunken customers were dutifully managed or promptly ejected.

At one time or another in American history the German beer hall cut diagonally across all levels of American society. Grover Cleveland spent many a happy evening in the German beer halls of Buffalo, especially at Schenkelbergers where he enjoyed the sausage and sauerkraut while playing cards with German voters. In Columbus, Ohio in 1844 the Germans celebrated the Fourth of July with such vigor, cannon fire, marching and drinking that the German newspaper chided the native Americans for not observing the birthday of their Republic. To demonstrate their own Republicanism, the editors printed a toast which their readers had repeatedly drunk and sung the day before:

> *Was wir lieben fern und nah;*
> *Jetzt an des Sciotos Strande,*
> *In dem neuen Vaterlande,*
> *Dir dies Glas, Amerika!*

> What we love far and near;
> Now on the shores of the Scioto,
> In our new father country,
> To you this glass, America!

Although it hardly needs to be said, Germans in America initiated and still dominate the brewery industry in the United States. Naturally, then, major beer manufacturing centers like St. Louis, Milwaukee, Cincinnati and Baltimore are precisely those cities where the German population once predominated and quite naturally composed a rich local outlet for the brewed products.

Whether eating or drinking, Germans have always liked company. Consequently, large numbers of drinking songs, *Trinklieder,* have been published as a natural by-product of their conviviality. Spurred on by the alcohol, lost in the anonymity of the beer hall, tables full of proud citizens will thunder out a gruff, rhythmic song often in rather uncertain unison. A good many *Trinklieder* have been handed down from the Middle Ages. In those raucous days, students bent more on drinking and being merry than on learning composed secular songs of a definite choral nature. Their hymns to pleasure and today's more explicit melodies all more or less praise the fraternal felicity of drunkenness.

In fact, the German language has developed precise terms that define the varying stages of alcoholic beatitude. If it is true as certain anthropologists tell us, that people have words for situations in proportion as they are important to us in life, then perhaps both Americans and Germans live in a strange light. Eskimos, for instance, have as many as fifty different words to describe snow and conditions of snow. We are told that this is because snow is such a vital thing for an Eskimo.

Counting the words in English that connote drunkenness, one should be able to come up with at least a dozen. That is true of German as well but there is an added dimension. Germans have words and phrases that distinguish between the degrees of inebriation. Euphemistically "*zu tief ins Glas gucken*" means that you "look too deeply into your glass;" you are therefore in the first stage of dizziness. Move on to the next stage "*Der hat einen Schwips,*" "he is a bit too high" and you can still belong to the human race. If you really go over the hump, people will say "*Der hat einen Affen*" which means roughly, "the guy is a monkey." Go all the way and you will probably be called simply *blau,* that is literally, "blue," a reference that seems to have penetrated the English language with such terms as blue Monday, to feel blue, etc. For whatever it is worth, we learn in Lichtenberg's *Mythologie der Deutschen* that there are 111 High German words for degrees of drunkenness, although in Low German there are only 56.

Once beer was strictly a winter drink, for without the icebox or the refrigerator there was little chance of preserving it. Then too, the actual brewing of beer was made difficult because of high summer temperatures. It was accomplished of course in limited quantities deep in the cool, vaulted cellars of the countryside where barrels of beer could be kept at lower temperatures. There are stories, in fact, that this was the beginning of the beer garden.

Tall, shady chestnuts and oaks were planted above the caves. Chairs and tables were brought in under the branches and the beer was simply served up from the ground in mugs—the birth of the outdoor *Biergarten.* Moreover, we come back again to the position that for the German, beer is nourishment. Accordingly, in these ancient tales, barrels of beer stored in the cellars were referred to as "casks of living bread." Did they mean that yeast is used in making beer just as for bread or did they mean to stress that beer is as fundamental to the diet as bread? Probably both implications are correct.

Over the centuries the beer garden tradition grew so that it is still a relaxing, out-of-the-way place to have refreshment even in the middle of huge cities. Many Germans on a Sunday afternoon drive out into the country just for a visit to their favorite beer garden. Even Goethe was thrilled by the atmosphere of the beer garden, writing, "Never before have I so easily found a spot so intimate and yet so homely; so I let the landlord bring my chair and table from out of the bar and set them up in the garden so that I could read my Homer in peace and tranquility." Scores of other poets have sung similar toasts to the garden way of drinking beer.

Sometimes beer-making even involved the powers of state. In 1372, Stephan, the Duke of Bavaria issued a permit to all citizens of Munich allowing them to brew their own summer beer to relieve the "ghastly" shortage in his country. At other times in the history of beer production there were beer revolutions. The year 1848 is primarily thought of as a time of political upheaval, but in at least one case it was no more than a beer revolt. When brewers raised the prices of beer that year, "pianos, pictures, clocks, linen, beds, clothes, chairs, tapestries, silver, and what have you were hurled by the angry mob out of the windows of a brewer's home; down and feathers, mixed with torn banknotes, fell to earth as if it were snowing."

Beer wars have not always coincided with political uprisings. Invariably though, an increase in the price of beer unleashed storms of protest. In 1885 the price rose by a mere half penny but the Bavarian demonstration of protest grew to such proportions that the militia had to be called out to suppress it. Earlier in 1865 several infantry units were ordered in to control the melee, and when they proved ineffectual against the mobs, the cavalry galloped to the rescue dispersing the rebellious beer drinkers. In Berlin merrymaking citizens on the Spree have been enjoying the delights of their beers for some three centuries. Before the war, in fact, their brands of *Schultheiss, Engelhardt* and *Schlossbrauerei* dominated both domestic and export markets. Since the war, however, the Bavarian beers have captured the spotlight with such titles as *Löwenbräu, Spatenbräu, Paulaner, Augustiner, Franziskaner,* and others.

Another brand, *Berliner Weisse,* belongs to the category of white beers or ales made of wheat malt and having a slightly acid taste as well as an alcoholic content of at least 11 percent. In 1806 Napoleon's soldiers expressed their admiration for the *Weisse* by christening it the "Champagne of the North." Around the year 1900 in Berlin there were over thirty brewers of "Berlin white" beer. Today it continues as a drink popular with mixed couples and is drunk sometimes with a straw. As earlier, both sexes often prefer to drink it with a shot of raspberry juice, calling the drink *"Weisse mit Schuss."*

When it comes to beer drinking, there is one saint who enjoys the highest cult of admiration among the Germans. He is Gambrinus, the inventor of beer and the patron saint of beer drinkers. A tour of the breweries, especially in Bavaria, will reveal short inscriptions in his honor on the doors and walls. Whether he is celebrated in the brewery, the tavern, or the seasonal party, his spirit has also wandered to America where at least one sizeable brewery in Ohio produces beer under the brand name of "Gambrinus." The fellow himself is legendary, of course, but there is some evidence to conclude that he may once have actually lived. They say his name is a corruption of "John the First," known in the Middle Ages by his Latin title Juan Primus (later corrupted to "Gambrinus"), the Duke of Brabant. Supposedly he reigned in the thirteenth century and came to fame because he could consume enormous quantities of beer—up to 144 pints at a single party.

As in so many good aspects of culture from the Middle Ages, the art of brewing the effervescent potion is derived from the monks, and even now many a monastery remains distinguished either for its fine beer, wines, or liqueurs.

Not far from Munich once stood the Benedictine monastery of Andechs. To this day *Kloster* Andechs boasts a beautiful baroque church but this is not the real source of its reputation. Today their brand of beer, *Andechs,* is what counts. It is served in many inns throughout Bavaria and from dawn till dusk at the monastery itself. Guests drive from miles around to sit in the former refectory on top of the 2,333 foot *Heiliger Berg* (Holy Mountain), munch *Würstchen* and gulp the wonderful *Andechs* beer.

A slightly different atmosphere exists about fifteen miles north of Munich in Freising. On the nearby heights stands the Weihenstephan Benedictine Monastery, now housing the School of Agriculture of the University of Munich. One of its present subdivisions is the Bavarian State Brewery which continues the fine brewing begun by the monks in the year 1146. According to the latest count, the state of Bavaria has 1,643 breweries whose output is thousands of gallons a day. An unknown percentage of it is for export abroad and to other cities in Germany but much of it never gets beyond the city limits of Munich.

Simply by looking at the official Munich seal one is reminded of the role played by the monks in the history of beer. Called the *Münchner Kindl,* the seal displays the image of a child dressed in the habit and cowl of the Franciscan Order of Monks. Literally translated, the words mean "the Monk child" because the word *München* itself has developed from the German *Mönch* meaning monk.

In Middle High German one finds the word written sometimes as *münch,* at other times as *münech,* thereby explain-
ing the English word for the city, Munich, and the German
word, *München,* meaning *"bei den Mönchen,"* at the home
of the monks.

A particular Munich monk called Barnabas has been
immortalized as the maker of *Salvator,* a strong beer produced especially for the lenten season. In fact, the big,
Salvator Keller on the Nockerberg retains its reputation as
the official headquarters for the strong-beer lenten celebrations. Traditionally at these festivals one must eat a special
fish broiled whole over open-pit fires, and drink *Starkbier,*
supposedly to tide oneself over the awful lenten fasts.
Needless to say, such other Munich brands as *Augustiner,*
and *Franziskaner* also perpetuate the prominence of monks
in the development of this particular beverage.

Beer was not the only potion discovered by those medieval men of God. Legend claims that the monks also discovered wine. One year during the Middle Ages, the Abbot
of Fulda sent a messenger to an outlying abbey commanding the monks to pick the grapes but the fellow got lost
on the way. When he finally did arrive at the abbey, the
grapes had become overripe. Nevertheless, the obedient
monks picked them and stored them in kettles. The happy
result, according to the story, was a delightful wine.

We know this tale is fictitious because wine is mentioned
even in Genesis IX, where it is ascribed to Noah. The
Greeks, too, had a highly developed wine culture, storing
it in casks, goatskins and earthenware, many of which
have been found in wrecked ships on the floor of the
Mediterranean. It is true, however, that during the Dark
Ages the production and quality of wine declined steadily.
In these dim times it was only the ecclesiastical communities, usually the monasteries, where the cultivation of

grapes continued strong simply because wine remained a requirement for the communion service.

In the twelfth century when the monastic culture was at its zenith, the planting of vineyards skyrocketed and soon came to have significant commercial importance. Medieval limitations on transport, however, compelled the growers to cling to the river banks for wine production. Hence, the generic names for wine brands frequently derive from rivers, especially the Rhine and the Mosel. It is true also that the climate, especially the direct sunshine, is a factor in determining the quality of a wine.

Monks again played a major role in developing and preserving good wines when they introduced their European vine stocks to the United States. The Christian Brothers of California, for example, have gained international recognition for their products. Thanks to their American transplants, Europeans today are still able to enjoy their centuries-old brands of wine. In the year 1863, millions of European winegrowing acres were devastated by an aphid-like insect called Phylloxera, which fed on the roots of the vines. In many areas this disaster ended wine making forever. Other ravaged sections recovered when bug-resistant stocks were reintroduced from America. Many older vines survive today only because they were cut from their defective roots and grafted on to American subcultures. Pre-aphid vines are extremely rare. If they exist at all, it is in Chile where the pest is not known to have penetrated. The only other disaster that threatened the very existence of wine was the enactment of prohibition in the United States in 1919, but here it was only a major market that was destroyed, not the vines themselves. Nevertheless it took a good thirty years before the industry got back on the road to recovery.

The major wine-growing regions of Germany are confined to the Rhine and the Mosel and their tributaries. According to ancient history, vineyards existed in these areas in Roman times. Roman viticulture disappeared in the Dark Ages but such vineyards as Johannisberg and Steinberg were planted originally in 1106 and 1131. They enjoy international fame today. Since those early years four basic districts of the Rhine variety of wine have developed: the Rheingau, the Pfalz or Palatinate, Rhein-hessen, and the Nahe valley.

Among the wines from the Rheingau is Rüdesheimer, the name of a small town along the river. Situated in the very heart of the most celebrated wine region of Germany, Rüdesheim boasts many a proud legend. At night, it is said, the spirit of Charlemagne himself strolls softly through the fields to bless and guard the precious vines. Another says that in the fourteenth century the Emperor Wenceslaus, witnessing the decline of his empire, eventually sold the whole thing along with his crown for a few casks of Rüdesheim wine. Other famous Rheingau brands are Johannisberger, Oestricher, Stienberger, Markobrünner, Bacharacher, Rauenthaler, and Hockheimer.

The region known as Franconia also produces wine but the products are less frequently exported. Just why, no-body seems to know but perhaps it is because the people of Franconia simply want them for their own consumption. In fact they express this opinion in a little poem:

> *Frankenwein ist Krankenwein*
> *Heissts im Lande auf und ab*
> *Auf Wein gestellte Frankenbeine*
> *Gehen nicht so schnell ins Grab.*

Franconia wine is for when you're sick
So they say throughout the country

Legs that stand on Franconian wine
Don't step so early into the grave.

From the Pfalz come brands such as Forster Ungeheuer,
Dükheimer, Michelsberger, Herrgottsacker (God's little
acre), and Kallstädter Saumagen (sour belly). From
Rheinhessen there is Nackenheimer, Niersteiner, Oppen-
heimer, and Liebfraumilch, which is really a generic label
for various wines from the greater Rhine area.

Originally *Liebfraumilch* (the Virgin's milk) was the
name given to wines from a vineyard situated near a church
in the city of Worms, called by the same name and dedicated to the Madonna. Now in use for more than two
hundred years, the label *Liebfraumilch* is a blend of good
quality wines from the Rhine area. The intention of the
shippers is to offer a consistently good product from various suppliers. Similarly the name *Moselblümchen* is a generic term for Mosel wine.

The Nahe valley is best known for such names as Nie-
derhausen, Kreuznacher, Nacktarsch (bare behind), Nar-
renkapp (fool's cap), and Schloss Böckelheimer. Most of
these names indicate the immediate areas from which they
come, and many like to tie in the name of some *Schloss*
(castle) or special *Berg* (mountain).

Usually the Mosel wines have a slightly lower alcoholic
content than the Rhine wines, often 11 percent versus 12
or 13 percent for the Rhines. Often too, the Rhines are
bottled in brown bottles while the Mosels have green flasks.
Once when I asked a connoisseur of German wines what
was the precise difference between Rhine and Mosel wines
he responded authoritatively: "The Rhine wines are more
grand; the Mosels are much more graceful." He did not
explain how to distinguish between the two adjectives.
There will be similar adjectives also: "full," "powerful,"

"youthful," "delicate," "fragrant," "flowery," and lots of others implying girlish charms. Yet the only conclusion seems to be that one really cannot describe wines.

German wines remain of high quality largely because the industry jealously guards its interests and has fostered strict German wine laws. Thus the better wines, "the liquid sunshine," are grouped by established categories and so labeled. On any high quality wine the following classifications may be found: *Spätlese,* picked late; *Auslese,* selected bunches; *Beerenauslese,* specially selected grapes; *Trockenbeerenauslese,* selected grapes picked when nearly dry. In certain years the weather is too poor to allow a meaningful breakdown into these groupings. Since the weather is such an important factor in the production of good wines, the year a wine is made must also be printed on the bottle. When the summer and fall are blessed with plenty of sun and not too much rain, it will be a good year for wine and those wines will bring fabulous prices on the markets for years to come.

To weather the storms of war and pestilence wine growers must count on an almost innate taste in man for wine. History tells us that German vineyards were under severe pressure in the fourteenth century because the German Hanseatic League imported large proportions of wine rich in alcohol from Spain and Italy. No sooner did they recover than Germany became embroiled in her devastating religious conflict, the Protestant Reformation. Instead of improving, this malady funneled into a far greater catastrophe, the Thirty Years' War. So disastrous was the Thirty Years' War for the German wine maker that it took him until the nineteenth century to recover. Barely on his feet, he was again struck, this time by the Phylloxera mentioned earlier.

In the United States, it seems, the calamities pursued

the viticulture just as furiously. Germans in Cincinnati, Buffalo and St. Louis tried to grow grapes on a grand scale with only partial success. One perpetual source of trouble was the weather which never seemed right in the eastern United States. Another more serious problem was the attitude of fundamentalist Americans toward alcoholic beverages. After struggling all through the nineteenth century, the German growers finally lost the battle in 1919. When prohibition became the law of the land, vast acres of imported German-stock grapevines simply met the fate of the plow. To cite but one example, the entire Kelley's Island in Lake Erie off the shores of Sandusky, Ohio was once covered by excellent grapevines. In compliance with the mood of the country in 1920, the owners uprooted every last plant. They had no other choice actually, for they had to sow other crops just to survive economically. In spite of their efforts to adapt, the wine farmers fell victim to the disasters and today the island is fallow, hauntingly empty, and covered with weeds and wild grasses.

As a national immigrant group, the Germans fought virtually alone against the blue laws and prohibition. Their lack of allies stemmed from their good fortune; none of the other immigrant nationalities in America stood on as solid a tradition of using liquor as food. It is true the French and Italians back in the mother countries had been raised on wine, but the habit had never been successfully transplanted in the United States. That left the Germans to wage their own war in behalf of the moderate use of alcohol, a war they were destined to lose eventually. What they had learned at their mother's knee had become overnight a matter of breaking the law.

Scholars who have studied the habits of the Scandinavians and the Irish, for example, observe that neither of these immigrant nationalities did very well in managing their use of liquor. In the mother country a principle of moderation in drink had never developed. These countries did not produce beer and whiskey and what a man does not have he cannot learn to use. When it came to the use of alcohol, Swedish immigrant farmers often drank to excess. Temperance habits grow only with deep roots stretching back many generations. Consequently, when the question of prohibition arose, the Scandinavians and the Irish along with many others were convinced that complete abstinence was the only alternative to drunkenness, character dissolution and economic ruin. As one old Norwegian immigrant told me, "We voted for prohibition to save us from ourselves."

That wine has survived all these onslaughts points to something basic about the relationship between man and wine. Stop and think for a moment how many religions lend special significance to wine. Frequently pre-Christian cults included one or more wine gods. The Greeks had their god Dionysus, and the Romans their Bacchus. Both Mohammed and Buddha strictly forbade the use of wine but in ancient rituals wine became a widespread offering to the gods in place of blood sacrifices. Thus the Christian use of wine in the sacrifice is not entirely without foundation in pagan practice.

The importance of wine for man and his religions seems to rest on the psychic effect it produces. Alcohol for early man was another way of reaching ecstacy and thereby a means of coming into close communion with his god or gods. In most mystic procedures wine and the symbolic dialogue connected with it play a significant role. Moreover, even in Germany today the many wine-harvesting festivals are often deeply religious affairs. In Jewish art, the vine is used as a symbol of their people. The Christians speak of their sacramental oneness through the metaphor of a vine; Christ said: "I am the Vine, you are the branches." In a much lighter mood, let us not forget the wisdom contained in the German proverb:

> *Wer nicht liebt Wein, Weib und Gesang,*
> *Der bleibt ein Narr sein Lebenlang.*
> Whoever doesn't like wine, woman and song
> Remains a fool his whole life long.

As might be expected, the profession of wine-making in Germany is firmly structured by the apprenticeship system. Accordingly there is an entire vocabulary to describe the steps. A *Winzer* is anyone who works at the profession in whatever capacity. Young grade school children can take up the subject of *Winzerlehre* for three years and then try to pass their *Winzergehilfenprüfung,* a test to become a wine-maker's assistant. Six years in this capacity will lead to the *Winzermeisterprüfung,* or if the lad is working in the cellars, to the *Kellermeisterprüfung.* He may go on to part-time schools for wine-making and take the state exams to become a *Weinbauer,* a viticultural expert. If he wants to climb still higher in the profession he will probably attend one of the technical institutes for wine-makers, the most prestigious being the one in Geisenheim. Upon completion he could take a more comprehensive state examination to become a *Weinbautechniker.* With three years in practice he could take a second state exam and subsequently serve as a *Weinbau-Kellerei-Inspektor.* With still more study the young man might eventually be a professor in a wine school, a researcher in grapevines, a vine louse commissioner, or even a *Weinbau-Direktor* of one of the major state vineyards or of one of the schools. Some of the better known wine schools are at Trier, Bad Kreuznach, Oppenheim, Ahrweiler, Neustadt, and especially Geisenheim on the Rhine.

In spite of all the care and concern for the production of wine, Germany is certainly not the world's largest maker. In an average year Germans grow only 10 percent of the amount grown in France, and just barely more than in the United States. For the most part the vineyards belong to small holders. Some 53,000 vineyard owners have less than two acres, 23,000 have less than four acres and there are only 730 holders whose wine acreage is over twenty acres.

The German growers have distinct problems. Germany is the northern-most wine producing area in the world. After all, the German wine district lies fully north of the Canadian border. Young vine plants must be protected from the winds, yet have exposure to the sun, and have soil that holds heat overnight. All summer in the wine districts, people worry whether the season will be long enough for the crop to ripen; for in Germany, the grapes are harvested later than anywhere in the world. For instance, in 1962, grapes were gathered as late as Christmas time, and harvesting usually runs into the middle of November. Naturally the German vintner must do all the work by hand if he is to practice selective harvesting to get the categories of grapes for *Spätlese, Auslese, Beerenauslese* and *Trockenbeerenauslese.*

Regardless of picking and of vintage year, here is a little bit of closing advice: all but the great, late picked varieties must be drunk while fairly young. If you are thinking of laying away a case of Rhine or Mosel wine for your grandson's twenty-first birthday, don't, if it is more than three years away. Far better to drink the wine yourself because it simply will not keep for more than a few years.

A German drink that is rapidly increasing in popularity in America is *Glühwein,* literally, glowing wine. Usually

Glühwein is a red wine that is heated to a near boil before serving. Unless the wine is very pungent to begin with, it is best to add cloves and cinnamon sticks and let the brew steep a while on the stove. The time for *Glühwein* is winter. In Germany it's sold along the streets and at outdoor public functions of every type. In the United States it's a favorite drink for after skiing hours or just in the evening after a cold day outdoors.

Before leaving the topic of beverages it should be mentioned that the Germans like *Apfelsaft* (apple juice) very much, and at the right time of the year, *Apfelwein,* an alcoholic apple cider famous especially in Sachsenhausen, a suburb of Frankfurt. For parties and seasonal feasts popular drinks are the *Bowle,* punch made of white wines, champagne, sugar and bits of fruit, frequently pineapple or strawberries.

Germans also like their *Schnaps,* or hard liquor, and commonly drink it using beer as a chaser. The word *Schnaps* is a generic name for the clear, strong liquors that are often somewhat crude. In Germany one can simply say *Korn* which means the liquor is distilled not necessarily from corn, but from any seeds in the grain family. Usually this is rye, the proper title of *Korn* being originally *Doppelstöckiger Münsterländer Korn.* In a way the liquor looks like gin but it tastes different.

That brings up another Westphalian drink, *Steinhäger,* which is very much like gin and which can hone a delicate edge on anyone's appetite. *Steinhäger* is made from grain alcohol and juniper berries, as is gin, only the juniper flavor is more pronounced. The original juniper patch was at the town of Steinhagen on the edge of the Teutoburg Forest. Steinhagen remains the center for production of *Steinhäger* although today the juniper berries come mostly from Italy. From the start, the liquor was stored in stoneware jugs and although it is available today in glass bottles the people still prefer those earthenware flasks. The origin of the drink dates from the Crusades when the juice of the juniper was thought to have medicinal value. The difficulty was that the extracts spoiled too rapidly. As a preservative, the doctors discovered they could add grain alcohol. Soon people who felt perfectly fine joined in the fun. Partly for this reason in 1688 the entire industry escaped the liquor tax imposed by Elector Friedrich Wilhelm of Brandenburg. Today Steinhagen's fifteen distilleries are the result of their former competitive advantage.

Another juniper *Schnaps* is *Doornkaat,* made in East Friesland, the German territory bordering on Holland. Although these two brands, *Steinhäger* and *Doornkaat* are popular throughout Germany, the juniper spirits are mostly confined to the north. In the south the people prefer brandies distilled from fruits. Possibly the most popular fruit brandy is *Kirschwasser,* a clear liquor made from cherries in the Black Forest. Plum *(Zwetschgewasser)* and raspberry brandies are also popular. Genuine *Himbeergeist* (raspberry brandy) is available only in limited quantities because the distillers do not resort to synthetic flavorings.

Our last classification of alcoholic beverages might be titled as cordials. These include the wide range of "monastery liqueurs" made from herb-flavored, aromatic concoctions. Generally the recipes are top-secret and handed down from monk to monk behind the cloistered walls. In the southern monasteries of the Bavarian Alps one can have the popular *Enzianschnaps* made from the roots of the blue gentian, *Benediktiner,* or *Kloster Ettaler* and many more.

The drink *Seehund* (meaning a seal, literally sea dog)

is a mixture of wine, rum and lemon juice. *Sylter Welle* combines red wine, brandy and spices and is drunk in the territory of Schleswig-Holstein. From Danzig in East Prussia there is *Danziger Goldwasser* (Danzig gold water), a sweet, syrupy, transparent liqueur with tiny flakes of gold suspended. Certainly a good recommendable brandy is *Asbach Uralt,* both tasty and mild.

In northern Germany where the people go in for strong drinks as well as tea they frequently reconcile the two by producing *Teepunsch* or tea with rum in it. This is also known as *Grog* or for those who prefer it extra strong, *Steifer Grog*—rum, with tea or hot water and sugar. *Steif* literally means stiff which really describes the gamut of German liquor.

MUSIC, THEATER, SONG

MUSIC, THEATER, SONG

DURING THE nineteenth century German music critics often referred to England and the United States as *"Länder ohne Musik,"* that is, countries without music. Whether or not this criticism was valid, American attitudes toward music are quite different from those prevalent abroad. One might say that the Germans take a kind of military approach to music. Famed conductors are titled *Herr Generalmusikdirektor* and frequently addressed as *Herr General* for short, just as in the Army. And some orchestra members are quick to point out that the directors are more "General" than "Director," and consequently feared for their military arrogance.

Music in itself, however, is not really military for the German; it is the joy of life, audible sunshine, something elemental in life like food, drink and love. The local population simply must subscribe to both the symphony orchestra and the opera. Going to the opera is a solemn ritual not unlike going to church. In fact once a performance has started no one is allowed to enter the auditorium and take his seat. Seating must wait until the end of the first act because ushers lock the doors to prevent even the slightest irreverent disturbance during a presentation. It goes without saying that one does not munch candy or hold his coat in his lap during the performance. Coats belong in the *Garderobe,* the check room.

The attitude toward great composers in Germany suggests that their music is also food for the soul. Germans
refer to Mozart's pieces as having an undertone of sadness and a silent current of sorrow. Truly great music
should always be sad according to the Germans. Bach is
admired for his granitic style, Beethoven for his stupen-
dous torment, Brahms for his melancholic melodies, and
Bruckner they say is basically "serious." It is rare, in fact,
to attend a concert where the big B's (Bach, Beethoven,
Brahms and Bruckner) are not represented.

In Germany music is also big business, for instance,
the recording industry. Germany's major electrical firm,
Siemens, backs one of the world's largest recording giants,
the *Deutsche Grammophon Gesellschaft,* to out-record all
others in the area of symphony and opera. To a considerable extent, therefore, top echelon managers of radio
stations and directors of leading orchestras can create
trends in taste or eliminate far-out styles of music. Besides
their good business sense, these men have excellent sub-
sidies from the federal government because the German
parliament is thoroughly *kultur*-conscious.

It is significant that in the whole world, where there are
only one hundred opera companies, more than thirty are in
West Germany. Ten more are in East Germany which
means that Germany has nearly half the world's opera.
In a sense even these figures are deceptive. Italy ranks
second in number of operas with eighteen, but all of them
operate for only short seasons each year. On the other
hand, the German companies perform at home or on the
road for ten or eleven months of the year and it is not
uncommon for a company to have more than 400 appearances in one season. The only city on earth to have
three permanent opera houses is Berlin. And what is
more, Berlin's only competition in respect to opera houses

also belongs to the German cultural entity, Vienna.

Germany is also the land of the summer music festival. Big, medium and small, there can be as many as a hundred in any one summer. Concerning the festival, the poet, dramatist and genius, Hugo von Hofmannsthal, wrote, "To hold a festival is merely breathing new life into something that has existed since time immemorial." Probably the quintessence of all summer music festivals is the Wagner theater of music and drama in the city of Bayreuth.

With all its cyclonic complexity, Wagnerian opera has also achieved a glorious reputation in countries other than Germany. Europeans have recently been great on Wagner, especially the English and the French. Writing about the Bayreuth festival some sixty years ago, however, the French writer Romain Rolland said, "The French flirt, the Germans drink beer, and the English read the libretto." If he had been writing today he would also have included some sly remark about the Americans who also attend the Bayreuth Festival by the hundreds each night.

At Bayreuth Wagner truly achieved what he called the *Gesamtkunst,* the perfect blend of music, acting and singing with poetry and drama—a complete artistic triumph. The achievement is supposed to bring an intellectual-emotional satisfaction. Thus, according to Wagner and a good many theorists since him, the highest form of art is the opera because it embodies all the others. Not just singing and acting, but orchestra and drama as well as painting and sculpture make up the stage settings.

When we are thinking of music or the theater in Germany, we are of course dealing with business. Yet taken from another angle it might be more correct to say that the theater, like the concert hall, is not just a business but a public service. In our country we may occasionally go to the theater for an opera, a play or a musical hit but we pay a price that immediately proves we are purchasing a luxury product. And the quality of the performance has probably been proved only by its ability to make a fortune at the box office. In Germany the playgoer is visiting a civic institution prized by local Germans much more highly than even our home baseball or football teams in the United States. To a German citizen it is his theater because his taxes have subsidized it dearly, just as any American city has taxed its inhabitants to install street lighting. Like the street lights, theater performances can-not be measured in strict values of dollars and cents, rather, the community as a whole profits from it and therefore must underwrite it.

Right now there are about 125 West German theaters subsidized with public funds in the sum of over $70,000,-000 annually. East Germany operates similarly, subsidizing eighty-six theaters for a population only one-third that of West Germany. The Germans, therefore, are operating on the principle that civilized people are entitled to the best in music and theater at public expense in the same way that all Americans are entitled to at least a high school education. In reality the comparison is quite valid, for in Germany it is expected that one comes to the theater to learn something as well as to be entertained.

As mentioned earlier, theater guests enter the building ceremoniously to wait for the beginning of a performance. Many arrive in time to sip a beer, study the program with its lavish notes, or nibble on a sausage. Once seated, though, there is a devout attentiveness, no coughing, no shuffling. So it remains until the intermission when the audience exits quickly and silently. Couples head for the food bar or the champagne stands if they are so inclined, others join arms to promenade in a clockwise circle around the foyer until the bells ring and all return quietly to their seats.

Thus are both theater and music viewed in Germany. It is not a matter of an exceptional and costly after-dinner gala treat but a normal everyday experience. The cultural nourishment is both cheap and available, like a visit to the neighborhood library in America. To the German, theater and music are just like books; they ought to be accessible to everyone. Wars and natural catastrophes may temporarily destroy them but ultimately they must be restored.

In a way the indestructibility of the German theater was confirmed during the Nazi period when it survived decapitation. That is, virtually all playwrights underwent twelve or more years in exile. The most famous of these was probably Bertolt Brecht who, like so many German political exiles for two hundred years before him, took refuge from oppression in the United States. Although Brecht died in East Germany in 1956, he is today recognized everywhere as the most influential playwright of the twentieth century.

Germany's great tradition of diversified theater, ironically, stems from the historical fact that for centuries the German nation simply did not exist. With no political center there was no center of gravity for writers, actors or elite audiences. Formerly the German nation consisted of over three hundred city-states of which thirty-nine still remained after Napoleon, and each of these sponsored a theater. Imbued with the German tradition of competitiveness, these theaters vied with each other causing the provincial quality to improve and the tendency toward decentralization to grow stronger.

With the rise of wealthy industrial centers, municipal populations grew prodigiously, soon demanding their own playhouses and proliferating more theaters. In a short time the city theaters outnumbered their aristocratic counter-parts and the big city centers, Hamburg, Munich, Düssel-dorf, Berlin, etc. also began to compete with one another. Court patronage thus turned into civil patronage. Even-tually civic patronage turned into something else. Citizens did not care to subscribe to what either playhouse was offering. In place of the "official" theaters they began to organize their own stages, called the *Volksbühne.* Financed either privately or by trade unions, these theaters flour-ished around the turn of the twentieth century. As it still functions today the *Volksbühne* has become a part of the regular theater system, offering subscriptions for cut-rate season tickets. According to this arrangement the specific plays to be seen are chosen by lot. Yet the lack of choice seems to be no deterrent, for sample attendances at Munich and Berlin show that the *Volksbühne* ticketholders account for a consistent 40 percent of the guests.

On whatever level, classical, comedy or contemporary, the guidelines call for a heavy subsidy. Payment to the theaters is based on the principle that theater is not a luxury but a right, similar to the right to knowledge. This arrangement seems to work toward the good of all. The bogeyman lurking in many an American's mind that fed-eral money means federal control is simply not con-firmed by the facts in a country like Germany. For ex-ample, a few years ago when Rolf Hochhuth's play *The Deputy* seriously offended Catholics because it indicted Pope Pius XII for his part in failing to stop Hitler's ex-termination of the Jews, certain Catholic organizations moved to secure a court order forbidding its showing in state-supported theaters. Wisely the government authori-ties replied that the repertoire was fixed by the artistic director, not by the politicians. Likewise, those who fear that subsidy makes for stale German repertoire have statistics against them.

Perhaps one price the Germans pay for good theater is poor television and poor movies. Good actors are drawn toward a life on the stage and unattractive pay in the other industries accounts for their poor quality. Theater, certain critics in Germany maintain, is not just theater, it is a way of life. No actor can shift from the stage to the movies without endangering his vocation. An actor in Brecht's company confirmed this view on acting; he responded to the master's question "Why do you act?" by stating, "Because people don't know what they are like and I think I can show them." That seems to come close to what modern theater seeks to do for the German population. The theater is a public place where a company presents working models of human behavior in order to find out about the causes and effects of human activity much as scientists make models to study planets and molecules. Always the desire to understand and to inform is paramount. Thus we come back to the attitude of the German community toward theater, that it is everyone's right just as we Americans believe use of the library is everyone's right.

Although the professional theater and symphony are the born right of every German citizen, there is no shortage of lesser musical endeavors. To illustrate, the Austrian Folksong Archive recently published a catalog listing all songs in their collection: over 150,000, and they are still collecting. There is hardly a circumstance, be it happy or sad, for which the German does not have a song. Songs put infants to sleep and wake them up, they encourage young lovers and inspire shy maidens, console aging women, bring nostalgia to old men, comfort departing soldiers and sustain beloved sweethearts and families during absences in the call of duty. There is, in fact, no stage in life that cannot be cheered by an appropriate song.

The *Wiegenlieder* or cradle songs soothe even adults as witnessed by the famous lullabies of Schubert and Brahms. The *Kinderlieder* likewise brighten the lives of grown-ups and what family celebrates the feast of Christmas without the popular *Weihnachtslieder*. The strains of yearning and longing in people of all ages are comforted by the eternal and unchanging *Liebeslieder*, songs of love, while the exalting joys of freedom with its endless horizons could not be complete without the accompanying *Wanderlieder*, the hymns of hikers. Hunters have their chases but not without their *Jägerlieder*, hunting songs, and the gymnasts cannot perform their cadences for long without a few *Turnerlieder*. And when the day's work is finished, what better way to relax than with gay company and a few *Trinklieder*.

Then there is that indispensable part of army life in Germany, the *Marschlieder*, sometimes also called *Soldatenlieder*. During one extended stay in Germany I lived west of Munich in the town of Fürstenfeldbruck where there is a large basic training camp for the German Air Force. When the *Bundeswehr* (Defense Department of the Federal Republic) was reconstituted in 1954, the world watched to see how this new "citizen's army" would handle its deep-rooted choral traditions. My experience suggests that the discipline may have mellowed a great deal but that the musical espirit de corps has not lessened to any degree. During almost any day and many nights at Fürstenfeldbruck we could sit in the living room or lie in bed, serenaded by the distant voices optimistically chanting the four-square *Marschlieder*.

American infantrymen never were so fortunate during their tough months of basic drilling. The German code of basic training has polished its marching songs with the same assiduity which other armies devote to rifle practice and shoeshining. A correct German *Marschlied* has a beginning, middle and end, can be counted out by numbers, stoutly resists syncopation, and generates a resounding choral effect.

Although a few German marching songs have been culled from the list, the old songs are still the mainstay of the military curriculum. Every recruit who enters the German army is carefully taught the art of singing while marching with full field pack. Accompanied by good singing habits from school, a draftee quickly adjusts to the "Sing out" barked by his corporal. The new recruits learn the melodies and words of the *Marschlieder* in the classroom, then move out to the back roads and byways *"im gleichen Schritt und Tritt."* In their back pockets is the handy, official, pocket-size *Liederbuch der Bundeswehr,* bound in waterproof plastic for inclement weather, which contains some 150 German marching songs.

In no time platoons manage considerable melodious finesse. To hear the *Bundeswehr* on the move can be a true delight. Close in, one even gets the feel of slogging feet drumming out the four-four beat while stalwart tones resound. Two-part harmony occasionally lends a certain filigree to the usual unison.

Auf der Heide blüht ein kleines Blümelein
Und das heisst, Erika.
Denn ihr Herz ist voller Süssigkeit
Lauter Duft entströmt dem Blütenkleid
Auf der Heide blüht ein kleines Blümelein
Und das heisst, Erika.

Out on the meadow there blooms a little flower
And she is called, Erika.
For her heart is full of sweetness
Pure fragrance flows from her gown of blossoms

Out on the meadow there blooms a little flower
And she is called, Erika.

The motorized units have adapted their singing to the
realities of mechanization.

Mit donnerndem Motor, so schnell wie der Blitz,
dem Feinde entgegen, im Panzer geschützt . . .

With thundering motor, as swift as the lightning,
out toward the enemy, protected by our tanks. . . .

No division is ever without its band. Formal occasions
call out armies of brass to glitter in the sun according to
precedents established by the flute-playing King Frederick
the Great. The band members are by no means the only
ones who enjoy the music; statistics show that LP's of the
German military band and the German *Marschlieder* are
among the perennial best sellers in Germany, Austria,
Holland, France, and even in the United States.

In deference to the NATO alignment the West Germans sometimes even sing such non-German assortments
as:

O Susanna! *O weine nicht um mich!*
Denn ich komm von Alabama, *bring meine Banjo*
nur für mich.

Surely when the *Bundeswehr* joined the alliance NATO
acquired her best brass players and her most song-con-
scious footsoldiery.

The *Lied* in Germany, then, is more than just a casual
folksong. Its influence on the concert music of the world
has become immeasurable. Whether in the symphonies of
Beethoven or Brahms or in the choral works and operas
of Wagner, the *Lied* is a top ingredient. The works of
Mahler, Schubert, Schumann and even Alban Berg are
unthinkable without them. Colleges and universities in the

United States as well as in Germany offer semester courses in the *Lied* while volumes and tomes try to explain its nature and importance. Great scholars have dedicated their lives to collecting *Lieder;* great composers have repeatedly sought to improve them, frequently being converted to the perfect simplicity already in the songs. Probably the greatest merit for compilation of the German folksong goes to the two literary romanticists, Clemens von Brentano and Achim von Arnim, for their three-volume collection *Des Knaben Wunderhorn* (The Boy's Cornucopia) published in 1805-08.

Musical instruments used to accompany the *Lied* have included almost everything, hunting horns, the long Alpine horns, drums, flutes, violins, the lyre, harp, xylophone, zither, and bagpipes. Equally popular companions are the accordion, guitar, mandolin and harmonica. Not to be forgotten, especially in the city of Berlin, is the old *Leierkasten,* a kind of barrel organ hauled around on a little wagon by wandering minstrels who played in the streets and courtyards for whatever pennies people cared to throw to them.

In the United States, the German contribution to our culture has certainly been evident in music, and it has been lasting. During the early period of our development, in fact, the Puritans in New England and the Quakers in Pennsylvania were highly distrustful of any kind of music —but for the prominence of music in the Old Testament the Puritans might have outlawed it entirely. Psalm-singing was about the only singing and the *Bay Psalm Book* of 1640 the only songbook. There continued to be no musical center in the United States until throngs of Germans began to arrive in Philadelphia, where the first concert in the United States was given at the Reformed German Church. Gradually where Germans settled, music had a homestead. Pretty soon Haydn, Händel, and Beethoven had a house and were appreciated in all the major cities. Orchestras eventually grew to prominence, the first of these being entirely German, so German in fact that its official title was "Germania." When "Germania" disbanded in 1854 it had done more in six years for musical taste in America than any similar organization before it.

The German-Americans were not only prominent in the establishment of orchestras and chamber music groups, but they also brought the folksong to life and made vocal music acceptable through the ubiquitous German *Gesangvereine*, singing societies. Every city in the United States where there was a substantial German contingent boasted its singing society. As they became more sophisticated these groups expanded from a simple diet of folksongs into the whole range of German composers, Händel, Haydn, Strauss, etc., for their programs. As early as 1837 when the German singing societies of Philadelphia and Baltimore paid each other visits we had the first *Sängerfest*, competitive singing meet, between the societies of different cities.

Eventually during the second half of the nineteenth century, the whole lot of German immigrants in America took to the Sängerfest as a means of getting together. The railroads encouraged this. Leaf through any back issues of a German-language newspaper in this country and you will see ads offering reduced rates for members of German singing societies going to *Sängerfeste*. Sites of major singing festivals were Baltimore, Buffalo, St. Louis, Milwaukee, Chicago, Cleveland, New Braunfels, Cincinnati, Columbus, Pittsburgh and Louisville. There even arose something akin to a National and an American League of singers, the one being the *Nordamerikanischer Sängerbund*, the other *Allgemeiner Deutscher Sängerbund von*

Nordamerika. Always the contests were enveloped in an aura of ceremony and solemnity. Lasting about three or four days, they generally were open to the public and usually attracted crowds larger than any hall could contain. Representatives of the city and state always wanted to welcome the visitors, if for no other reason than because the political impact on such huge audiences of Germans was a matter to be reckoned with.

Eventually, of course, all of this crumbled with the hysteria triggered by the First World War. It would have been a normal response for the singing societies to rally to the cause of the Fatherland in her time of need, but there is no evidence that such indeed happened. It is true that many presidents of societies received propaganda bulletins issued by the German government calling for support, but while the officers felt emotionally stirred they were never converted. Eventually such efforts on the part of the Kaiser proved futile. Furthermore, as hostilities increased direct lines of communication between the United States and Germany were cut off. Yet when counter-propaganda issued by the British government totally aroused the Anglo-Americans against the German singing societies, the German-Americans had no choice but to fight for their lives. The pro-British bias in time grew so strong that the German singing societies were forced to disband. Today, in a few scattered strongholds of German immigration there still are German *Gesangvereine* and *Sängerfeste,* but these are anachronistic. Most of the singers have not the slightest clue about the historical significance of the event, nor even about the meanings of the words they are singing.

As with music, the German immigrants in the United States largely created the theater. During the nineteenth century the big cities of the East had regular German stock theaters. New York had its own as did Philadelphia, Cleveland, and Cincinnati. In Milwaukee the Pabst brewery family endowed the German theater. Often the singing societies offered their hall for at least an embryonic German theater and frequently they even tried their hands at opera. In the final analysis, however, it must be said that during the nineteenth century when the influence of Germans in America was strongest, the theater as an American cultural phenomenon was at its weakest. Therefore, even though German inspiration was significant the lasting effects have proved to be Cinderella-like.

An aspect of German music in the United States that should be mentioned at least in passing is the so-called "old time" or "oompah" style of polkas, waltzes and schottisches. Known only in the midwest states of Wisconsin, Minnesota, Iowa, the Dakotas and Nebraska, it is nowhere so entrenched as in the Turner City—New Ulm, in Minnesota. With a population of around fifteen thousand the city boasts from twenty to tweny-five polka bands, depending on the month they are counted, and observes an annual Polka Days festival. The music is distinctly Bavarian (Ulm is on the border between Bavaria and Württemberg) or Austrian, particularly as is common in rural Austria and in the Tyrol.

The instrumentation is Bavarian-Austrian, the beat simplified tyrolean, and the lyrics of the singing parts are frequently German folksongs. Curiously the yodeling has never been transferred to the United States even though the yodelers' melodies have been adopted. By far the majority of the polka band programs would not be recognizable in Germany today. The German folksong and rural melodies have changed and those in America have likewise veered off in different directions. In America there have been a great many "composers" who have tinkered with one or more of the basic German melodies to produce new polkas and waltzes. Virtually all of these polka and waltz numbers now have American names.

As for who listens to the bands, New Ulm is more German than the Germans. On radio station KNUJ polka band selections make up one-third of the daily programming. Many, many other stations in the six state area present a spicy diet of the same numbers. Not all, but in great part, the audience for polka music is rural, as is generally the case in Germany. Iverson in his sociological study *Germania, U.S.A.* observes that the polka style of music is not strictly the product nor the love of the Turners who have always considered themselves slightly higher-classed, but of extraneous German folk in the community.

Similar to the polka-waltz love affair in America, are phenomena like the Schnitzelbank song. In the Thirties and Forties German-Americans sang the ditty with feelings of identification and nostalgia for their Fatherland. It originated as the product of Mader's Restaurant in Milwaukee; along with the restaurant's German-style cooking went also its German-style song. In reality of course both were artificial. The song of the Schnitzelbank has never been sung on German soil, except perhaps by some disillusioned tourist or misinformed American G.I.

One aspect of theatrical-musical life that has long been popular in Germany but that has never caught on in the United States is the *Kabarett,* or cabaret. The cabaret is really a hybrid of theater, nightclub and street clowning. It is going to an elegant bar to sip a drink and watch the comic-satirical act on a small stage. Generally the cabaret is highly charged with political allusions and unless one is well-informed on the political issues of the day, chances are he will miss the subtle innuendos. Although there is a very old tradition of cabaret in Germany, it did not really gain widespread recognition until after 1900, which explains also why it was not imported with German immigrants to the United States. Likewise, today's best cabaret remains in the cities of its birth, basically in Vienna, Munich, and Berlin.

In concluding this chapter let us note a paradox, especially about German music. There seems to be a parallel between the rise of German music and the evolution of German philosophy. The earliest great German composers were Protestants while the Catholics remained for a longer time caught up with the popular baroque and its naive fondness for ceremony and smiling faith. A whole nation sang with Bach to the Lord, and individual souls were magnified. Yet at the end of it all Northern Germany seemed exhausted by the effort. Germany quit singing, taking pleasure rather in a rebirth of the pagan classics of Greece and Rome, especially with the triumph of Goethe and Schiller at Weimar. They no longer sang, they recited.

Then music found a new home in the Catholic south where life was more sentimental and less purely spiritual. Thus Beethoven, Haydn, and Mozart conducted an uninterrupted concert from the baroque to the romantic, but all of them lived in Salzburg, Munich, or Vienna. Then along came Schubert and Schumann, the former from the north and the latter from the south, who, in spite of their short lives, incarnated in their music a unity which bridged the many gaps in German culture. Unlike their predecessors, Schubert and Schumann took virtually all their music from the folk and by that token appealed to the folk in a dramatic way. Thus, despite the decentralization of theater and the apparent north-south cleavage of the musical tradition, the German heritage of music and theater proved to be the mortar that welded the people of *Deutschtum* into a bond of unity.

CONCLUSION

MOMENTOUS CHANGES in one's life chisel permanent impressions into the mind. Marriage, the birth of a child, or the adoption of a new mother country are truly burned into our consciousness. Years and generations later, detailed etchings of some far-off fateful drama arise and instantaneously scenes begin to talk. Between the years 1820 and 1925 the U.S. Census Bureau indicates that nearly six million Germans disembarked on our shores, the highest number of immigrants from any country in the world including Ireland and England. This enormous immigration dropped off when the quota system took effect in the 1920's and fell to a trickle during World War II, although temporary spurts occurred in the 1930's and again in the late 1940's.

In the minds of countless other millions who were sons and daughters of German stock, engravings of the Old Country endure vividly today. Grandchildren imagine pictures from stories told by their parents about their parents. Some tales still excite dreams of great fulfillment while others are chilling nightmares of uncertainty and dismal disappointment. The majority, however, have been simply woven into the smooth tapestry of modern America. Individuals think there is German blood in their family background, but from the sound of their names who can tell? Others have authentic German names but that is the only claim they can muster to a German identity. Under the impact of two World Wars, some Americans have become ashamed of their German parentage. Yet for most, the worst enemy of all has been the age-old one, time. In time, the German immigrants to America found success—a formidable enemy to any links with the mother tongue and the fatherland. My hope is that this book shall breathe vicarious life-roots into some of these countless millions of Americans whose heritage has been German.

Many things are not in this book that might have been included. History is occasionally present, but always through a backdoor entry. Government is always absent, for government policies are unwelcome in a book of this nature. There are no organized guidelines for the tourist, no list of do's and don'ts for the uninitiated. There are no tips on how to look for a job in Germany, nor even the best way to shop. Prospective visitors will still have to find out about visas and the *Aufenthaltserlaubnis,* the residence permit issued by the local police for all but transient tourists, and mothers will not know whether it is safe or not for their babies to drink German water. Incidentally, it is completely safe.

Readers have found no explicit treatment of the famous German arts and crafts, nor the comparative advantages of the Mercedes over the Volkswagen automobile. There is no speed limit on the German highways and *Autobahns* that could be mentioned, nor is there much point in looking back in the text for parking regulations or the store hours for shoppers. The revolving world of fashion precludes a meaningful entry about what the American visitor should wear, and who knows what the future holds in store for the merits of rail over air travel. Leaving all these practical matters to the guide books (a good one is Eugene Fodor, *Germany,* Mouton & Co., The Hague,

Netherlands) and the travel agencies, I have concentrated instead on what constitutes the German way of life.

There are good German cookbooks in print, fine histories, even splendid picture books about Germany, but few of them successfully measure the pulse of German life. My purpose in writing this book could be compared to a television picture tube. The information is available. It is constantly being sent out in all directions, but it is seldom reconverted into an image for the American viewer. Therefore, I have also brought in smatterings of facts about the lives of Germans in the United States and have tried repeatedly to focus my information about Germany by comparing it to situations in our home country. To what extent I have succeeded depends on you, the reader.

LA VERN RIPPLEY